CORNELL STUDIES IN INDUSTRIAL AND LABOR RELATIONS

VOLUME XIX

Value Judgments in Arbitration

CORNELL STUDIES IN INDUSTRIAL AND LABOR RELATIONS

Cornell Studies in Industrial and Labor Relations and International Reports are research monographs published by the New York State School of Industrial and Labor Relations.

CORNELL INTERNATIONAL INDUSTRIAL AND LABOR RELATIONS REPORTS

IN THIS SERIES

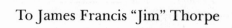

To James Francis "Jim" Thorpe

CORNELL STUDIES IN INDUSTRIAL
AND LABOR RELATIONS

Value Judgments in Arbitration

A Case Study of Saul Wallen

by Brook I. Landis

New York State School of Industrial and Labor
Relations, A Statutory College of the State University at Cornell University, Ithaca, New York

1977

Price: $10.00

ORDER FROM

Publications Division, New York State School
of Industrial and Labor Relations
Cornell University, Ithaca, New York 14853

Library of Congress Catalog Card Number: 77-8131
International Standard Book Number: 0-87546-063-1
International Standard Serial Number: 0070-0053

Library of Congress Cataloging in Publication Data
Landis, Brook I   1945–
Value judgments in arbitration.
(Cornell Studies in Industrial and Labor Relations; 19)
Bibliography: p.
Includes index.
1. Arbitration, Industrial—United States.
2. Wallen, Saul.   I. Title.   II. Series.
HD5504.A3L3   331.89'14   77-8131
ISBN 0-87546-063-1

Composed by Utica Typesetting Company
Printed in the United States of America by
Cojac Printing Company

Contents

Foreword

AMERICAN labor policy encourages the arbitration of contract labor grievances. Moreover, professional labor arbitrators have displayed a high level of competence and morality. Among labor arbitrators, Saul Wallen was an outstanding technician and a luminous human being. His decisions, so thoughtfully and precisely exhibited in this book by Brook I. Landis, will serve as target flares for future generations of arbitrators and advocates.

Labor arbitration, used properly, is among the most highly principled and humane of judicial systems. Unlike judges and juries, arbitrators are able to blend into their decisions a wide range of normative considerations, not excluding their sympathy for the individuals caught in the contractual matrix within which the grievance erupted. Arbitrators need not choose between conflicting or colliding legal principles which might be deemed mutually exclusive. Their scale of justice is commodious and affords room to weigh the human needs of the workers against the institutional demands of the employer.

There are tensions between systems which regulate by democratic methods of agreement and those which rule through bureaucratic intervention. Collective bargaining is a contractual system, used to establish employment relationships between workers and management, balancing employees' interests against the firm's need for efficient allocation of

resources. The grievance procedure makes it possible for parties to re-
nounce economic sanctions by agreeing to a process for resolving disputes
arising during the term of their contract. The arbitrator is the final
referee of such disputes, providing a backstop for settlement discussions,
deciding only grievances that resist settlement. The arbitrator must act in
accordance with the duties assigned under the submission agreement.
Frequently, the arbitrator is carefully instructed as to the issues, the scope
of consideration, and the remedy power. At other times, the arbitrator's
authority is less settled. In such cases, the arbitrator's operating approach
will determine how the issues will be decided.

Saul Wallen was particularly sensitive to the rights and interests of the
individual worker. At the same time, he recognized that the workers had a
continuing interest in the prosperity of the enterprise. Many of the
Wallen opinions show this good man wrestling with the hard task of
balancing asserted interests, seeking a solution that would reflect the
parties' reasonable expectations and would provide substantial justice for
all concerned. He believed in reconciliation through peaceful negotiations. He was patient, thoughtful, and fair.

He was convinced that a negotiated agreement was preferable to one
imposed upon the parties. He often directed the parties back towards
each other, for yet one more effort to achieve a settlement. His penchant
for compromise, seeking solutions to mutual problems, and insisting
upon human justice was well known to his peers and to the labor-
management community. As Byron Yaffe pointed out in *The Saul Wallen
Papers: A Neutral's Contribution to Industrial Peace,* Wallen sought "a common ground between disputing parties that often contributed to a constructive change in their relationship." He was flexible, recognizing that
arbitration could quietly adapt to the industrial relations environment
within which it was to be used.

Saul Wallen learned to pick his way around the artificial boundaries of
the contract. He became adept at identifying the realities of the underlying problems. As a working model, the Wallen technique deserves close
study.

While still the most humanistic system of adjudication, arbitration is
always in danger of being stamped into the mold of a formal judicial
process, of being converted into a totally adversary, polar, legalistic arena
for trial lawyers. Saul Wallen understood that labor arbitration could be a
powerful engine for justice, where irreconcilable differences would be
converted into mutually beneficial solutions, with equity and fair consideration for all concerned.

Wallen's view of arbitration matured through more than two decades of
arbitral service. As Brook Landis testifies, Wallen learned how to impose
his own high vision of humanity upon the parties. Those he touched

gained a better understanding of the value of impartial voluntary justice.

In his final years, Saul Wallen wanted to expand the benevolence of contractual justice into novel areas. He sought out new fields where collective negotiating techniques and conciliation and impartial arbitration could take root, offering previously impotent groups an opportunity to seek social justice at the bargaining table. He was a farsighted idealist. The fruits of his thinking, as analyzed in this important book, are worth close study.

Wallen was a prolific writer. His articles and opinions provide insight into the practice and purpose of grievance arbitration.

We are all in debt to Brook Landis for dissecting the Wallen writings with great sensitivity. Saul would have been pleased. He was legendary for his willingness to lend a hand to students of labor arbitration, helping them to learn the trade and to become established in their own right. Arnold Zack and Marcia Greenbaum are among the well-established young arbitrators whom Saul helped to launch. For this, too, labor and management owe him their gratitude.

It is hoped that other labor arbitrators will encourage young people to prepare themselves for this exacting profession. The use of arbitration to resolve labor-management disputes has increased in recent years. And, as arbitration systems expand into other areas of institutional conflict, there will be a growing demand for professional peacemakers in further fields. The writings of Saul Wallen will shine ever more widely, leading the way toward a society ruled by reason.

ROBERT COULSON
President
American Arbitration
Association

Preface

THE ROLE of personal value judgments in decision making is an issue that has troubled labor arbitrators for several generations and probably will continue to do so in the future. Most of the literature on the subject admonishes the labor arbitrator to base decisions solely on presented evidence of the parties' intent in reaching an agreement. A vocal minority, however, considers this view to be either self-deceiving or impractical.

My interest in this issue began when, as a graduate student at the New York State School of Industrial and Labor Relations, Cornell University, I assisted Byron Yaffe in selecting and editing materials for his book, *The Saul Wallen Papers: A Neutral's Contribution to Industrial Peace,* which was published by the School in 1974. It was readily apparent in reading the labor arbitration decisions of Saul Wallen that he did not fit into the usual mold. He relied upon and readily expressed his own values in reaching his decisions. Yet, he undeniably was a very successful and sought-after arbitrator. This raised questions about the validity of the commonly described limits of "appropriate" arbitral behavior.

While this book was written with the goal of providing answers to these questions in mind, it is hoped that it can also stand as a fitting tribute to an outstanding man. Saul Wallen was unique. The parties who used him and his fellow arbitrators knew this. Future practitioners and students of arbitration also should be reminded of his contributions.

The efforts of many people went into making this book a reality. Mary Wallen, Arnold Zack, and Marcia Greenbaum provided much needed information. Professors Frederic Freilicher, Byron Yaffe, Kurt Hanslowe, and Felician Foltman, all of the ILR School, provided advice and criticism.

A special debt of gratitude is owed to Professor Jean T. McKelvey for encouraging the submission of this publication. Thanks are also due to typists Anna Lane and Charmaine Moore and to Charlotte Gold for editing. The Saul Wallen Fund for Minority Studies provided partial funding for this volume and part of the proceeds and profits will be returned to the fund to support its future programs.

Finally, a special note of thanks goes to my parents, William and Ruby Landis, and to my wife, Cherry, for their ever-present support and encouragement.

Chapter I

The Historical
Link

The purpose of this book is to clarify the role of the modern-day labor arbitrator. In particular, several questions concerning the appropriate function of the arbitrator as a decision maker are raised and ultimately answered: (1) To what extent can arbitrators forsake the limited role of judge, basing their decisions on factors other than evidence presented by the parties in explanation of their intent in originally reaching agreement during contract negotiations? Specifically, to what extent can arbitrators rely on their preconceptions and personal values, born out of expertise developed in the field, in making their decisions? (2) If the arbitrators' personal values play a significant role, what are these values? (3) To what degree can arbitrators force or persuade the parties to accept their principles and rely on their expertise through the use of remedy powers? How creative can arbitrators be in fashioning solutions to problems before them, and how forceful can they be in assuring the implementation of these solutions?

The answers to these questions are provided through an in-depth analysis of a successful arbitrator, Saul Wallen. Before analyzing Wallen's career, however, or even justifying his selection as the focus of this study, it is important to understand the historical context in which these questions are raised.

The word *arbitration* has had many meanings in the course of American labor relations history. Even today, while there is a broad consensus that it necessarily implies that a third-party neutral hears and decides a labor dispute, there is still considerable divergence of opinion about how this neutral person should perform that decisionary role.

THE NINETEENTH-CENTURY VIEW OF ARBITRATION

During the nineteenth century, the term *arbitration* generally was applied to any settlement of a labor dispute without a strike. It was often used to describe those negotiations between parties, involving no third party, that today would be called *collective bargaining*.[1] *Arbitration* was also used to describe intervention by a third party who was not empowered to decide the dispute; today this would be called *mediation*. The boards of arbitration that were established in many states and localities in the late nineteenth century to aid in the settlement of labor disputes were for the most part mediation agencies.[2]

There were a few instances, however, in which *arbitration* was used in the narrower meaning of a binding third-party determination of a dispute.[3] In most of these situations, this arbitration was what would today be termed *interest arbitration,* that is, the third-party determination of a dispute over those terms and conditions of employment which constituted the labor agreement or contract itself. This stands in contrast to *grievance* or *rights arbitration,* which involves the determination of a dispute over the interpretation and application of already existing contract terms.

As an example of early interest arbitration, in 1871 the Pennsylvania coal industry's Anthracite Board of Trade and the miners' Workingmen's Benevolent Association selected a neutral umpire to decide the industry's terms and conditions of employment, including the issues of wages, hours, and union recognition. The Ohio coal industry and its miners similarly submitted their dispute to a third party in 1874. A few other industry and labor organizations, such as the Massachusetts shoe and boot industry, had provisions for third-party dispute settlement, but rarely used them.[4] For the most part, their "arbitrations" were actually collective bargaining activities conducted without third-party intervention.[5] As a general rule, arbitration as we know it today simply was not practiced to any measurable extent in the nineteenth century.

ARBITRATION IN THE EARLY TWENTIETH CENTURY

In the years before World War I, third-party labor arbitration was rare. The most publicized instance of its use was in the anthracite coal strike of 1902. Here, President Theodore Roosevelt intervened after a five-month strike and obtained the parties' agreement to submit their dispute to an Anthracite Coal Strike Commission, whose members were appointed by the president. As part of the arbitration award settling the strike, the commission established an Anthracite Conciliation Board to settle any future disputes over the interpretation and application of the industry's labor agreement. This was the first real use of what is now termed *grievance arbitration*. While the board was bipartisan, its machinery provided for the appointment of a neutral umpire to render a decision in the event that the parties could not settle their grievances themselves. In the first nine years of the board's functioning, 25 grievances were submitted to a neutral umpire for a decision.[6]

Third-party arbitration was also used as a strike substitute to settle interest disputes in a few other industries, most notably in the settlement of railroad labor disputes. A far more significant development in the evolution of American labor arbitration, however, was the introduction of grievance arbitration machinery in the clothing industry. Procedures were established in the New York cloak and suit industry in 1910 by the Protocol of Peace, as the settlement of the industry's long and bitter strike was termed. Under this agreement, Louis D. Brandeis served as the impartial chairman of the arbitration board that was set up. Since the protocol agreement had no time limit, the board frequently settled interest disputes over new contract terms, as well as grievances over the interpretation of already-existing contracts. Similar arbitration machinery was established in the cloak, dress, and waist industries of Boston and Philadelphia and in the men's clothing industries of New York and Chicago.

In most instances, renewed labor warfare caused the arbitration machinery to collapse frequently; in one case, however, the arbitration process was an outstanding success. This occurred under the Chicago Hart, Schaffner, and Marx men's clothing agreement. Here, the labor agreement was of a limited duration and the arbitration board involved itself solely with grievance arbitration. It never had anything to do with the determination of contract terms. The success of this type of grievance arbitration amid the widespread failure of interest arbitration machinery elsewhere in the clothing industry was a portent of things to come.[7]

ARBITRATION BETWEEN THE WORLD WARS

In the 1920s and early 1930s, arbitration remained for the most part centered in the garment industries, although it did spread to hosiery and bookbinding.[8] Most arbitrators still did not clearly differentiate between grievance and interest arbitration. This was especially true where, instead of a full, written labor agreement, there was an oral understanding or a sketchy written agreement of unlimited duration covering only the basic wage scales and the issue of union recognition. In most situations when arbitration was called for, the parties generally appointed a permanent arbitrator to settle all disputes arising during the life of their agreement. The popular present-day practice of selecting a different ad hoc arbitrator for each case that arises was uncommon. Since most of the arbitrators of this period had a close, continuing relationship with the parties, it consequently was easy for them to become involved with interest disputes as well as with questions of contract interpretation.

Comparatively little was written at this time about the nature of arbitration, although two works reflect generally prevailing attitudes. The first was by one of the most experienced of the early arbitrators, George W. Taylor, who, in the 1930s, served as a permanent impartial chairman for the hosiery and garment industries. As such, Taylor had a broad grant of authority from the parties to settle disputes and was involved with the parties on a continuing basis. Taylor, who considered both interest and grievance arbitration to be aspects of the collective bargaining process, commented on both in a 1938 article in the *Arbitration Journal*.[9] While he expressed a willingness to arbitrate a grievance on its own merits—that is, strictly according to the existing contract terms — if an employer demanded that he do so, he stated that in these cases "it is evident that the employer has not actually accepted collective bargaining as the basis for his industrial relations." Taylor added that "one frequently has a feeling of futility about the accomplishment of an arbitration award made under these circumstances." He preferred, where possible, "not solely to settle an individual dispute, but to assist in the development of procedures to dispose of such types of disputes in the future.[10]

While Taylor contended that this assistance was really a facilitation of negotiations between the parties and not an external imposition by fiat of the proper industrial relations, administrative, or economic principles, it is clear that he envisioned his role as something more than a mediator. The typical arbitration issue was a "problem in economics that has complex psychological aspects" that called for an "economically sound" decision.[11] He believed that the arbitrator had the opportunity to apply economic expertise to arbitration problems, that he should factually appraise the problem and establish appropriate principles as a solution, and that the parties would "customarily accept its inevitability if the underlying facts are secured and properly analyzed."[12]

Frances Kellor, a member of the Board of Directors of the American Arbitration Association from its founding in 1926 through the 1940s, discussed industrial grievance arbitration in 1934 in her book *Arbitration in the New Industrial Society*.[13] She stated that "industrial arbitration involves the complicated subject matter of human relations and public welfare; it involves class consciousness and prejudice, economic beliefs and doctrines, social philosophies and a wide array of intangibles." She contended further that "in an industrial arbitration, it is of the very essence of the proceeding that the arbitrators take into account everything which will help them to arrive at a settlement." She believed that grievance arbitrators having a continuing relationship with the parties under an agreement should be "men of bargaining minds and familiar with sales tactics."[14] The role she describes is primarily that of a wide-ranging mediator rather than that of Taylor's industrial relations expert or consultant.

THE WAR YEARS

As the incidence of written collective bargaining agreements increased in the years just before 1941,[15] and as experimentation with arbitration to settle differences arising out of these contracts became more common, some criticisms were voiced about the notion that arbitration was either a mediatory process or an interjection of the arbitrator's own values and ideas into the parties' management of their affairs.[16] These same complaints were much more prevalent in the postwar era.

A significant change in popular perceptions of the arbitrator's proper role did not occur until World War II. As a means to prevent strikes and lockouts over grievances, the National War Labor Board (NWLB), the government agency responsible for ensuring peaceful industrial relations during the war, encouraged the use of arbitration as the final step in the settlement of employee grievances under collective bargaining agreements. The board went so far as to order the inclusion of clauses requiring grievance arbitration to be inserted into agreements in several cases before it.[17]

To increase the voluntary use of grievance arbitration and decrease management resentment where its use was ordered, the NWLB attempted to reduce fears that grievance arbitration would impinge upon traditional managerial prerogatives that the employer may have successfully defended during negotiations with the union. The board did this by encouraging the careful definition of the jurisdiction of the arbitrator and the nature of arbitrable grievances when the collective bargaining agreements were drawn up. Contracts specifically excluding from arbitration all matters not mentioned in the written agreement were approved by the NWLB. The board gave such restrictions full force when deciding cases involving complaints over arbitrability of subjects or the jurisdiction of the arbitrator. Where it was reasonably clear that the arbitration clauses meant to exclude a subject from arbitral review, the NWLB denied arbitration. The only exception was the issue of discharge for cause, which the board held arbitrable regardless of the contract language. Where the arbitration clause failed to define adequately the arbitrator's jurisdiction and a dispute later arose, the board's policy was to confine jurisdiction to disputes over working conditions or the interpretation of specific contract language. The NWLB made it clear that the arbitrator could not modify, alter, or amend contract language. It further specifically defined grievance arbitration as a judicial process, limited in jurisdiction and limited to an award based solely on the evidence presented at a hearing.[18]

POSTWAR VIEWS

The limited, judicial style of grievance arbitration fostered by the NWLB succeeded in meeting wartime needs of both unions and management. The popularity of this type of arbitration continued after the war. At the Labor-Management Conference called by President Truman in 1945 to chart postwar industrial relations, representatives of unions and management unanimously supported a resolution recommending that all labor agreements should provide for grievance arbitration, with the limitations that: (1) arbitrators could decide only those issues specifically submitted to them, (2) they were required to base their decisions solely on evidence presented at the hearing, and (3) they could not add to, subtract from, or modify existing contract provisions.[19]

The legislative or consultative approach, the approach exemplified by George Taylor's work in the 1930s, was specifically disavowed. Postwar labor agreements reflected this changing trend in thought as the majority of labor contracts began to call for ad hoc arbitration systems in which the arbitrator was chosen on a case-by-case basis and did not have the continuing relationship with the parties necessary to establish a consultative approach.[20]

A large segment of the arbitration profession in the early postwar years also echoed these sentiments, supporting limited judicial arbitration. In 1948, Frances Kellor, in differentiating grievance arbitration from mediation, said that "arbitration, on the other hand, is a judicial process. ... Upon the evidence submitted the arbitrator makes his award." In her book *American Arbitration,* she continually referred to the arbitrator as a judge.[21] J. Noble Braden, tribunal vice president of the American Arbitration Association, called for, and reported that most arbitrators favored, a judicial concept of arbitration in which the arbitrator interpreted the contract language legalistically, considered only the evidence presented, and remedied only the issue at hand.[22] Arbitrator Douglass Brown, in describing appropriate arbitral conduct, stated that the arbitrator's "duty is and can only be to interpret the agreement. In the absence of specific instructions from both parties, he exceeds the bounds of his office if he substitutes his judgment for the apparent judgment of the parties. Whatever itch he may feel to 'help the parties out,' he must bear his frustrations manfully."[23] Arbitrator Harold W. Davey stated that "the essential function of an arbitrator is an adjudicatory one," that "arbitration is a judicial process," and that "the arbitrator has a professional obligation to base his award strictly on the merits as shown by the weight of the evidence made available for his consideration."[24]

These authorities rejected the view that arbitrators should base their decisions on their own values, or that they should attempt to solve any of the parties' problems other than the immediate, specific issue submitted. The arbitration process was considered to involve the evaluation of *past* events in light of the contract and the remedying of *past* violations of said contract. The process did not involve the governing of the *future* conduct of the parties. Any guidance for the future that the parties gained was to be by their own choice, not at the direction of the arbitrator.

There were probably many reasons for the development of this judicial philosophy of grievance arbitration. Undoubtedly, many of those involved in the process desired to make arbitration a salable commodity and were simply responding to the perceived demand for this type of arbitration. Arbitration still had many skeptics in labor and management ranks, and our society was used to a legal system that possessed the safeguards of both appellate review of decisions and a reliance on legal precedent, neither of which was a feature of ordinary grievance arbitration. Many authorities thought that in this environment only a limited arbitral function carefully controlled by the parties could gain widespread industrial popularity.[25]

Some authorities, however, were concerned with more than just making grievance arbitration, or their own services, a marketable commodity. Harold Davey and Lloyd Garrison, former vice-chairmen of the National War Labor Board, believed that the public interest could not tolerate industrial strife in the form of strikes over grievances and called for mandatory grievance arbitration as a substitute.[26] A limited, judicial style of arbitration would infringe the least on the liberties of the parties in governing their own affairs.

Advocates of nonjudicial, problem-solving or consultative grievance arbitration did not become extinct after World War II. George W. Taylor still did not view himself as an industrial judge, although his later statements differed in some significant aspects from those he voiced in the 1930s. He still relied on mediation and mutual exploration as a technique, but contended that his arbitration decisions were best based not on his own values or expertise, but upon the criterion of mutual acceptability.[27] Taylor claimed that in using this criterion, he was basing his decisions solely on the desires and needs of the parties that were expressed to him at the time of the arbitration hearing and not those expressed in an agreement reached in the past, which were probably now outmoded. He was not antagonistic to judicial arbitration where the parties or necessity demanded it. As vice-chairman and later as chairman of the National War Labor Board, he had recognized the need for such arbitration during the war. He even suggested this judicial approach after the war to managements and unions reluctant to implement grievance arbitration.[28] Taylor expressed no desire to foist nonjudicial arbitration onto unwilling parties,[29] and in fact opposed any sort of mandatory grievance arbitration schemes or legislation. He maintained, however, that judicial, ad hoc arbitration ideally should be only a transitory method along the path toward mature industrial relations relationships that were best serviced by permanent arbitrators who would base their decisions on mediated mutual acceptance.[30]

Arbitrator William Simkin, a colleague of Taylor and a former president of the National Academy of Arbitrators, also supported the notion of mutual acceptability as an appropriate basis for arbitration decision making. Simkin argued that "no arbitrator in his right mind wants to change the clear-cut terms of an agreement, whatever may be his personal views on the subject matter," but that cases involving clear-cut contractual direction seldom reach the arbitration stage. Simkin believed that, lacking clear-cut language, arbitrators were better off ascertaining and basing their decisions on present needs rather than on imperfect past intent. Simkin argued, however, that ideally arbitrators should attempt to base their decisions on the same general criteria, whether it be equity, past practice, the literal contract terms, or something else, that the parties themselves had relied upon in the past when settling grievances short of arbitration.[31] It was through the determination of an acceptable process that Simkin thought the arbitrator could reach Taylor's goal of acceptability.

Arbitrator Emanuel Stein also criticized the concept of the arbitrator as a judge, terming this process a "frustrating kind of legalism." In a manner similar to Taylor's, he viewed industry as being too dynamic to permit a labor agreement to remain meaningful in all aspects for even a limited time.[32]

Despite voices to the contrary, it became increasingly evident in the immediate postwar years and through the 1950s that the so-called judicial school was the more predominant. The nonjudicial point of view was often described as a "Messianic conception, a patent abuse of power, a substitution of one-man rule for the rule of law"; arbitrators of the nonjudicial school were said to "think they can 'play God' though the actual motive of their actions is usually a base instinct to meddle in other people's affairs."[33]

While all advocates of the judicial approach did not have an identical view of the process they supported, there were common elements in their views of the appropriate role of the arbitrator. First, the labor agreement was considered the basic source of the parties' rights and its language or intent was the fundamental criterion on which the arbitration decision was to be based. Second, the agreement's intent was to be determined solely on the basis of evidence presented at the arbitration hearing. Arbitrators were judges, evaluating only the evidence presented and ignoring their own ideas of what was proper, best, or fair. Finally, the decision and award were to answer only the question submitted and were only to make the aggrieved party whole in the event of a contract violation. The arbitrator had no mandate to control or attempt to control the future conduct of the parties.

While those who subscribed to this school of thought described this type of decision making as judicial, legal scholars since before the turn of the century have been reluctant to claim that court judges possessed such self-restraint. Even a superficial analysis of the available legal literature reveals that great debates over the nature and sources of judicial decision making have taken place among legal scholars for decades and that, whatever these scholars' viewpoints concerning the processes judges should use in rendering decisions, they are virtually unanimous in admitting that judges do not make decisions solely on the basis of the evidence and to the total exclusion of their personal values, beliefs, and perception of prevailing social attitudes.[34]

THE TRILOGY AND AFTER

The debate over the appropriate role of the arbitrator was intensified in 1960 when the Supreme Court issued its famous Trilogy decisions.[35] In these three decisions, the Court severely limited the role of the lower courts in arbitration. This was especially true with respect to the issue of arbitrability, the question of whether a particular dispute was required to be submitted to arbitration if one of the parties sought to have the case heard. Before the Trilogy, many lower courts followed what was commonly termed the *Cutler-Hammer* bona fide dispute doctrine, which required that where one party refused to submit a grievance dispute to arbitration, the other party, when seeking a court order to arbitrate, had to establish that (1) an agreement to arbitrate grievances did exist, (2) the issue grieved was covered by some specific contract language, and (3) the contract language in question was sufficiently unclear or ambiguous to require arbitral clarification.[36]

In the Trilogy, the Supreme Court specifically disavowed this approach and directed the lower courts to order the parties to undertake arbitration wherever (1) an agreement to arbitrate was shown to exist and did not specifically exclude the type of grievance issue being raised, and (2) an assertion was made that some contract provision was violated, even if the assertion was patently frivolous.[37] Any doubt as to whether a claim was arbitrable was to be resolved in favor of arbitrability.[38] The purpose of the Supreme Court's approach was to involve the lower courts only in the determination of whether the parties had agreed to arbitrate the type of dispute that had arisen, and to prevent the lower courts from deciding the dispute itself. This latter task was left solely to the arbitrators.

Although the Trilogy decisions dealt specifically with the appropriate role of the courts in arbitration, the Supreme Court also outlined its view of the arbitrator's appropriate role in extensive and in some ways conflicting dictum. On the one hand, the Court stated that, in rendering a decision, the arbitrator should take more than the collective bargaining contract into consideration.

The labor arbitrator's source of law is not confined to the express provisions of the contract, as the industrial common law — the practices of the industry and the shop — is equally a part of the collective bargaining agreement although not expressed in it. The labor arbitrator is usually chosen because of the parties' confidence in his knowledge of the common law of the shop and their trust in his personal judgment to bring to bear considerations which are not expressed in the contract as criteria for judgment. The parties expect that his judgment of a particular grievance will reflect not only what the contract says but, insofar as the collective bargaining agreement permits, such factors as the effect upon productivity of a particular result, its consequence to the morale of the shop, his judgment whether tensions will be heightened or diminished.[39]

When the arbitrator is commissioned to interpret and apply the collective bargaining agreement, he is to bring his informed judgment to bear in order to reach a fair solution of a problem. This is especially true when it comes to formulating remedies. There the need is for flexibility in meeting a wide variety of situations. The draftsmen may never have thought of what specific remedy should be awarded to meet a particular contingency.[40]

On the other hand, the following admonition was included:

Nevertheless, an arbitrator is confined to interpretation and application of the collective bargaining agreement; he does not sit to dispense his own brand of industrial justice. He may of course look for guidance from many sources, yet his award is legitimate only so long as it draws its essence from the collective bargaining agreement. When the arbitrator's words manifest an infidelity to this obligation, courts have no choice but to refuse enforcement of the award.[41]

Whether one viewed grievance arbitration as properly being mediative, consultative, or adjudicative, there was at least some dictum that could be construed as support for one's position, although the adjudicative approach probably received the least support in the Court's opinions. These cases evoked as much comment over the issue of the appropriate role of the arbitrator as did the decisions about the appropriate role of the courts.

The judicial school of arbitration did not abandon its views in light of the Trilogy, although its members at least were forced to admit the existence of, and legal sanction for, alternative schools of practice. Professor Lon Fuller analyzed the existing schools of arbitral thought, comparing the arbitral judge, whose "object is not to do justice, but to apply the agreement," with the "labor-relations physician," whose "task is not to bend the dispute to the agreement but to bend the agreement to the unfolding needs of industrial life." Fuller observed that "even those arbitrators who purport to adhere to a fairly extreme position at one end or the other of the scale seldom practice entirely what they preach." He also recognized that judges generally do not exhibit the behavior attributed to them by the judicial arbitration school, and in fact frequently add to, subtract from, or modify contract language to a greater degree than do even the most nonjudicial arbitrators. He saw a variety of modes of judicial conduct and stated that "if the arbitrator were to pattern his conduct after the worst practices of the bench, arbitration would be in a sad way."[42]

The remainder of Fuller's article supported the logical corollary that if arbitrators followed the best practices of the bench, they would be much better off. He expressed alarm that, because of the Trilogy dicta, "by a single stroke the arbitrator-physician is largely relieved both of the restraints of judicial office and of any undue concern to find justification for what he does in the words of the agreement." He admonished the arbitrator who would reach decisions on the basis of his own values or concepts of right and wrong to "ask himself whether the argument for bending his powers for good is not like that of the man who, in order to give to a worthy charity, embezzles funds entrusted to his care for an undeserving nephew." In both cases, Fuller felt that preserving the integrity of the process was a more worthy goal than achieving ends at the cost of ignoring the means.[43] While he recognized the existence of arbitrator-physicians, his advice to them could be construed as "Physician, heal thyself."

Arbitrators Paul Prasow and Edward Peters were less conciliatory in their remarks concerning nonjudicial types of arbitration. In admonishing those who used their own expertise or ideas of justice in solving cases and formulating remedies, they emphasized the restrictive portions of the Trilogy dicta, but primarily based their arguments on the concept of professionalism. They argued that the "quasi-judicial character of the process must be maintained if its usefulness is to be preserved," and that while some procedural flexibility was not undesirable, flexibility "becomes license when the arbitrator imposes his own subjective notions of justice on the parties rather than seeking to ascertain their mutual intent." The mediation or consensus school of arbitration was not criticized as much as the consultant school, for the former was not perceived any longer as a real threat to judical arbitration. Prasow and Peters wrote that, while in the early days of arbitration the "guideposts evolved by influential consensus arbitrators provided the minimum uniformity of contract interpretation necessary for the transition to judicial arbitration," a "process of 'natural selection' has all but eliminated the 'human-relations' consensus arbitrators."[44]

Paul Weiler, a Canadian observer of American arbitration, found several models of arbitration in existence: the arbitrator as mediator, the arbitrator as industry policymaker, and the arbitrator as adjudicator. While recognizing the legitimacy of the formulation of creative remedies by the arbitrator to effectuate adequately the contract's provisions, Weiler saw the proper role of the arbitrator as an adjudicative one, in which decisions were based on contract language and discernible intent. Where the search for the document's intent became strained or artificial, as in the case of a problem not at all envisioned by the contract negotiators, Weiler recommended that the arbitrator decline jurisdiction.[45] He offered this advice:

Hence I conclude that, even on pragmatic grounds, there is no justification for the arbitrator stepping outside his appropriate adjudicative role and donning the cloak of industrial policy-maker. There is no intrinsic likelihood that he will furnish a solution to the problem of industrial change that is substantively adequate and fair or that his efforts to impose such a solution will be more than intermittently successful. He is best advised to restrain his exercise of judgement and originality to problems where this is widely conceded to be legitimate.[46]

Warnings that anything but a limited, adjudicative role for arbitrators is an abuse of their appropriate function and is sure to result in professional suicide continue to be voiced to the present time. In a paper presented to the twenty-fifth annual meeting of the National Academy of Arbitrators, arbitrator Louis Crane delivered a forceful defense of the strictly adjudicative role.[47] Several other arbitrators issued statements in agreement with his views.[48] Crane concluded that arbitrators should properly decide disputes solely on the basis of the evidence presented to them:

If there are weaknesses or gaps in the proofs, or if one party or the other did less than what the arbitrator feels should have been done under the agreement, then the party responsible for the weakness or the gap in the proofs or the party who failed to do what should have been done must stand the consequences in the final decision.... The arbitrator's role is to decide disputes on the basis of what has been presented to him.[49]

He argued that the powers of arbitrators do not appropriately allow them to base decisions on their own values or expertise. The power to decide a case "is not a roving commission. It is not a solicitation for industrial relations advice." The arbitrator was to answer only the narrowly defined issue submitted.

Where the agreement was unclear or the evidence scanty, Crane did not foresee that the search for intent would become strained or artificial, as did Weiler, or, if he did, he considered it a lesser evil than not providing an answer to the question submitted. Crane considered the policy of remanding the case to the parties, as Weiler recommended, to be an abdication of arbitral responsibility.[50]

Crane recommended that the power to remedy be exercised as cautiously as he would have the decision-making process performed. The submission of the issue was not "a request for a magic formula for handling all future problems which may arise under the disputed contract provision." Dictum should be similarly limited: "Gratuitous observations about what should not have been done, or what should be done in the future, or such palliatives as what the arbitrator would have done if the facts were different, have no place in the arbitration decision."[51]

Crane stated that not only should the remedy not include principles governing future conduct, but that it should not even call for the prohibition of future contract violations through the use of what he termed arbitral cease-and-desist orders. He considered such orders not so much an abuse of arbitral power as a "waste of power" and "more shadow than substance," as the arbitrator has no special contempt powers to insure compliance.[52] Crane concluded his article with the stern admonition that arbitrators themselves, as well as the process, are being continually evaluated and appraised by the participating parties, and, as a result, perceptive arbitrators will best insure their professional survival by avoiding abuses of power.

The adjudicative view of arbitration thus either denies or places strict limitations on the use of personal views in decision making and opposes creative or affirmative remedies and unsolicited guidance. Although the adjudicative approach appears to predominate (at least among those who write about the process), it is by no means the only view of either how grievance arbitrators do or should operate.

Arbitrator Edgar Jones, Jr., in a post-Trilogy article, described the following arbitral dilemma:

What criteria of judgment does the arbitrator use as he formulates his decision? He sits in the halfway house between the legislator and the judge, neither expected to create a policy out of his own conception of what is wise, nor to rely on past usage to avoid present inquiry. The key is routinely said to be consensuality, but the key is either so often mislaid or purposefully concealed that quite often the arbitrator must fashion his own method to gain access to the wisdom and prudence necessary to resolve the dispute. According to the existing uses of propriety he is then supposed to call that conclusion "the intent of the parties."[53]

To answer this dilemma, Jones offered the following resources for arbitral judgment:

The decisions of the labor arbitrator, in the ancient tradition of his peers, (1) should conform to the clearly expressed intent of the parties to the agreement, but (2) should conform only so long as that intent remains within the bounds of generally deducible public policy, but (3) absent the guidance of the parties, and on occasion despite it, should reflect contemporary community attitudes of what is fair in procedure and equitable in result.[54]

He claimed that such a role is not an abuse of proper function, guaranteed to gain censure by the parties, but rather a reasonable fulfillment of the parties' expectations:

The parties who have left their arbitrator (as the legislators who have left their courts), without specific guidance in the collective agreement (as when they indicate he shall be "just") must expect him to form his judgment from *some* source or sources external to the silent agreement. They have joined in the creation of his office and thereby the necessity of his decision.[55]

Jones further stated that such a reflection of the "contemporary conscience of the community" was the "unique contribution of the arbitral processes to the Anglo-American system of justice."[56]

Arbitrator Gabriel Alexander also saw the arbitrator's values and expertise as playing an important role. In addressing the National Academy of Arbitrators in 1971, he stated that "decision making by arbitrators is a dynamic mental and emotional process which includes nonrational, as well as rational, elements." The ambiguity and frequent silence of the labor agreement compels the arbitrator to "exercise his will with little or no specific contractual restraint." Alexander argued that where the contract or its intent is ambiguous or totally absent and the outcome dependent on "value judgements, the arbitrator has no alternative to making his choice on the broad basis of experience and wisdom."[57]

CURRENT ANALYSES OF ARBITRATION

Some students of arbitration have analyzed published cases to discover evidence of the effects of personal values on arbitral decision making, and instances of arbitral attempts to influence the long-run behavior of the parties. In a study examining procedural due process in arbitration, Arbitrator Robben Fleming concluded that arbitrators' value judgments influenced not only their decision making and the conduct of the hearing, but also affected the procedures employed by managements for in-plant discipline: "It should be noted that the development of a 'rule of law' within the plant is in substantial part due to the decisions of arbitrators through which the parties have come to lay down and accept regularized procedures governing their conduct." This development was not contractually contemplated through the intent of the parties, but rather an imposition of the arbitrators' values and expertise: "It may be seriously doubted whether such a development could have taken place had arbitrators not to a certain extent imposed their ideas of constructive labor relations on the parties."[58]

Arbitrator John Teele did a case study of the following hypothesis concerning arbitral decision making and the effect of the Trilogy:

> Clearly an arbitrator, even before these provocative new opinions of the Supreme Court were published, has in close cases always had to bring to the proceedings something of his own — even if just his own simple judgment as to the realities of the situation in the shop. This need for him to contribute something personal to the solution stems from the inability of any contract to cover all of these realities.[59]

Teele's examination of 295 discharge decisions showed that in 90 arbitrators relied primarily on contract language in reaching their decisions; in 112, the arbitrators relied either on local or general practices or else on arbitral and court precedent, all construable as indicators of the parties' intent; and in 93 cases, arbitrators relied clearly on their own personal standards and judgment. He concluded that these results lead one "to suspect that labor unions and company managements may have less to say about running things in their joint sphere of influence than they might wish."[60]

Professor James Gross analyzed the following hypothesis:

> The basic assumption underlying this study is that labor arbitrators are influenced by values or predilections which not only condition their thinking but also provide them with ultimate standards for judgement. These conditioning factors are not prejudices in the narrow sense of the word. They are the prevailing ideas at the basis of the contemporary social order, which serve as guiding principles for the individual.
>
> Attachment to these values results in the prepositioning of an individual whenever he engages in the "practical conduct" of his affairs. Consciously or unconsciously, arbitrators bring these ideas about ethics, man, law, private property, economics, and so forth to their cases.[61]

His study was limited to ad hoc arbitration cases involving subcontracting and out-of-unit transfers of work. The purpose of the study was to find evidence of the existence of such value judgments, not to draw conclusions concerning their social effects or the fate of arbitrators whose decision making continually draws heavily on noncontractual values. Gross found the dominant value in the type of cases he examined to be a consideration of efficiency, the "prevailing ideology concerning the benefits of unrestricted technological change," of which he said:

> The presence of this value judgement, which has influenced significantly the experience of labor arbitration, has been verified in this article. Arbitrators appropriated and applied these value premises at least from the very beginning of published opinions, long before the Supreme Court "trilogy."[62]

He stated that the value aspects of the arbitral decision-making function required more analysis to draw more precise conclusions:

Studies of arbitrators are needed. The opinions of individual arbitrators should be followed down through topical areas and across area boundaries. Analyses of arbitrators ought to include not only surveys of their social and educational backgrounds, professions, attitudes, and opinions, but also in-depth biographies which will aid in understanding their philosophies and techniques.[63]

It is this need for study and understanding that prompted the in-depth case analysis of arbitrator Saul Wallen.

Notes

1. Edwin E. Witte, *Historical Survey of Labor Arbitration* (Philadelphia: University of Pennsylvania Press, 1952), pp. 1 and 4. See also Vernon H. Jensen, "Notes on the Beginnings of Collective Bargaining," *Industrial and Labor Relations Review* 9 (1956): 230–31.

2. Witte, pp. 1 and 8.

3. See, for example, Witte, p. 11; Jensen, p. 231; and United States Congress, Senate Committee on Education and Labor, *Report of the Committee of the Senate Upon the Relations Between Labor and Capital, and Testimony Taken by the Committee* (Washington, D.C.: GPO, 1885), vol. II, pp. 23 and 85.

4. Witte, pp. 11–13.

5. Jensen, pp. 233–34.

6. Witte, pp. 21–23.

7. Ibid., pp. 23–26.

8. Ibid., pp. 37–38. See also Morton Gitelman, "The Evolution of Labor Arbitration," *DePaul Law Review* 9 (1960): 182.

9. George W. Taylor, "The Factual Approach to Industrial Arbitration," *Arbitration Journal*, o.s. 2 (1938): 343.

10. Ibid., p. 345.

11. Ibid., p. 346.

12. Ibid., p. 347.

13. Frances Kellor, *Arbitration in the New Industrial Society* (New York: McGraw-Hill, 1934), pp. 133–60.

14. Ibid., pp. 135–36.

15. Paul Prasow and Edward Peters believe that the NLRB's decision in the *Inland Steel* case of 1937, making the refusal to reduce an agreement to writing an unfair labor practice, did much to influence the growth of grievance arbitration. "The Development of Judicial Arbitration in Labor-Management Disputes," *California Management Review* 9 (1967): 11.

16. Wayne Morse, "The Judicial Theory of Arbitration." In Wight Bakke and Clark Kerr (eds.), *Unions, Management, and the Public* (New York: Harcourt, Brace, 1948), p. 489.

17. Jesse Freidlin and Frances Ulman, "Arbitration and the National War Labor Board," *Harvard Law Review* 58 (1945): 344.

18. Ibid., pp. 346–48 and 355.

19. J. Noble Braden, "The Function of the Arbitrator in Labor-Management Disputes," *Arbitration Journal* 4 (1949): 35.

20. Ernestine Moore and James Mix, "Arbitration Provisions in Collective Agreements," *Monthly Labor Review* 76 (1953): 264.

21. Frances Kellor, *American Arbitration* (New York: Harper and Bros., 1948), pp. 84–85.

22. Braden, p. 35.

23. Douglass Brown, "Management Rights and the Collective Agreement," *Proceedings of the First Annual Meeting of the Industrial Relations Research Association* (New York: IRRA, 1949), p. 152.

24. Harold Davey, "Hazards in Labor Arbitration," *Industrial and Labor Relations Review* 1 (1948): 389 and 393.

25. Harry Shulman, "The Role of the Impartial Umpire." In Wight Bakke and Clark Kerr (eds.), *Unions, Management, and the Public* (New York: Harcourt, Brace, 1948), p. 485.

26. Davey, "Hazards in Labor Arbitration," p. 400; Lloyd Garrison, "Proposal for a Labor-Management Board and a Charter of Fair Labor Practices," *University of Chicago Law Review* 14 (1947): 358.

27. George W. Taylor, "The Voluntary Arbitration of Labor Disputes," *Michigan Law Review* 49 (1951): 787.

28. George Taylor, "The Arbitration of Labor Disputes," *Arbitration Journal* 1 (1946): 414.

29. Taylor, "The Voluntary Arbitration of Labor Disputes," p. 798.

30. George Taylor, "Effectuating the Labor Contract Through Arbitration." In Jean T. McKelvey (ed.), *The Profession of Labor Arbitration* (Washington, D.C.: BNA, 1957), p. 40.

31. William Simkin, *Acceptability as a Factor in Arbitration under an Existing Agreement* (Philadelphia: University of Pennsylvania Press, 1952), pp. 40 and 43.

32. Emanuel Stein, "Arbitration and Industrial Jurisprudence," *Monthly Labor Review* 81 (1958): 867.

33. Lon Fuller, "Collective Bargaining and the Arbitrator." In Mark Kahn (ed.), *Collective Bargaining and the Arbitrator's Role* (Washington, D.C.: BNA, 1962), p. 9.

34. See, for example, Roscoe Pound, "Jurisprudence." In Harry Barnes (ed.), *The History and Prospects of the Social Sciences* (New York: Knopf, 1925); Roscoe Pound, "Justice According to Law," *Columbia Law Review* 13 (1913); Oliver Wendell Holmes, *The Common Law* 35 (1881); Oliver Wendell Holmes, "The Path of Law," *Collected Legal Papers* 181 (1920); Benjamin Nathan Cardozo, *The Nature of the Judicial Process* (New Haven, Conn.: Yale University Press, 1921); Jerome Frank, *Law and the Modern Legal Mind* (1930); Jerome Frank, "Mr. Justice Holmes and Non-Euclidean Legal Thinking," *Cornell Law Quarterly* 17 (1932); Joseph Hutcheson, Jr., "The Judgement Intuitive: The Function of the 'Hunch' in Judicial Decision," *Cornell Law Quarterly* 14 (1929); and Nathan Isaacs, "The Limits of Judicial Discretion," *Yale Law Journal* 32 (1923).

35. USWA v. Am. Mfg. Co., 363 U.S. 564 (1960); USWA v. Warrior and Gulf Navigation Co., 363 U.S. 574 (1960); USWA v. Enterprise Wheel and Car Corp., 363 U.S. 593 (1960).

36. IAM Dist. 15, Local 402 v. Cutler-Hammer, Inc., 271 App. Div. 917, 67 N.Y.S. 2d, 317 (1947).

37. American Mfg., 363 U.S. at 568.

38. Warrior and Gulf, 363 U.S. at 585.

39. Id. at 582.

40. Enterprise Wheel, 363 U.S. at 597.

41. Id.

42. Fuller, pp. 10, 14, and 29.

43. Ibid., pp. 11 and 28.

44. Prasow and Peters, "The Development of Judicial Arbitration in Labor-Management Disputes," pp. 13–14.

45. Paul Weiler, "The Role of the Labour Arbitrator: Alternative Versions," *University of Toronto Law Journal* 19 (1969): 19, 23, 28, 37, and 39.

46. Ibid., p. 43.

47. Louis Crane, "The Use and Abuse of Arbitral Power." In Barbara Dennis and Gerald Somers (eds.), *Labor Arbitration at the Quarter-Century Mark* (Washington, D.C.: BNA, 1973).

48. Comments by Stuart Bernstein, Stephen Vladeck, Lawrence Kearns, and Robert Manning accompanied the article.

49. Crane, p. 68.

50. Ibid., pp. 69–70.

51. Ibid., p. 70.

52. Ibid., p. 73.

53. Edgar Jones, Jr., "Power and Prudence in the Arbitration of Labor Disputes: A Venture in Some Hypotheses," *UCLA Law Review* 11 (1964): 709.

54. Ibid., p. 741.

55. Ibid., p. 742.

56. Ibid., p. 712.

57. Gabriel Alexander, "Discretion in Arbitration." In Gerald Somers and Barbara Dennis (eds.), *Arbitration and the Public Interest* (Washington, D.C.: BNA, 1972), pp. 85, 92, and 94.

58. Robben Fleming, "Problems of Procedural Regularity in Labor Arbitration," *Washington University Law Quarterly* 1961 (1961): 249.

59. John Teele, "The Thought Processes of the Arbitrator," *Arbitration Journal,* 17 (1962): 85.

60. Ibid., pp. 92 and 95.

61. James Gross, "Value Judgements in the Decisions of Labor Arbitrators," *Industrial and Labor Relations Review* 21 (1967): 55. Gross examined approximately 150 ad hoc arbitration decisions issued between 1945 and 1966 concerning subcontracting and approximately 120 decisions dealing with out-of-unit transfers of work.

62. Ibid., p. 71.

63. Ibid., p. 72.

Chapter II

Why Saul Wallen?

The few studies to date that have attempted to explore the question of personal values in arbitration have done so by analyzing the decisions of many arbitrators who have dealt with the same topic, such as discipline or subcontracting. Studies of this type are useful and more should be undertaken on yet other subjects. But while such a technique is helpful in identifying the prevalence of personal value judgments in the decisions of arbitrators, it provides little information about the extent to which particular arbitrators can rely on their own values or use their remedy powers to force their views and values on the parties and still remain acceptable to them.

An alternative approach, that of examining one arbitrator's personal values and their influence on his or her decisions, opens up new avenues of exploration. Through this method, it is possible to gauge the degree to which certain attitudes had an impact on the handling of different issues encountered throughout that arbitrator's career. Changes in personal values over time or changes in the manner of applying these values to particular types of cases can be examined. In addition, the impact of such an approach on an individual's career in terms of the arbitrator's acceptability to the parties can be understood.

At first glance, such an approach appears to suffer from an important drawback. Information is generated about only one arbitrator and thus it may be assumed to be difficult to draw conclusions about the arbitration process in general. If, however, the individual arbitrator selected for examination is one who relied extensively on personal value judgments in decision making, conclusions can be drawn about acceptable limits in applying such values. The analysis of the career of just one successful arbitrator, successful in terms of remaining acceptable to a large number of parties for a long period of time, cannot establish how an arbitrator *must* act, but it can demonstrate how he or she *may* act. Furthermore, if the successful style analyzed and described falls outside those limits of acceptability as defined by the conventional wisdom of arbitrators and scholars, something has been learned about the true limits of acceptable style and about the validity of those limits presently espoused. New limits can be defined. Future studies of other successful arbitrators could conceivably expand these limits even further.

The selection of Saul Wallen as the arbitrator to be studied was not a random choice. Wallen contributed his personal papers and case files to the Labor-Management Documentation Center at Cornell University's Martin P. Catherwood Library at the New York State School of Industrial and Labor Relations.[1] Wallen had the reputation of an arbitrator with strong personal values, of relying on these values in his decision making, and of introducing creative, problem-solving remedies. Even a superficial analysis of his writings and of some of his more publicized cases substantiates this reputation. In addition, Saul Wallen was one of the most successful full-time arbitrators in the nation, at least to the extent that success can be measured by his remaining acceptable to both labor and management during his entire career, which spanned more than 22 years. It is this aspect of arbitral success, the ability to remain acceptable to the parties, that this study seeks to illuminate.

Inasmuch as the commonly accepted view of the arbitrator renounces or discourages reliance on personal values and rejects attempts to influence the future behavior of the parties, it is of particular interest to analyze an arbitrator who did not follow this generally recommended course of conduct, but nevertheless was successful. His success in itself raises serious questions concerning the validity of the prevailing point of view.

A BRIEF BIOGRAPHY

Saul Wallen was born on June 29, 1910, in New York City's upper East Side and was reared in the White Plains section of the Bronx.[2] His father, a painting contractor, and his mother both emigrated from Russia in 1907, met in New York City, and were married in 1909. Wallen graduated from Morris and James Monroe High School in New York City in 1928 and enrolled that year in New York University's Washington Square College of Commerce, undertaking a curriculum in statistical economics. His goal at that time was to prepare for a statistical career with the New

York Stock Exchange. Although the depression forced him to withdraw from full-time schooling after two years and to work as a house painter, he attended night school and received his bachelor of science degree in economics in 1933.

Wallen's initial entrance into the field of labor relations and arbitration was largely accidental and a result of the conditions of the time. Unable to find a job on Wall Street, he heard of a job opening from a relative and was hired as a labor adjuster for the New York City United Association of Dress Manufacturers. As a representative of the employers, he worked with his union counterpart in settling disputes over the wages to be paid for various dress-making operations. Unsettled disputes were submitted to a neutral arbitrator.

In 1936 Wallen left his job as a labor adjuster for the greater job security afforded by a civil service post as a research investigator for the New York State Department of Labor, investigating the treatment of women in the state's "sweatshop" industries. In 1940, he left this post for a similar position with the United States Department of Labor in Washington, D.C., investigating hazardous children's occupations. Because of his previous labor relations experience, the newly formed National War Labor Board hired him as a mediation officer in 1942. Given a ten-day assignment to set up a regional office in Boston for the board's First Region (New England), Wallen was named the chairman of that regional board when the position unexpectedly opened. Wallen remained in this post until November 1945, directing the board's efforts in settling New England labor disputes and in administering the wage stabilization program.

In 1946, Wallen began his career in Boston as a full-time labor arbitrator and mediator, a career that covered 22 years and approximately 6,200 separate grievance arbitrations.[3] He became the permanent arbitrator for several unions and companies, including the Ford Motor Company and the United Auto Workers, General Motors and the United Auto Workers, General Tire Corporation and the United Rubber Workers, B. F. Goodrich and the United Rubber Workers, Firestone and the United Rubber Workers, Eastern Airlines and the International Association of Machinists, Sylvania Electric and the International Union of Electrical Workers, and the Massachusetts Leather Association and the Leather Workers' International Union. He was a charter member of the National Academy of Arbitrators and was its president in 1954.

Wallen left full-time arbitration in 1968 to take the position of director of the New York City Urban Coalition, an organization devoted primarily to the creation of employment opportunities for minority groups. He died in August 1969.

Saul Wallen's career is especially suited to an analysis of the role of personal values in arbitration because Wallen operated successfully near the bounds, and even beyond the bounds, of what the profession assumed to be the appropriate limits for value judgments in decision making.

WALLEN'S PRINCIPLES

Saul Wallen was not a private man; in his extensive career of public service, he placed himself on the record on most of the significant social issues of his time. Throughout this record run several consistent strands of thought and belief concerning the manner in which industrial society should conduct its affairs and the goals toward which it should strive. In several statements, he outlined the goals that an arbitrator, as a participating member of industrial society, should advance.

In brief, these goals were the promotion of (1) equity and justice for all members of industrial society; (2) efficiency, productivity, and technological innovation; and (3) stable collective bargaining.

The first goal involves the concept of fundamental justice and fairness, a recognition of the basic rights of all those at the workplace. Even before Wallen entered the arbitration profession on a full-time basis in 1946, he expressed his belief in moral and ethical reasons for the settlement of labor disputes and grievances on the basis of justice rather than on strict economic and political grounds of self-interest. He stated that a fair disposition of grievances was necessary to create the good will necessary for successful industrial relations.[4]

Wallen's concept of justice was more basic and far-reaching than that of most arbitrators. In general, employees are insured a full measure of their contractual rights under the collective agreement through the "covenant of good faith" that nearly all arbitrators require of the parties in their fulfillment of contractual obligations. Even where there was no union or collective agreement, however, Wallen believed that simple justice could be discerned. To this end, he saw usefulness in, and looked with favor on, the "few nonunionized companies with advanced personnel policies" that have implemented arbitration procedures to solve employee grievances.[5]

Wallen's concept of justice might simply be termed fair dealing. He envisioned as an ideal the distribution of the rewards of industry not on the basis of arbitrary caprice, favoritism, or prejudice, but on the basis of merit, with the appropriate yardstick of merit depending on the particular situation involved. This concept included a recognition of the human investment of individual workers in their employment, an investment that increased the longer they were employed.

In 1966, Wallen defined his concept of justice as "establishing a rule of law rather than arbitrary power at the workplace."[6] He cited with obvious approval Professor Eli Ginzberg's attempt to "uncover the wellsprings from which this great impulse toward a rule of law at the workplace flows," which described the human need that Wallen felt arbitration could and should help to fill:

During his formative years, the [American] ... is indoctrinated with ideas of equality and freedom — with the belief that every man is as good as every other man. ...

Nurtured on this heady drink of freedom and equality, of liberty and justice, he cannot fail to become restive, disturbed, antagonistic by what he finds in the employment situation. From the moment the starting whistle blows, his freedom is in suspense; justice is in jeopardy; one man is clearly the superior of another; power and authority permeate the work place. ...

The average man ... sees his life as a whole. He cannot live without tension by one set of values in the hours during which he works and live by an entirely different set of values during the hours when he is off the job.[7]

Wallen believed that the basic right of the employer to manage was "hemmed in by the responsibility to manage with due consideration for the interests of all of the elements of the enterprise — the employees, the owner, the public, and the management."[8] He contended that the *process* of management should consider these factors, and if it did not, the process of arbitration should correct the situation. Wallen, however, did not consider the extension of fair treatment to affected individuals to be just a duty of management. This concept applied to unions in their industrial relations dealings as well.

Wallen held as a fundamental tenet the fact that this justice could only be assured in a two-party dispute by allowing a disinterested third party to settle the issues in conflict. He stated that

When two parties meet as equals and draw up an agreement, one party cannot in good conscience insist that if there is a dispute over what it means, his decision will be determinative. It is elementary that there must be a referee or an umpire to judge disputes over the application of the rules of the game.[9]

He termed the insistence by one party on retaining the final say "tantamount to the home team insisting on the right of its manager to call balls and strikes."[10]

This hard-to-define concept of justice was so basic to successful industrial relations that he promoted its effectuation not only when working as an arbitrator, but also while engaged as a mediator of contract disputes. In an article on the role of the mediator in the collective bargaining process, Wallen discussed the situation in which one party is vastly more powerful economically than its opponent. He described the mediator's appropriate role in this situation as more than one of helping to "arrange surrender terms." The mediator should help the weaker party to advance its cause in those instances in which its cause is the "right and just thing in the light of prevailing conditions."[11] Wallen's advocacy of this role indicates a strong belief in the concept of basic, elementary justice. Most practitioners of mediation consider this role to be dangerous and potentially ruinous to the mediator's credibility as a disinterested party. As a result, they restrict their interest in the substantive outcome of negotiations, at most, to the exclusion of terms that violate statutory public policy.[12]

A second goal of arbitration was the protection of the productive nature of the enterprise which exists in a competitive business environment. This is the theme of "efficiency, as the 'summum bonum,'" in the words of James Gross.[13]

Wallen justified consideration of arguments about economic growth, efficiency, and technological change on two grounds. He supported the concept of "a larger pie leading to a larger slice for everyone," the idea that the economic well-being of workers and of management are intertwined in the long run. Wallen stated that collective gains for workers were "made possible by the continued growth and prosperity of the employer. The growth of production and the enhancement of efficiency were the sources of the gains in wages and benefits for the man engaged in production."[14]

A second justification for considering aspects of efficiency and productivity was industry's role in society as the producer of goods and services. Just before entering the arbitration profession, while still the New England regional director of the War Labor Board, Wallen spoke of the industrial sector's obligation to provide maximum production for society to insure prosperity.[15] Similarly, in an article written toward the end of his arbitration career, he wrote that "society needs the benefits of management's productive radicalism."[16]

One widely publicized statement by Wallen seemed to belie his concern, as an arbitrator, for productivity. In an article written shortly after the Supreme Court's Trilogy decisions, Wallen commented on the Court's dicta that the arbitrator's judgment should reflect not only the contract, but also factors such as effects on productivity, morale, and tensions. Here, Wallen reflected a view similar to that expounded by the judicial school of arbitration:

It has been my experience that American labor relations have achieved that state of maturity in which the parties want me or my colleagues to decide only what the contract says, or to give them a fair construction of what it says unclearly or implicitly. They most emphatically do not seek my views on what will raise productivity. Nor do they ask me to make that decision which will be best for morale. Whose morale? Some of our decisions cause worker morale to soar, while acting as a terrific depressant on the morale of managers, and vice-versa.[17]

In offering this statement, Wallen left much unsaid. What of the situation in which the contract says nothing about efficiency or productivity, but such considerations are offered in evidence by one or both of the contesting parties? This happens frequently in arbitration. Here, an opinion on these considerations is being sought. It is precisely because of problems connected with the issues of efficiency and productivity, never contractually spelled out, that Wallen called arbitration "a highly complex field of its own that deserves the attention of specialists who will combine impartiality with technical competence and business realism."[18]

The third and final goal the process of arbitration should promote was, for lack of a better term, the stability of reasoned, codetermined rule making in the industrial relations sphere. To understand this concept, one must first understand some of Wallen's views concerning the process of collective bargaining. Wallen believed, ideally, that unions and managements were capable of creating a system of self-government that met the needs and basic rights of all governed by it. This was a goal to be worked toward. He did not, however, share the belief of some that any agreement reached by the parties through the trial by fire of economic conflict necessarily produced the best possible solution or even one that met the needs of the governed. His view was not the same as that held by George Taylor, who, for two reasons, deemed the end results of a clash of economic power to be satisfactory. First, Taylor stated that any agreement reached was by definition acceptable to the parties, otherwise agreement would not have been reached. Taylor wrote that "the results of a work stoppage are not necessarily fair and equitable by some objective standards. Nor is it required that the acceptance of terms by each party be enthusiastic. But the terms must be mutually preferable to a continuance of the work stoppage and the costs of idleness." Second, Taylor held that, over time, a more reasoned style of industrial rule making would evolve out of this system of strife. He described the optimal style of collective bargaining as follows:

The real test of collective bargaining lies in the ability and willingness of union and management representatives in the great majority of cases, to reconcile their differences through peaceful negotiations. Mutual acceptability of the terms of employment has to be arrived at principally by analysis of the facts, persuasion, modification of extreme positions by one or both parties, compromise, and agreement.[19]

Another view of collective bargaining and its functioning that differed from Wallen's was that expressed by George Brooks, an authority on the American labor movement and a critic of arbitration, who stated approvingly that "the principal function of collective bargaining is to produce a consensus among wage earners and supervisors about the conditions under which they are going to work" and that "while collective bargaining may not produce the most 'just' system, or the one freest of 'inequities,' it will almost certainly produce the arrangement which has the maximum amount of consent."[20] Wallen might have conceded that in practice maximum consent might be the practical result of bargaining and economic warfare, but he did not approve of this end in itself if the basic rights of those in the minority or in an economically weak position were ignored in the process of reaching a consensus.

Wallen was concerned about the shortcomings of the internal communications processes of unions and managements that prevented the aspirations, complaints, and rights of individuals from receiving proper consideration,[21] and was even more concerned about the shortcomings of collective bargaining where economic power was the primary determinant of the bases for agreement. Wallen once stated,

These are moral as well as practical reasons for the imposition of self-limitations on the use of economic force in the settlement of labor disputes. Very often strikes and lockouts bring about settlement of issues in dispute on the basis, not of justice, but of the relative strength of the contesting parties.

If it is conceded that the interests of our society are best served by the finding of just solutions to our economic problems, rather than solutions based primarily upon the superior strength of one of the contestants, then it must also be conceded that the picket line or the lockout are not always the best means of securing justice. A way must be found to insure that the answer to a particular problem is not based primarily on the brawn of the contestants.[22]

This concept of collective bargaining does much to explain the activist role that Wallen advocated for mediators in situations in which one party in bargaining was much weaker economically than the other.

Wallen held this view not only in connection with collective bargaining over contract terms (interest disputes) but also with bargaining over grievances under a contract.

Managements and unions are composed of human beings, subject like all of us to opposing pressures from the desire to be fair and the desire to protect or advance one's self; and from all those urges that produce conflict between justice and self-interest. The company executive caught between a cost-conscious top management and a costly though reasonable grievance of the men frequently, but not always, rules on the side of justice. The union leader caught between a militant rank and file clamoring for results and an inner knowledge that their position is unfair frequently, but not always, has the courage to tell his own people the truth.[23]

One should not infer from these reservations about the practical results of collective bargaining that Wallen condemned the process. He recognized that some form of collective bargaining was necessary for a representative form of industrial self-government and for the achievement of justice. He had no illusions that the arbitrator could in some way replace collective bargaining as the primary guarantor of the individual rights of workers and management: "The agreement is the basic law of the plant—

but it was legislated by labor and management themselves through collective bargaining and not by a third party. The agreement is the touchstone from whence the arbitrator's decision springs."[24]

Since grievance arbitration is a totally voluntary process, he realized that it would not exist unless there was some sort of two-party conflict to be arbitrated. He also recognized that the absence of collective bargaining would deny people their individual rights in many industrial enterprises. Without bargaining in these places, the power of management would be completely unfettered and the rights of employees completely unprotected. As a result, Wallen accepted collective bargaining, realizing its shortcomings, and set as the goal for himself as an arbitrator the transformation and stabilization of collective bargaining from a process based on economic power to one based primarily on reason. Wallen frequently termed this goal the promotion of stability in industrial relations.[25]

He advanced this goal in many ways. First, although he detested the loss of productivity and frequent inequity of economic warfare waged in reaching agreement over contract terms, he advocated the granting of a large measure of respect for the resulting agreement, and did not advocate the compulsory replacement of economic warfare with any other system that might be less costly and more just. He recognized that through such warfare, or the likelihood of it, the "union is reinvigorated; its solidarity is enhanced."[26] In disputes over the basic contract, this restorative quality added more to protecting the rights of all in the long run than that which was subtracted by the presence of unreasoned self-interest. Wallen did not hold the same belief about economic warfare during the life of an agreement, however. Here, he termed economic conflict improper and unnecessary.[27] In this case, he considered arbitration not only desirable but necessary. On one occasion he said that grievance arbitration "is as necessary for peaceful relations between worker and manager as courts of law are for the maintenance of peaceful relations between citizen and citizen."[28] Along these same lines much later in his career, he termed the concept of totally voluntary, judicially unenforced arbitration of grievances as impractical.[29]

Why was Wallen so firm about the need for grievance arbitration? He alluded to two important reasons in his writings. The first was that, unlike contract negotiations, the lack of reasoned consideration of basic individual rights would outweigh any additional salutary effect that economic warfare might have. Second, he believed that grievances often were primarily a reargument of issues already settled in negotiations rather than an exploration of new issues. A settlement of these issues by economic warfare would destabilize the entire industrial relations system, insuring one party's rights only so long as the party had the economic muscle to back them up. Even where the issue in question was undeniably a new matter not previously discussed, Wallen believed that the grievance procedure allowed sufficient opportunity for bargaining. In the interest of stability, should bargaining fail, a determination by the arbitrator would be better than economic warfare.[30]

Wallen saw grievance arbitration as a process by which the parties were assured of continued production and income and one's just rights already gained through bargaining for a fixed period of time (the life of the agreement). Grievance arbitration was a means of increasing participation in collective bargaining and faith in the process. Through the promotion of reason in bargaining, justice and productivity would be ensured in the long run.

An essential ingredient in a system of representative industrial government was an effective communication system in management and the union. This was especially important in the latter case to ensure that minority viewpoints were heard and adequately represented. He saw this as an especially relevant problem where the minority involved was not just a political minority in the union, or the workers of one shop or on one shift, but a racial minority.[31] The long-run preservation of the union as a stable, self-governed organization and as an institution willing to rely upon arbitration rather than economic force in the settlement of grievances placed certain limitations, however, on the role that arbitration could play in assuring an individual's rights within the union. In such situations, as an arbitrator, Wallen would face a clear-cut conflict between his goals of stability of institutions on the one hand and justice for the individual on the other.

Along with others, the following issues were closely connected with the question of stability for Wallen: reasonably clear contract language (especially in those cases where the language was inequitable), arbitral case precedent, treatment of wildcat strikers, and the rights and duties of the union as the workers' representative. These issues are explored in ensuing chapters. Of particular interest are those situations in which the question of stable relations in the long run comes into conflict with immediate considerations of individual justice or productive efficiency. Wallen once voiced the following view of arbitration, hinting at the problem of achieving a balance among these considerations in a particular case:

Labor arbitration is more than the interpretation of contracts. It involves their interpretation in the context of an on-going relationship in which the rights and the wrongs are weighed against the parties' needs and aspirations which may transcend the immediate cause. It requires of the decider a sensitivity to the parties' whole relationship precedent and antecedent to the case at hand. This is not to say that such considerations dominate arbitral decisions. It is to say only that they may temper them in cases where other factors are in balance.[32]

While Wallen's goals of individual justice, production efficiency, and industrial relations stability are examined in this study when they come into conflict with one another in specific arbitration cases, the reader should not assume that Wallen thought that these goals were antagonistic to one another in the long run. On the contrary, Wallen regarded them as reinforcing one another over time — stability ensuring reasoned consideration of matters of justice and efficiency, as well as providing for continued production;[33] individual satisfaction from fair treatment and increasing economic well-being ensuring the stability of the system;[34] and fairness and justice leading to increased efficiency.[35]

Many of these opinions were not new, nor was Wallen the only one in the field to hold them. A brief survey of the writing of other arbitrators reveals a concern with these same goals to varying degrees, as well as a concern with others. Arbitrators Willard Wirtz, Ralph Seward, and Robben Fleming have written at length about the necessity for the development of due process in grievance handling as a matter of elementary justice, not only at the arbitration hearing stage of the grievance procedure but also during in-plant discussions of the grievance.[36] Arbitrator Harry Platt called for a standard of justice in the decision-making process, stating that "perhaps the best that an impartial arbitrator can do is to decide what reasonable men, mindful of the habits and customs of industrial life and of the standards of justice and fair dealing prevalent in the community, ought to have done under similar circumstances."[37]

One student of arbitration, Joseph E. Finley, has said that justice is not only a relevant goal, but the primary goal of arbitration, pointing out that "the real test of the inherent value of labor arbitration, it would seem, is in whether or not it affords a result that comports with the demands of justice."[38]

Others have spoken of the need for encouraging productivity, efficiency, and economic growth. Gross found an interest in efficiency to be the guiding force in numerous cases involving subcontracting and work transfer.[39] Harry Shulman, referred to as the dean of arbitrators, noted that "the effects of efficiency, productivity, and cost are important factors to be considered" in decision making.[40]

Arbitrators Harold Davey, Frederic Meyers, and Harry Shulman also considered the goal of stability through the encouragement of reasoned, bilateral rule making.[41]

Some of those involved in arbitration have been less ready to judge what is good for the parties or for the process itself. William Simkin stated that "there are few subject matters in grievance arbitration in which anyone can afford to be very dogmatic in distinguishing the good from the not good." He believed that an arrangement which Wallen would have termed stable would evolve in any collective bargaining relationship without the help of arbitral interference and would contain the proper amount of concern for productivity or justice according to the parties' standards.[42] George Brooks has been even more adamant in his condemnation of such arbitral interference with collective bargaining, declaring that whenever "arbitrators insidiously insert the notions of justice, equity, and fairness," they are doing more harm to the long-term vitality of the process than they are gaining any immediate benefit.[43]

There can be a wide disparity between what arbitrators say are desirable or beneficial goals for the arbitral process and what they are willing to do to further these goals through their decision making. The real test comes in incorporating these values in the logic they use in reaching their decisions. Undoubtedly, arbitrators as a group, just as any other group of individuals, possess widely varying degrees of courage. Any such disparity, if it exists, can only be discovered through a case-by-case analysis of a particular arbitrator's decisions in a large variety of circumstances.

The following chapters of this study are just such an attempt to discern to what degree one man, Saul Wallen, had the courage of his convictions and based his decision making on an interest in justice, efficiency, and stability. Were these his primary goals as revealed in his decisions, were his decisions at least consistent with, if not specifically based upon, these values, or was he willing to ignore his own values and somehow, in a totally disinterested manner, rely solely on the intent of the parties' agreements?

Chapters III through VI provide a detailed analysis of his decisions. Chapter III demonstrates the influence of his principles on his treatment of the issue of arbitrability — the decision to hear and decide a case. Chapter IV shows the effect of his values on decision-making criteria, that is, the importance he ascribed to the various types of evidence in support of the parties' intent versus the importance he gave his own concepts and values. Chapters V and VI analyze basic extra-contractual rights and obligations that Wallen accorded to management, unions, employees, and the public where these rights and obligations were (a) not mentioned in the labor agreement or in any supporting evidence of the agreement's intent or (b) specifically abrogated by the agreement. The extent to which Wallen sought to force or persuade the parties to accept his solutions to specific cases, either through advice and explanation or more directly through the use of his arbitral remedy powers, is explored in Chapter VII.

Although this is not a comparative study of arbitrators, Chapters III through VII also indicate where Wallen stood in comparison to his contemporaries. This is done by examining whether the majority of arbitrators reached conclusions and solutions much like Wallen's when dealing with similar topics. The question of whether their decisions were based on value judgments similar to those of Wallen's or on dissimilar ones or whether they relied strictly on evidence of the agreement's intent is also examined. The purpose here is not to draw conclusions about arbitrators in general, but rather to see where Wallen stood relative to the rest of the arbitration community and to assess the importance of particular values to Wallen. In those cases where Wallen was ahead of his times or in a distinct arbitral minority, it can be argued that he was taking at least some risk with respect to his future acceptability as an arbitrator. To have accepted such risks, he must have held those values rather strongly.

The final chapter, Chapter VIII, discusses those conclusions that can be drawn concerning the reliance on personal principles and experience in arbitral decision making, both in terms of Saul Wallen in particular and of arbitration in general. Areas for additional study are also outlined.

Notes

1. Wallen's personal files are located in the Documentation Center. Unless noted otherwise, arbitration awards cited are from these files. See also Byron Yaffe (ed.), *The Saul Wallen Papers: A Neutral's Contribution to Industrial Peace* (Ithaca: New York State School of Industrial and Labor Relations, Cornell University, 1974).

2. In general, biographical data presented in this chapter were obtained in a December 6–7, 1973 interview with Mrs. Mary Wallen, the widow of Saul Wallen. This information was supplemented and verified through correspondence with the Office of the Registrar, New York University, and the National Personnel Records Center, General Services Administration, as well as through a check of Wallen's personal records and various newspaper reports.

3. A count of his files reveals records of 4,717 separate arbitration hearings. At many hearings, however, especially those involving the leather working industry, Wallen heard and decided two or more separate and unrelated grievances at one sitting, delivering separate opinions and awards for each grievance, but then filing the entire record of the proceeding in one folder. It is estimated that this would increase the actual number of cases heard and decided upon by at least 30 percent. This increase would yield a figure of approximately 6,200 decisions. This estimate appears conservative in light of a report in *The New York Times* on May 4, 1962 (p. 18, col. 5) that at that time he had decided over 5,000 cases. This was more than seven years before the end of his career.

4. Saul Wallen, "A Formula For New England Prosperity," *Toward Better Labor-Management Relations in New England, New England Council 80th Quarterly Meeting, September 14, 1945* (Boston: New England Council, 1945), p. 14; Saul Wallen, untitled speech, 1945, personal files, pp. 3–4.

5. Saul Wallen, "Arbitrators and Judges—Dispelling the Hays' Haze," *Southwestern Legal Foundation Labor Law Developments, Proceedings of the 12th Annual Institute on Labor Law* (Washington, D.C.: BNA, 1966), p. 160.

6. Ibid.

7. Ibid., p. 161.

8. Saul Wallen, "The Arbitration of Work Assignment Disputes," *Industrial Labor Relations Review* 16 (1963): 193.

9. Saul Wallen, "Decision of Fact Finder — Lowell School Committee and Lowell Teachers Organization," May 19, 1967, 48 LA 1044 at 1049.

10. Id.

11. Saul Wallen, "The Role of the Mediator in the Collective Bargaining Process," speech delivered to the Air Line Pilots Association Negotiating Committee Seminar, Chicago, Illinois, December 13, 1967, personal files, p. 4.

12. Kurt Braun, *Labor Disputes and Their Settlement* (Baltimore: The Johns Hopkins Press, 1955), p. 53; John T. Dunlop and Neil W. Chamberlain, *Frontiers of Collective Bargaining* (New York: Harper and Row, 1967), pp. 281–82; Arthur S. Meyer, "Function of the Mediator in Collective Bargaining," *Industrial and Labor Relations Review* 13 (1960): 165; William E. Simkin, *Mediation and the Dynamics of Collective Bargaining* (Washington, D.C.: BNA, 1971), pp. 36 and 39.

13. James Gross, "Value Judgements in the Decisions of Labor Arbitrators," p. 70.

14. Aluminum Co. of Am., Warrick Works and Aluminum Workers Int'l Union, Local 104, December 18, 1963, p. 8. See also Trailways of New England and Div. 1318, Amalgamated Transit Union, AFL-CIO, December 22, 1965, p. 10.

15. Wallen, "A Formula for New England Prosperity," pp. 14 and 16.

16. Saul Wallen, "How Issues of Subcontracting and Plant Removal Are Handled by Arbitrators," *Industrial and Labor Relations Review* 19 (1966): 266.

17. Saul Wallen, "Recent Supreme Court Decisions on Arbitration: An Arbitrator's View," *West Virginia Law Review* 63 (1961): 306.

18. Saul Wallen, "The Place of Arbitration in Labor Disputes," a speech delivered to the Institute of Industrial Relations, University of Minnesota, November 29, 1945, personal files, p. 6.

19. George W. Taylor, "The Voluntary Arbitration of Labor Disputes," *Michigan Law Review* 49 (1951): 790.

20. George W. Brooks, *The Sources of Vitality in the American Labor Movement* (Ithaca: New York State School of Industrial and Labor Relations, Cornell University, 1960), Bulletin No. 41, p. 35.

21. Saul Wallen, "Lessons from Arbitration in Dealing with Minority Problems," a paper presented to the Collective Bargaining Forum, New York City, May 12, 1960, personal files, p. 10.

22. Wallen, "A Formula for New England Prosperity," p. 14.

23. Wallen, untitled speech, 1945, p. 3.

24. Ibid., p. 6.

25. Ibid.

26. Wallen, "The Place of Arbitration in Labor Disputes," p. 5.

27. Wallen, "A Formula for New England Prosperity," p. 15.

28. Wallen, "The Place of Arbitration in Labor Disputes," p. 3.

29. Wallen, "Arbitrators and Judges — Dispelling the Hays' Haze," p. 171.

30. Wallen, "Recent Supreme Court Decisions on Arbitration," p. 296.

31. Wallen, "Lessons from Arbitration in Dealing with Minority Problems," p. 10.

32. Saul Wallen, Book Review of Paul R. Hays, *Labor Arbitration: A Dissenting View,* in *Harvard Law Review* 81 (1967): 510.

33. Wallen, "A Formula for New England Prosperity," pp. 14–16; Borden Chem. Co. and Int'l Chem. Workers Union, Local No. 553, December 9, 1959, p. 8.

34. Wallen, "Lessons from Arbitration in Dealing with Minority Problems," p. 9; Wallen, untitled speech, 1945, p. 4.

35. Wallen, "Decision of Fact Finder — Lowell School Committee and Lowell Teachers Organization," p. 1049.

36. W. Willard Wirtz, "Due Process of Arbitration." In Jean T. McKelvey (ed.), *The Arbitrator and the Parties* (Washington, D.C.: BNA, 1958); Ralph Seward, "Arbitration in the World Today." In Jean T. McKelvey (ed.), *Labor Arbitration* (Washington, D.C.: BNA, 1957); Robben W. Fleming, "Due Process and Fair Procedure in Labor Arbitration." In Spencer D. Pollard (ed.), *Arbitration and Public Policy* (Washington, D.C.: BNA, 1961).

37. Harry H. Platt, "The Arbitration Process in the Settlement of Labor Disputes," *Journal of the American Judicature Society* 31 (1947): 57.

38. Joseph E. Finley, "Labor Arbitration: The Quest for Industrial Justice," *Western Reserve Law Review* 18 (1967): 1098.

39. Gross, "Value Judgements in the Decisions of Labor Arbitrators," pp. 60–62, 65–67, and 70.

40. Harry Shulman, "Reason, Contract, and Law in Labor Relations," *Harvard Law Review* 68 (1955): 1018.

41. Harold W. Davey, "The Arbitrator Views the Agreement," *Labor Law Journal* 12 (1961): 1167; Frederic Meyers, "The Task of the Labor Arbitrator," *Personnel Journal* 22 (1959): 26; Shulman, "Reason, Contract, and Law in Labor Relations," pp. 1016–17, 1019, and 1021.

42. William E. Simkin, *Acceptability as a Factor in Arbitration under an Existing Agreement* (Philadelphia: University of Pennsylvania Press, 1952), pp. 42, 43, and 66–67.

43. Brooks, p. 27.

Chapter III

Arbitrability

Challenges to the arbitrator's power to decide a case can arise where it is asserted either that the subject matter of the grievance is outside the scope of issues that the parties had previously agreed to arbitrate or that the grievance was not processed in accord with the time limits or other procedural requirements of the agreement. The manner in which Wallen treated this problem and the degree to which his approach was predicated on personal values are explored here. Did he construe his powers narrowly, asserting them only where the parties' labor agreement specifically granted jurisdiction to him; did he believe he had broader powers, declining to decide a case only where the agreement clearly denied him the right; or did he choose a middle-of-the-road approach? What was his rationale or justification in doing so and to what degree did he attempt to further those goals toward which he thought the arbitration process should strive?

Jules J. Justin has defined arbitrability as follows:

By arbitrability, I simply mean: Did the parties agree to make the arbitration process available for a particular dispute under their arbitration clause? That is, is a particular grievance or dispute that arises during the contract term subject to the arbitration system that the parties set up under their contract? As one court aptly put it, arbitrability seeks to answer the question: "Is the subject matter (of the grievance or dispute) comprised within the agreement to arbitrate made by the parties?"[1]

The issue of whether the decision to arbitrate should properly be determined by the arbitrator or by a court of law has been argued for years.[2] The question can be raised in either the arbitration or law forum. While many arbitrators believed that this question should be determined only by the arbitrator, Wallen felt the decision did not fall within the sole province of the arbitrator. He believed that the arbitrator should decide this issue only if specifically empowered to do so by the parties. He approved of court rather than arbitral determination of arbitrability, but also agreed with Trilogy limitations on such court determinations, requiring a granting of arbitrability where doubt existed rather than allowing an examination by the courts of the merits of the specific case.[3]

Some authorities have divided the question of arbitrability into two issues, the question of arbitrators' jurisdiction and the question of their authority. The issue of jurisdiction involves those subjects over which the parties have agreed to empower the arbitrator to decide. This is to be contrasted with the authority afforded the arbitrator under the agreement to award affirmative remedies to rectify contract violations. For example, assume that employees terminated because of a plant shutdown claimed that their terminations violated rights due them under the contract's layoff clauses. Assume also that, since reinstatement could not be the remedy where the plant no longer existed, the employees demanded severance pay as appropriate compensation. This hypothetical case poses two questions: first, does the arbitrator have jurisdiction to determine if the layoff clause of the contract was violated, and second, if the arbitrator does find a violation, has he or she the authority to award severance pay as requested? The wording of the specific arbitration clause, as well as the inclusion or exclusion of specific contract clauses dealing with layoffs and severance pay, would have much to bear on the determination of the arbitrator's jurisdiction and authority. The above example, incidentally, was a case decided by Saul Wallen. He found that the issue was within his jurisdiction to determine, but that he lacked the authority to award the remedy requested.[4]

Some authorities have found the distinction between jurisdiction and authority to be unrealistic or else too difficult to distinguish from one another since these issues are frequently intertwined, as are the merits of the particular case in question.[5] In part, this confusion exists because any determination by arbitrators of their jurisdiction necessarily determines also to some extent their authority. One writer has stated, "The arbitrator's authority—even when narrowly limited, as is indeed the case under the standard clause—can never intelligently be construed as involving less power than that needed to preserve the guarantees of the basic document."[6]

This power is nothing more nor less than the authority to award an appropriate remedy for contractual violations. The asserting of jurisdiction by the arbitrator is also the assertion of some type of authority. While the determination of appropriate jurisdiction over, say, a discharge case might automatically carry with it the authority to remedy a violation with reinstatement and backpay, it would not automatically carry with it the authority to award cash damages of a million dollars. If such damages were the remedy requested by the grievant, the arbitrator would, in all likelihood, under the typical labor agreement find that he or she had jurisdiction to hear the grievance but lacked authority to grant the remedy requested. There is a clear theoretical difference between the issues of arbitral jurisdiction and authority: the difficulty lies in the factual separation of these two issues in an actual case.

The issue of arbitral authority is dealt with in depth in Chapter VII, which covers Wallen's views on the remedy process and powers. In this chapter, only Wallen's views and treatment of the problems of jurisdiction are analyzed.

SUBSTANTIVE ARBITRABILITY

The first major problem of jurisdiction is the question of arbitrability of substantive issues, that is, whether the subject matter of the grievance is arbitrable. This is distinguished from the arbitrability of procedural issues—the question of whether a grievance was filed on time or was filed by the appropriate person. Wallen's general criteria for determining substantive arbitrability will be discussed in order of complexity.

Unless otherwise noted, the contracts in the cases mentioned here all contain the prevalent standard or narrow arbitration clause, typically limiting the arbitrator's jurisdiction to "any disputes involving the interpretation or application of any provision of this agreement."[7] The question of jurisdiction for all practical purposes does not arise under the less common broad arbitration clause allowing arbitration of "any dispute, difference, disagreement, or controversy of any nature or character" arising between the parties during the life of the agreement, although some interesting issues of arbitral authority can arise under this type of clause.[8]

The simplest, most basic rule that Wallen followed throughout his career was to respect clear contractual exclusions from arbitration, regardless of the possible effects of such exclusions on considerations of justice, productivity, or the stability of the parties' relationship. For example, Wallen in 1946 did not dispute an expressed limitation on his jurisdiction only to examine if an employee was disciplined for cause and not to examine whether the penalty administered was appropriate in relation to the offense committed.[9] Other typical examples included a refusal to review the discharge of probationary employees in a 1948 case,[10] refusals to review the propriety of management's actions in combining jobs and subcontracting in two 1961 cases,[11] and denial of review of the appropriateness of penalties for wildcat strikers in a 1963 case.[12] In each of these instances, clear contract language prohibited arbitral review and Wallen refused to violate these prohibitions.

It can be argued that in such clear-cut situations, he had virtually no other choice. While the determination of whether an issue was expressly or clearly excluded from the agreement to arbitrate involved some degree of subjective judgment, Wallen considered this issue much easier to resolve in cases where the contract limited the no-strike clause only to those items found arbitrable, thus clarifying the handling of the issues found nonarbitrable. In these cases, Wallen was willing to exclude from arbitration problems that he normally found arbitrable, such as subcontracting, where the contract was totally silent about the matter.[13]

Similarly, if the written submission agreement was narrowly framed, delimiting Wallen's jurisdiction to an examination of the violation of only one or a few particular clauses, Wallen claimed that he would respect this limitation on his jurisdiction, even though the particular clauses might miss the point and other relevant contract language might be thus ignored. While Wallen argued that the arbitrator might forestall this occurrence by taking an activist role in the framing of the submission, he stated that he would respect any signed submission, even if it was manifestly incorrect.[14] An examination of Wallen's decisions reveals no cases in which he clearly violated a signed submission, although it is apparent from the dicta of several that he believed his arbitration under these circumstances was almost an exercise in futility, neither solving the true problem at hand nor granting a measure of justice or equity.[15]

Wallen's second rule of jurisdictional arbitrability was to hold an issue arbitrable if the grievant asserted, and could make a reasonable case, that a specific contract clause or right was either violated or nullified, or that an oral modification of the agreement existed and was similarly violated or nullified. Wallen, as previously noted, supported the Supreme Court's viewpoint in the Trilogy decisions that the courts essentially should accept as valid any claim to arbitrability based on the alleged violation of a specific contract clause, even if the claim was patently frivolous. Wallen also approved of the court's over-ruling in these cases of the so-called *Cutler-Hammer* bona fide dispute doctrine, discussed in Chapter I, which required that the court determining arbitrability be convinced that the contract language in dispute was in fact subject to more than one interpretation.[16] This type of examination by the courts frequently involved an examination of the actual merits of the case and a decision on the merits by the court.

Wallen, however, did not believe that the method used by the courts in determining arbitrability should necessarily be the one employed by the arbitrator in making a similar determination. The arbitrator should attempt to dispel doubts about arbitrability by a deeper examination of the merits, rather than by simply finding the issue to be arbitrable if a violation of a specific clause was asserted. In those cases where arbitrability was not the sole issue, but the case was to be decided on its merits if found arbitrable, Wallen preferred to reserve judgment on arbitrability until after the entire case was heard, unless he was immediately convinced of its absolute nonarbitrability.[17] Before holding a case arbitrable, Wallen applied a standard not dissimilar to that used by the court in *Cutler-Hammer*, at least to the extent that a mere allegation that a specific clause was violated was insufficient to guarantee a ruling that the dispute was arbitrable. Throughout his career, both before and after the Trilogy decisions, Wallen required that a reasonable argument be made that the action grieved in some way violated or nullified a specific contractual right or that there existed a "substantial question of contract interpretation"[18] in order for the dispute to be ruled arbitrable.

In at least one case, Wallen denied arbitrability on the grounds that "because of the crystal clarity of [the article in question], no dispute can exist as to its meaning in relation to the facts of the claims here presented and no arbitrable controversy is therefore involved." This particular case involved a very explicit contract clause which required that employees had to work at least one shift during a week on which a holiday fell to be eligible for holiday pay. The grievant was ill the entire week containing the holiday and claimed that the denial of holiday pay to him was unfair, a claim that Wallen said presented no arbitrable controversy over the terms of the agreement.[19]

In the vast majority of cases that reached Wallen for his decision, however, there did exist disputes over interpretation sufficient to merit arbitration, and arbitrability was granted in nearly all cases alleging violation of, or dispute over, specific contract language.[20] In one such case, a female employee grieved that a foreman had sworn at her for loitering, even though he had issued no formal disciplinary reprimand. Management claimed that no arbitrable controversy existed because no formal disciplinary action was taken. Wallen held that such actions by foremen had "disciplinary connotations," even if no record of the incident was entered into the employee's personnel file, since the matter would probably be cited by management in the event of any future misconduct by the employee. As a result, Wallen declared that the dispute was arbitrable.[21]

If, after an in-depth examination of the issue, Wallen still entertained doubts over arbitrability, he then resolved them in favor of granting arbitration or asserting jurisdiction. In such situations involving post-Trilogy cases, namely, those after 1960, Wallen occasionally made reference to the Supreme Court's doctrine supporting the resolution of doubts in favor of arbitrability, but he did so only after he had made a considerable effort to resolve those doubts through consideration of the evidence and merits of the case.[22] Wallen went through the same process in pre-Trilogy cases as well and resolved doubts in favor of arbitrability. Although Wallen used the court's dicta occasionally after the Trilogy decisions to support his philosophy concerning arbitrability, this dicta does not appear in any way to be the basis for his philosophy. Even in the post-Trilogy years, he declined to find patently frivolous grievances to be arbitrable,[23] even though the Supreme Court directed the lower courts to declare them such.

Where an aggrieved party alleged the existence of an oral agreement or mutually accepted past practice that either modified or added to the written agreement, Wallen, as a rule, found the dispute arbitrable.[24] Only where the arbitration clause specifically limited the arbitrator's jurisdiction to the written agreement did Wallen consistently deny the arbitrability of the claims.[25] Such action is consistent with his first rule of arbitrability, that of honoring specific exclusions. Under such circumstances, however, a claim of a controlling past practice related to contract provisions or illuminating ambiguous language could still be held an arbitrable subject.[26]

Wallen's third rule of arbitrability, his most complex and controversial, was to assert jurisdiction in some situations if an aggrieved party claimed that some action violated the entire contract, the contract's basic underlying purposes, or the intent that the parties had when drafting the agreement, even though the aggrieved party could point to no specific contractual language that was violated by the action in dispute. Wallen's philosophy in this area is best understood by an examination of several cases he decided in which the issue was whether to assert jurisdiction under these circumstances.

In 1948, Wallen was asked to rule on the arbitrability of discharges under a contract that did not explicitly require that management discharge employees only for cause. In this case, a narrow arbitration clause allowed arbitration only "in the event no agreement is reached in any matter involving the application or interpretation of any provision of this contract." The company argued that no provision specifically mentioned the requirement of discharge for cause and hence no arbitrable dispute existed. It also cited a former arbitration award under the contract in which the arbitrator ruled against the arbitrability of discharges. The union argued that the wording in an article titled "Procedures on Disputes," listing the pre-arbitration grievance steps, contemplated or at least implied the requirement of discharge only for cause. Wallen, admitting uncertainty as to whether the clause on procedures could be read to mean discharge only for cause, found for the union on the basis of two factors.

First, although the requirement of discharge for cause was not stated clearly or even implied clearly — and in fact the title of the clause in question pointed otherwise—he found that it would "hardly be consistent with justice" to deny the logic of contemplating the requirement of just cause for discharge, inasmuch as such a denial would also tend to reduce the effect of the arbitration clause. Second, while "the parties were, of course, free to contract that discharges would not be subject to arbitration except if both agreed in each case," to do so would require a positive, clear disclaimer. Silence on the issue should be considered to be intended as assent to the "commonly prevailing practice" in industry of recognizing the "propriety and essential justice" of subjecting discharges to arbitral review. Wallen noted that no evidence was introduced at the hearing of any agreement on the nonarbitrability of discharges, although the limited arbitration clause would seem to require that the burden of evidence be placed on those asserting the arbitrability of the issue.[27]

In 1949, Wallen found for the arbitrability of discharges in an even more controversial case involving the Coca-Cola Bottling Company of Boston. The contract contained provisions stating that arbitration should be the final method of determination of "any dispute as to the meaning of this agreement," that "except as there is contained in this agreement an express provision limiting the discretion of the Company, nothing herein contained shall be deemed to limit the Company in the exercise of the rights, functions, and privileges of management," and that "this contract contains the entire agreement between the parties and disposes of all issues open between the parties."[28] There was no mention in the agreement of a requirement of just cause for discharge, nor was such a clause discussed in contract negotiations.

Wallen determined that the dispute was arbitrable, again basing his reasoning on two points. The first was that if there was no requirement of just cause for discharge, several contract provisions could be reduced to a nullity, in particular the layoff and recall provisions and the provision calling for the adjustment of grievances. The union did not claim, however, nor was any evidence presented, that the company had used its discharge powers to defeat any of these contract provisions. This danger was potential, not actual. Wallen's second and primary reason was much more far reaching. He stated that the collective bargaining agreement was "an instrument one of whose basic purposes is job security," and said furthermore that

In our opinion, the meaning of the contract, when viewed as a whole, is that a limitation on the employer's right to discharge was created with the birth of the instrument. Both the necessity for maintaining the integrity of the contract's component parts and the very nature of collective bargaining agreements are the basis for this conclusion. Inasmuch as this limitation is an implied term of the contract, discharges are subject to the grievance procedure and arbitration.[29]

He also said that the denial of arbitrability of discharges could be upheld only if the contract specifically contained such an exclusion, and that the provision stating that "this contract contains the entire agreement between the parties" did not accomplish this purpose.

Later, Wallen encountered a similar situation. In a 1967 case, the company contested the union's claim that discipline short of discharge was reviewable by arbitration. The contract required that discharges not related to "an express provision" of the agreement were not arbitrable, and while the contract required that discharge be for cause, it mentioned nothing about discipline short of discharge. Wallen stated that

The proposition that the company may discharge only for just cause but may discipline by suspension for other than just cause runs counter to logic. Parties are free to make illogical bargains. But if they choose to make a bargain that flies in the face of logic and runs counter to universal custom and practice, it must be so clearly expressed as to evidence that intent unmistakably and unequivocally.[30]

He also wrote that common sense and equity require the submission of such discipline to arbitral review. Wallen related his reasoning to the contract by also finding that a disciplinary suspension could be construed as a layoff, for which there was contractual language requiring "lack of work or other legitimate reason."[31]

Wallen was willing to claim a broad grant of jurisdiction in cases involving the integrity of the bargaining unit as well as those involving individual job security. For example, under restrictive arbitration clauses, he found for the arbitrability of disputes over subcontracting where the contract did not mention the issue, again basing his reasoning on the existence of inherent rights created with the birth of the contract. Two cases are particularly revealing of his philosophy, inasmuch as, unlike the above discharge cases, the issue of some limitation on subcontracting had arisen during contract negotiations and was rejected by management. In a 1959 case, the contract permitted arbitration of grievances "if and to the extent, and only if and to the extent, that the same relates to the interpretation of any provision of this agreement," and also contained language stating that "this agreement contains and constitutes the entire agreement between the parties hereto." The contract further stipulated that "no arbitrator or arbitrators shall have the right to disregard any of the provisions hereof or to consider as binding upon either party any terms or provisions not expressed either in this Agreement or in a formal supplement hereto signed by the parties hereto."[32]

The union claimed, first, that there existed an oral supplement to the agreement limiting subcontracting, a contention that Wallen ruled

against, and, second, that the contracting out of work violated an obligation implied in the agreement, but not stated in it. It was agreed by the
parties that the union had introduced a clause in negotiations to ban
subcontracting only when employees were either on layoff or would be
laid off as a result of the subcontracting, but this partial limitation was
rejected by management and the matter dropped by the union. The
company had subcontracted work in the past without protest from the
union, although the extent of this subcontracting was unclear.[33] Wallen
ruled that subcontracting could undermine the purpose of the entire
agreement, as well as render meaningless the seniority and recognition
clauses, as well as others. On the basis of this possibility, he declared the
dispute arbitrable and proceeded to the merits.

As with the discharge cases, the contract's arbitration clause would seem
to indicate that evidence of such damage be shown *before* the dispute
could be declared arbitrable. In deciding on the merits of the case, one of
the touchstones or principles that Wallen relied on in his finding for
management was that no personnel would be laid off because of the
subcontracting, the precise limitation that was denied in negotiations.[34]

Wallen's criteria for deciding issues of subcontracting are explored later
in this book; the matter is mentioned here simply to demonstrate that the
granting of arbitrability in this case on the basis of potential and not actual
nullification of some contract provision enabled Wallen to impose his own
notion of the importance of job security and basic bargaining unit integrity on the parties. This clearly was not the notion implied in the agreement and in fact was precisely the concept that was denied inclusion in the
agreement. Had Wallen insisted on evidence supporting the contention
that the subcontracting in question was violative of or threatening to any
contract provision, he would have had a much more difficult time justifying his assertion of jurisdiction.

In a 1961 case, similar narrow constraints limited the arbitrator's jurisdiction to written provisions, and a ban on subcontracting was sought in
negotiations by the union, denied by management, and dropped. Wallen
outlined the reasons that led him to declare the dispute arbitrable and
assert jurisdiction:

Under a contract silent on the point management unquestionably retains a wide
latitude in the matter. But even in such a case its powers are not unlimited. If it
engages in contracting out in such a scale so massive as to jeopardize the very
existence of the Agreement; or if it contracts out solely for the purpose of evading
the very wage, seniority or other provisions it contracted to observe, it may engage
in a violation of the Agreement *as a whole* without specific reference to any of its
parts. In short, an agreement silent on the subject implies, at most, a right to
contract out work reasonably and without intent to evade contractual obligations.
An allegation not patently frivolous that a particular case of contracting out
exceeds these limits is arbitrable and deserves scrutiny of the merits.[35]

Once again, Wallen declared the dispute arbitrable on the basis of possible contingencies and then explored these contingencies when ruling on the merits, rather than hearing them as evidence of the arbitrability of the dispute. The standard he required to gain arbitrability in serious matters involving individual job ownership, bargaining unit integrity, and the existence and stability of the entire agreement was much less demanding than the standard of a reasonable argument that Wallen required to gain arbitrability for the violation of specific, less serious contract clauses. The standard used for these more serious cases was nowhere stated in an agreement. In fact, the cases presented here involving job security and unit integrity contain some of the most restrictive arbitration clauses that Wallen faced. This easier standard of gaining arbitrability was based solely on Wallen's own concept of what was important to him and what he believed was important for the parties' well-being.

PROCEDURAL ARBITRABILITY

It is impossible to advance common criteria for the determination of procedural arbitrability, due to the literally thousands of different types of procedural challenges that can arise. The challenges themselves, however, for simplicity's sake, can be categorized into four major types. Challenges arise in cases in which: it is asserted that the grievance has been filed improperly or is untimely; it is asserted that the person pressing the grievance is ineligible to do so; it is asserted that another forum, such as the National Labor Relations Board (NLRB), may have primary jurisdiction; and a firm asserts that it is not obligated to undertake arbitration because it has changed owners, because it has closed down operations, or because the agreement has expired.

In dealing with the first category of cases, Wallen did not automatically deny jurisdiction simply because of a violation of procedures or time limits. For example, one case involved a request for arbitration filed more than 45 days after management's answer at the next lowest grievance step. The contract required that written notice of a request for arbitration be filed within that 45-day period. Wallen upheld the arbitrability of the grievance on the basis of a tradition of looseness in the handling of grievances. While he declared that the company could "pull the pin" and tighten up the grievance handling to match the contract's requirements, it could not do so without first giving the union adequate notice of its intentions.[36]

In another case, Wallen similarly denied a management claim of untimeliness because management had itself violated a time constraint in the handling of the grievance.[37] In a third involving the correctness of procedures used in grievance processing, Wallen found that the union's executive committee and the company had settled the grievance at a lower step, but that the rank and file of the union had voted to reject the settlement. Although Wallen ruled that the executive committee had the power under the contract and the union's constitution to make such a settlement, he granted arbitrability on the merits for special reasons, namely that this was the first grievance to reach this stage of the process in 20 years, and hence the procedures were unfamiliar. He also concluded that the grievance issue was subtle.[38]

Where it was asserted and proven that contractual grievance requirements or steps short of arbitration were not exhausted, Wallen denied arbitrability.[39] Similarly, cases involving the question of whether the contract *would* be violated by some future action were generally denied arbitrability as being premature or hypothetical.[40] In one of these cases, Wallen asserted that arbitration of a future problem should be undertaken "only as a last resort," since the parties were in a better position than the arbitrator to decide the issue and possessed intimate knowledge of the problem that the arbitrator lacked.[41] Wallen's concern that the rule-making process of the parties remain viable is apparent in reading these particular cases.

In another unusual procedural case, Wallen refused to assert jurisdiction in a case involving the meaning of a disputed clause, where it was apparent from the evidence that the parties never had agreed upon the meaning of the clause, and hence there was really no agreement to interpret. Wallen declined jurisdiction and directed that the parties settle the issue themselves because contract negotiations were in progress and he feared that a decision by him at that time could prejudice the on-going negotiations.[42] This was the only case in which Wallen declined jurisdiction for this reason. As a rule, he asserted jurisdiction in this situation and discounted challenges to arbitrability on the grounds that no agreement existed. He once stated that

Such a finding might be appropriate in the case of a commercial contract. But this is a labor agreement with a no-strike provision and an agreed-upon machinery for deciding disputes over the meaning of its terms. In these circumstances it is incumbent on the arbitrator to interpret or construe the disputed clause rather than declare either clause or the whole Agreement nonexistent because the parties differed over its meaning from the moment it came into being.[43]

Wallen recognized that in these situations the threat of economic conflict created "pressure to have some agreement rather than none," that "the parties have a continuing relationship which they thought they stabilized," and that since "they do not relish having to do the job again," he should undertake the task.[44]

The second type of procedural issue on which Wallen had to rule were challenges to arbitrability on the grounds that the grievant was for some reason ineligible to process or pursue the grievance. As a general policy,

Wallen allowed union stewards or officers to file and press a grievance even if they were not aggrieved and the aggrieved person did not wish to pursue the matter. Wallen reasoned that otherwise the rights of other employees and of the union could be endangered. If the contract specifically required that the aggrieved party file or at least sign the grievance, however, Wallen denied arbitrability if these requirements were not met.[45]

In those cases where an employee heatedly resigned over a dispute and later, thinking more clearly, attempted to grieve the issue through arbitration, Wallen generally denied challenges to arbitrability on the grounds that the grievant was not an employee. Wallen stated that a quit required intent, as well as the physical act of saying "I quit" or filling out a resignation form.[46] Where the evidence showed that acts were not ill-considered, but thought-out and intentional, and that the grievants simply changed their minds or tactics later, however, he denied arbitrability.[47]

In another case involving grievance eligibility, Wallen allowed a retired pensioner to pursue a grievance through arbitration, although the contract limited access to employees, on the grounds that the grievant would have pressed the matter before his retirement if he had been fully aware of the company's position on the matter in question (pension policy). Wallen found the company at fault for not adequately relating its policy to him either before or at his retirement, and ruled that the company therefore could not rely on the limitation of arbitration to employee's grivances in this case.[48] In a somewhat similar case, but one in which the arbitration clause was not as specifically delimited, Wallen allowed the union the right to press pensioners' grievances through arbitration, calling that right logically similar to the well-recognized right of unions to bargain for pensioners.[49]

In a somewhat different dispute involving grievance eligibility and access to arbitration, a second union wished to participate in an arbitration case between another union and their common employer over the assignment of work. Wallen ruled that the contract did not provide for such three-party arbitration, but he did allow the second union to participate as an interested observer at the proceedings. The hearing was conducted under American Arbitration Association auspices, and Wallen declared that the voluntary labor arbitration rules of the association allowed him to determine and decide any claim of direct interest in an arbitration proceeding. He further stated that

In a case where an employer and several unions have contracts covering employees in the same plants, it is the height of fantasy to regard each such contract as embracing an utterly isolated and self-contained relationship. Just as the work functions they cover are inevitably integrated, so must the contracts be integrated and meshed if the objectives of the national labor policy are to be achieved. Those objectives are furthered, not thwarted, by an exercise by an arbitrator of his discretion to permit an observer from a local union that can show a color of an interest to observe the proceeding between his employer and another union.[50]

Wallen generally was hesitant to assert jurisdiction in that category of procedural cases in which it was asserted that the dispute might more appropriately be decided in another forum, particularly those problems involving potential violations of the Wagner and Taft-Hartley Acts. In a 1950 case,[51] for example, he declined to rule on a grievance which asserted that employment applicants were required to answer queries concerning their previous union activity. He stated that no applicable agreement provision was violated. He similarly declined jurisdiction and referred the parties to the NLRB in cases involving insufficient bargaining before subcontracting in 1963,[52] the unprotected status of wildcat strikers under Taft-Hartley in 1965,[53] and the rights of employees to have representation when being disciplined and protesting discipline in a 1969 case.[54] In all of these cases, no specific contractual rights were violated or diminished by the actions complained of, said Wallen. Where the NLRB declined to rule, he would assert jurisdiction and consider the national labor policy implications as well as the contractual questions. In a 1966 case involving the exclusion of certain job classes from the bargaining unit, Wallen asserted jurisdiction after the NLRB had dismissed a unit clarification petition on the matter and in doing so had commented that the matter was better suited for arbitration.[55] He also asserted arbitral jurisdiction over claims of discrimination for union activity, initial jurisdiction over which the NLRB specifically ceded to arbitration in *Spielberg Manufacturing Company* (1955). In these cases, Wallen specifically attempted to meet the standards required by the NLRB if deference to the arbitrator was to be final in the cases involved.[56]

In the fourth category of procedural cases, those involving arbitrability where the firm has closed down or changed ownership, Wallen, as a rule, declared that the arbitrability of a dispute survived the change, provided that the rights involved similarly survived. For example, rights that vest, such as vacation pay and pension rights, survive a closing of operations and hence disputes over these rights remained arbitrable to Wallen.[57] This obligation existed even if the particular agreement had expired, inasmuch as the obligation to provide such benefits as pensions continued. Wallen similarly ruled that the right to arbitrate survived changes in business ownership. The range of potentially arbitrable topics in this situation greatly exceeded those that survived a closing down of operations, including more than just those rights that were vested.[58] Wallen, however, denied that the right to arbitrate such nonvested matters survived a change in ownership of the firm's site and physical assets, where the new owner planned to use them for an entirely different purpose than did the original owner. Wallen considered this situation to be more nearly a plant closing and sale of the physical assets rather than a change in ownership of an on-going organization.[59]

COMPARING AND ASSESSING WALLEN'S VIEWS ON ARBITRABILITY

A comparison of Wallen's decisions on arbitrability with the decisions and writings of other arbitrators reveals, for the most part, that his findings were not at serious odds with most of his contemporaries. For example, express substantive exclusions from arbitration have been almost universally honored by arbitrators,[60] although there has been a considerable range of thought as to exactly how clear and applicable to the immediate facts an exclusion must be before it is deemed controlling.[61] Also, subjects specifically included in the agreement to arbitrate, issues over the interpretation, violation, or nullification of specific provisions or words in the agreement, claims of a clearly established past practice, and claims of the existence of a binding oral agreement modification or addition are all generally found to be arbitral subjects by the vast majority of arbitrators.[62] In evaluating such claims, most arbitrators have required a reasonable showing of evidence of the particular claim, withholding arbitrability if there was simply the assertion of such a claim without any logical substantiation or if the claim was patently frivolous.[63] Most arbitrators employing such a standard have also tended to resolve doubts in favor of arbitrability if such doubts remain after the issue has been thoroughly explored; this tendency has been particularly evident in cases since the Supreme Court's Trilogy decisions.[64] Some, a minority, have held since the Trilogy that any doubts as to arbitrability should require that the case be ruled arbitrable and decided on the merits.[65] The majority also appear to agree with Wallen that arbitrators are free to rule on the issue of arbitrability without relying on the court's determination, if the issue is raised before them after arbitration of the case in question has been directed by a court.[66]

Arbitrators, both before and especially after the Trilogy decisions, have also tended to grant arbitrability where procedural challenges are raised, unless the procedural defect was in violation of expressly stated and historically followed contract language and, in addition, was a serious defect or violation.[67] This is not to say that some arbitrators are not very strict in procedural matters,[68] but that they appear to be in a distinct minority. The majority of those contemporary with Wallen were probably even more likely than Wallen to assert jurisdiction in cases that might also fall within the province of the NLRB.[69]

One aspect of Wallen's treatment of the issue of arbitrability, however, was at times considered bold, radical, or on the fringe of arbitral thought, and even "reaching toward the limit of what is appropriate in labor arbitration."[70] This was his assertion that there existed inherent or implied obligations to undertake arbitration in spite of restrictive contract language, prevailing counter past practices, prior arbitration decisions to the contrary, and evidence that the precise issue sought in arbitration was sought but refused in contract negotiations.

Arbitrator Archibald Cox analyzed perhaps the most controversial grant of arbitrability by Wallen, that in the *Coca-Cola Bottling Company* case, and seriously questioned Wallen's rationale. Finding Wallen's secondary argument, the endangerment of the contract's seniority provision, to have "little force," Cox then attacked the main assertion that the mere act of signing a collective bargaining agreement somehow automatically subjected management to arbitral scrutiny of actions nowhere limited, especially in light of the restrictive arbitration constraints in the agreement. Cox asked, "where is the limit?"[71]

At least for Wallen, this was the limit, or near to it. This limit was not that different from the limits reached in the decisions of many other arbitrators in cases involving individual job security or bargaining unit protection, as an analysis of published arbitration opinions readily shows. Several arbitrators found for arbitrability in situations where the arbitration clause was very restrictive and the contract silent on the matter at hand, be it discharge for cause or the subcontracting or removal of work. Most of these arbitrators, however, based their decisions on stretched interpretations of the intent of the recognition, layoff, or seniority clauses present in the contracts.[72] A minority declared such disputes nonarbitrable, even where the issue at hand was discharge.[73]

Similarly, Wallen's finding for arbitrability provoked more controversy in cases in which arbitration was restricted, the contract silent on an issue, and there was also evidence that a specific clause limiting the company's actions had been sought and denied in negotiations, or there existed a clear past practice of the act that was the subject of the complaint. While most of his contemporaries might have agreed, for example, that an abortive attempt to gain a *total* ban on subcontracting during negotiations would not necessarily negate a later claim of an implicit or implied partial ban, a specific failure in negotiations to gain that same *partial* ban would be valid evidence for many that the contract did not and could not imply such a ban.

In the last fifteen years, however, the trend has been toward the assertion of jurisdiction in these situations regardless of the negotiation history. In most decisions up until the early 1960s involving subcontracting or work removal, the majority of arbitrators so ruling justified their decisions on the potential violation of other specific clauses, such as the recognition clause. Only a minority used a logic similar to Wallen's reasoning that the meaning of the contract as a whole could be endangered by subcontracting or work removal, even where there existed a past practice of such an action or where the union was unsuccessful in gaining specific contractual prohibitions of such an action during negotiations. In the post-Trilogy years, some of the arbitrators who ruled for arbitrability under these circumstances simply justified their stand by reference to the court's dicta favoring the granting of arbitrability.[74]

Inasmuch as the results of a majority of Wallen's rulings on arbitrability on most issues were similar to those of a great many other arbitrators, the question arises as to why his rulings were sometimes considered somewhat radical. The key to this question lies in the reasons he gave for his rulings. While he sometimes discussed the potential nullification or violation of specific seniority or recognition clauses, he did not rely on the possible infringement of these rights to explain his actions. Instead, he stated that his primary reason for granting arbitrability, even though the contract was silent, was the belief that the "essential justice" of basic individual job security and bargaining unit integrity were created automatically with the birth of the agreement and the assumption by the parties of the responsibility of collective bargaining. The creation of these rights did not necessarily require that the parties in any way express their intent in writing, or even discuss or mention these matters. These basic precepts could be negated only by a specific and clear disavowal by both parties.

It was his candor on these issues that rankled some and surprised others. The explanations he gave for his rulings indicate how important Wallen considered these goals of justice and fair dealing to be and show his willingness to stand by these precepts as an arbitrator. They also reveal his faith that these precepts were shared by others, namely, the framers of the agreements in question. There is evidence that other arbitrators have been similarly guided by such considerations in granting arbitrability, even if they did not say so. Many have been inclined to resolve doubts in favor of arbitrability, particularly in discharge and subcontracting matters, both before and after the Trilogy decisions. As arbitrator Louis Crane has commented,

Perhaps, all things being equal, arbitrators would tend to hold a grievance "arbitrable." But, without an extensive and intensive study, it would be difficult to say whether this is due to arbitrator's concepts of the nature of the collective bargaining agreements, the Supreme Court's declarations or a feeling that any doubt should be resolved in favor of giving a man his "day in court."[75]

Such a policy in the extreme, however, potentially can be destructive to the stability of the bargaining relationship by diminishing the faith held by the parties in the integrity of the written agreement. Wallen realized this fact. He was willing to deny the individual, the union, or the employer essential justice if it was abundantly clear that this was the true agreement reached by the parties and that that agreement was clearly expressed. Without exception in those cases in which discharge and subcontracting were declared to be arbitrable in the absence of specific inclusionary language, he noted that he would respect specific exclusionary language on the matter if it were in the agreement. Thus, he let the parties know that they still retained primary control over their collective bargaining destinies. Wallen also ignored contrary past practice and negotiation history only in those situations in which the issue was the individual's investment in a job or the integrity and stability of the bargaining unit. In all other matters, he considered these factors relevant in determining arbitrability and he further required a reasonable case supported by evidence or logic, not simply an allegation or something pointing to a possibility, to sustain a ruling of arbitrability.

Thus, the evidence indicates that Wallen's treatment of the issue of arbitrability was at least partially predicated on his view of the necessity of pursuing the dual goals of justice for the employee and stability for the bargaining relationship, as well as the necessity for balancing these considerations where they were in conflict. Wallen gave a party asserting a contractual violation its day in court, unless by doing so he would clearly undermine the validity or integrity of the written agreement and hence also undermine the stability of the agreement-making process. In result, this treatment of the issue of arbitrability is not different from the treatment given it by other arbitrators, although the reasons that he advanced for doing so might be different from theirs.

Notes

1. Jules J. Justin, "Arbitrability and the Arbitrator's Jurisdiction." In Jean T. McKelvey (ed.), *Management Rights and the Arbitration Process* (Washington, D.C.: BNA, 1956), p. 3.

2. Ibid., p. 17; Archibald Cox, "Reflections Upon Labor Arbitration in the Light of the Lincoln Mills Case." In Jean T. McKelvey (ed.), *Arbitration and the Law* (Washington, D.C.: BNA, 1959), p. 56; Russel A. Smith, "Arbitrators and Arbitrability." In Mark L. Kahn (ed.), *Labor Arbitration and Industrial Change* (Washington, D.C.: BNA, 1963), p. 83; Frank Plaut, "Arbitrability Under the Standard Labor Arbitration Clause," *Arbitration Journal* 14 (1959): 56; Herbert Schmertz, "When and Where an Issue of Arbitrability Can Be Raised," *Labor Reporter Bulletin* 3 (1966): 2; Benjamin Aaron, "Arbitration in the Federal Courts: Aftermath of the Trilogy," *UCLA Law Review* 9 (1962): 363; Russel A. Smith, "The Question of 'Arbitrability' — The Roles of the Arbitrator, the Court, and the Parties," *Southwestern Law Journal* 16 (1962): 10.

3. Wallen, "Recent Supreme Court Decisions on Arbitration," pp. 297–98 and 302.

4. Textron, Inc., Esmond Mills and Textile Workers Union of Am., CIO, April 8, 1949, 12 LA 475.

5. Smith, "Arbitrators and Arbitrability," p. 78.

6. Plaut, p. 52.

7. Ibid., p. 51.

8. Textron, Inc., 12 LA at 476.

9. Landers, Frary, and Clark and United Elec., Radio, and Mach. Workers of Am., CIO, Local 207, April 29, 1946.

10. Connecticut Light and Power Co. and Int'l Bhd. of Elec. Workers, Local B-420, April 28, 1948.

11. Aluminum Co. of Am., Lancaster Plant and Aluminum Workers Int'l Union, Local No. 415, August 30, 1961; Aluminum Co. of Am., Massena Plant and Aluminum Workers Int'l Union, Local No. 420, June 5, 1961.

12. Yale and Towne Mfg. Co. and Int'l Ass'n of Mach., Lodge 1717, May 24, 1963, 41 LA 1100.

13. Aluminum Co. of Am., August 30, 1961; Aluminum Co. of Am., June 5, 1961.

14. Saul Wallen, "Procedural Problems in the Conduct of Arbitration Hearings: A Discussion." In Mark L. Kahn (ed.), *Labor Arbitration – Perspectives and Problems* (Washington, D.C.: BNA, 1964), p. 24.

15. Fafnir Bearing Co. and United Auto., Aircraft and Agricultural Implement Workers of Am., Local No. 133, AFL-CIO, May 27, 1957; Connecticut Light and Power, April 28, 1948.

16. IAM Dist. 15, Local 402 v. Cutler-Hammer, Inc., 271 App. Div. 917, 67 N.Y.S. 2d 317 (1947).

17. Wallen, "Procedural Problems in the Conduct of Arbitration Hearings," p. 2.

18. The Stanley Works, Stanley Tool Div. and Int'l Ass'n of Mach., Hardware Lodge No. 1249, September 9, 1954.

19. Union Hardware Co. and Int'l Union of Elec., Radio, and Mach. Workers, CIO, Local 247, March 16, 1954, p. 2.

20. Bell Tel. Laboratories, Inc. and Communications Workers of Am., Cobb-Finch Grievance, May 4, 1967; Stanley Works, September 9, 1954; Trans World Airlines, Inc. and Int'l Ass'n of Mach., October 10, 1959, 34 LA 420; CBS-Hytron and Int'l Union of Elec., Radio, and Mach. Workers, AFL-CIO, Local No. 270, March 25, 1958; and Sylvania Elec. Prod., Inc., Huntington Plant and Int'l Union of Elec., Radio, and Mach. Workers, AFL-CIO, Local No. 608, June 9, 1957.

21. Sylvania Elec., June 9, 1957, p. 2.

22. Gregg and Sons, Inc. and Int'l Bhd. of Teamsters, Door and Window Div., Local Union No. 379, April 7, 1965, p. 5.

23. Chase Brass and Copper Co. and United Auto. Workers of Am., Local No. 1565, November 30, 1961, p. 3.

24. Container Corp. of Am. and United Papermakers and Paperworkers, Local No. 68, April 12, 1967; General Tire and Rubber Co., Ashtabula Plant and United Rubber, Cork, Linoleum, and Plastic Workers of Am., Local No. 595, October 14, 1960.

25. Aluminum Co. of Am., Warrick Works and Aluminum Workers Int'l Union, Local 104, May 24, 1965; Aluminum Co. of Am., Vancouver Works and Aluminum Trades Council, AFL-CIO, November 6, 1961.

26. Aluminum Co. of Am., Massena Works and Aluminum Workers Int'l Union, Local 420, June 13, 1962.

27. General Elec. Co. (East Boston) and United Elec., Radio, and Mach. Workers of Am., CIO, March 3, 1948, 9 LA 757 at 759 and 752.

28. Coca-Cola Bottling Co. of Boston and Retail, Wholesale, and Dep't Store Union, Local 513, August 1949, p. 2.

29. Ibid., p. 4.

30. Draper Corp. and United Steelworkers of Am., February 7, 1967, pp. 4–5.

31. Ibid., p. 5.

32. The Murray Co. of Texas, Boston Gear Works Div. and United Steelworkers of Am., AFL-CIO, December 3, 1959, p. 4.

33. Ibid., p. 5.

34. Ibid., p. 8.

35. Chase Brass and Copper Co., November 30, 1961, p. 3.

36. The Firestone Tire and Rubber Co., Pottstown Plant and United Rubber, Cork, Linoleum, and Plastic Workers of Am., Local No. 336, May 18, 1959.

37. Trailways of New England, Inc. and Amalgamated Transit Union, March 29, 1965, 46 LA 369.

38. General Insulated Wire Works, Inc. and Int'l Bhd. of Elec. Workers, Local 1242, September 18, 1961, 38 LA 522 at 523-24.

39. Allegheny Ludlum Steel Corp. and United Steelworkers of Am., Local No. 2478, January 27, 1964; Consolidated Chem. Indus. and Int'l Fur and Leather Workers Union, CIO, December 27, 1948.

40. The B. F. Goodrich Co., Riverside Plant and United Rubber Workers of Am., Local 434, October 26, 1966; General Tire and Rubber Co. and United Rubber, Cork, Linoleum, and Plastic Workers of Am., Local No. 9, October 5, 1959.

41. General Tire and Rubber Co. and United Rubber, Cork, Linoleum, and Plastic Workers of Am., Local No. 9, October 5, 1959.

42. Merrow Mach. Co. and Int'l Union of Elec. Workers, Local No. 249, November 8, 1961.

43. Threadwell Tap and Die Co. and United Elec., Radio, and Mach. Workers of Am., Local No. 274, April 15, 1957, p. 9.

44. Wallen, "Recent Supreme Court Decisions on Arbitration," p. 296.

45. BLH Electronics and Int'l Ass'n of Mach., Dist. 38, Lodge No. 1836, June 5, 1968.

46. Firestone Tire and Rubber Co., Firestone Store and United Rubber Workers of Am., Local No. 7, January 14, 1964, pp. 4–6; Boston Record Am., Advertiser Div., and Am. Fed'n of News Writers, Reporters, and Editorial Workers Union No. 21432, February 7, 1968, pp. 7–10.

47. Aluminum Co. of Am., Warrick Works, and Aluminum Workers Int'l Union, Local 104, April 29, 1965, p. 2.

48. Waterbury Farrel Foundry and Machine Co. and United Steelworkers of Am., CIO, Local Union No. 3381, June 19, 1951, pp. 8–13.

49. G. Levor and Co., Inc. and Amalgamated Meat Cutters and Butcher Workmen of North Am., Local 41-L, November 30, 1967, p. 12.

50. Radio Corp. of Am. and Int'l Union of Elec., Radio, and Mach. Workers, Local 103, January 29, 1968, p. 9.

51. Taller and Cooper, Inc. and Amalgamated Mach., Instrument, and Metal Workers, Local No. 475, UERMWA, Issue No. 5, January 12, 1950, pp. 8–10.

52. Fafnir Bearing Co. and United Auto. Workers, Local No. 133, April 15, 1963.

53. Trailways of New England, March 29, 1965, 46 LA 369.

54. Texaco, Inc., Westville Plant and Oil, Chemical, and Atomic Workers Int'l Union, January 16, 1969.

55. Allegheny Ludlum Steel Corp., Brackenridge Plant and United Steelworkers of Am., Local Union No. 2984, April 15, 1966.

56. Hoague-Sprague Corp., Converter Div. and Int'l Chem. Workers Union, Local 553, January 10, 1967.

57. The Bridgeport Rubber Co. and United Rubber, Cork, Linoleum, and Plastic Workers of Am., Local No. 176, October 27, 1958; Bonin Spinning Co. and Indus. Trades Council, May 6, 1963; G. Levor and Co., Inc., November 30, 1967.

58. Supreme Embossing Co. and Int'l Fur and Leather Workers Union, Local No. 21, CIO, November 11, 1947.

59. Stop and Shop, Inc. and Amalgamated Meat Cutters and Butcher Workmen of North Am. and Retail Clerks Int'l Ass'n, July 31, 1964.

60. Plaut, p. 70.

61. Robben W. Fleming, "Arbitrators and Arbitrability," *Washington University Law Quarterly* 1963 (1963): pp. 209–14.

62. Plaut, pp. 68–70.

63. Ibid., pp. 54–55. See also Russel Smith and Dallas Jones, "The Impact of the Emerging Federal Law of Grievance Arbitration on Judges, Arbitrators, and Parties," *Virginia Law Review* 52 (1966): 873–74.

64. Smith and Jones, p. 873; Fleming, "Arbitrators and Arbitrability," p. 220; Continental Air Transp. Co., Inc. and Auto. Livery Chauffeurs, Local 727, Int'l Bhd. of Teamsters, June 1, 1962, N. Eiger, arbitrator, 38 LA 778 at 780.

65. Smith and Jones, p. 873.

66. Ibid.; Aaron, "Arbitration in the Federal Courts," p. 363. Even in the landmark *Warrior and Gulf* case, the arbitrator, J. Fred Holly, made an independent assessment of the arbitrability of the dispute after the Supreme Court had referred the case to arbitration. See Warrior and Gulf Navigation Co. v. USWA, 61–2 ARB 8401 (1961).

67. Fleming, "Arbitrators and Arbitrability," p. 220; Smith and Jones, pp. 881–83; Forse Corp. and Int'l Union, United Auto., Aircraft, and Agricultural Implement Workers of Am., Local No. 635, AFL-CIO, July 21, 1962, H. Dworkin, arbitrator, 39 LA 709.

68. Potash Co. of Am. and Int'l Ass'n of Mach., Local 1265, June 30, 1964, R. Ray, arbitrator, 42 LA 1106.

69. Smith and Jones, pp. 831–32.

70. Lon Fuller, "Collective Bargaining and the Arbitrator." In Merton Bernstein (ed.), *Private Dispute Settlement* (New York: The Free Press, 1968), p. 303.

71. Cox, "Reflections Upon Labor Arbitration in the Light of the Lincoln Mills Case," pp. 48–49.

72. General Portland Cement Co., Trinity Portland Cement Div. and United Cement, Lime, and Gypsum Workers Int'l Union, Local No. 124, December, 1961, W. Quinlan, arbitrator, 62-1 ARB 8172; The Atwater Mfg. Co. and United Steelworkers of Am., Local 3456, CIO, December 7, 1949, J. Donnelly, M. Svir doff, and W. Clark, arbitrators, 13 LA 747; Whitney Chain Co. and United Auto., Aircraft and Agricultural Implement Workers of Am., Local 1199, CIO, March 16, 1955, R. Stutz, S. Curry, and W. Mottram, arbitrators, 24 LA 385; Tubular Products Co. and Allied Indus. Workers of Am., March 5, 1957, R. Stutz, W. Mottram, and S. Curry, arbitrators, 28 LA 255; Maclin Co. and Miscellaneous Warehousemen, Drivers, and Helpers, Local 986, Int'l Bhd. of Teamsters, April 24, 1969, A. Koven, arbitrator, 52 LA 805.

73. Plaut, p. 70; Smith and Jones, p. 881; American Oil and Supply Co. and Int'l Bhd. of Teamsters, Local 478, October 6, 1960, M. Berkowitz, arbitrator, 36 LA 331; Columbian Carbon Co. and Int'l Union of Operating Engineers, Local 404, AFL, July 23, 1947, C. Potter, arbitrator, 8 LA 634.

74. Allegheny Ludlum Steel Corp., Ferndale Plant, and United Auto., Aircraft, and Agricultural Implement Workers of Am., Local No. 157, March 3, 1961, M. Ryder, arbitrator, 36 LA 912; Celanese Corp. of Am. and United Mine Workers of Am., Dist. 50, United Constr. Workers, Local 153, September 28, 1959, G. A. Dash, Jr., arbitrator, 33 LA 925 at 948; General Tel. Co. of Kentucky and Communications Workers of Am., September 24, 1960, J. Murphy, arbitrator, 36 LA 677 at 679.

75. Louis A. Crane, Discussion of "Arbitrators and Arbitrability." In Mark L. Kahn (ed.), *Labor Arbitration and Industrial Change* (Washington, D.C.: BNA, 1963), p. 101.

Chapter IV

Interpretation of
the Agreement

In this chapter, the methods by which Wallen interpreted the provisions of labor agreeements and applied these provisions to cases at hand are examined. Among the questions raised are what specific techniques did Wallen use to interpret the agreement's provisions? At what point did Wallen generally find that the plain written words of the agreement were not fully dispositive of the issues before him? When he determined that the agreement's provisions were ambiguous, what other factors did he rely on to discover the intent of the parties? What was the relative importance of the parties' negotiating history, their past practices, prior arbitration findings, and considerations of equity and fairness? In cases involving issues that were covered by statutory law, as well as by provisions of the agreement, what was the effect of the law on his decision making? On whom did Wallen place the burden of proving a case or issue, and how much proof did he require?

Relatively little has been written about the means and criteria by which decisions are reached and the influence of personal values on arbitral decision making. It is hypothesized here that arbitrators' approaches to these issues—their personal choices in selecting criteria on which to base their decisions — reveal a personal value orientation, given the great number of choices open to them. It is possible that these choices could be made randomly or on the basis of what arbitrators think is fashionable among other practitioners, but the evidence presented in this chapter proves overwhelmingly that Wallen's approach to interpreting and applying the agreement was planned, purposeful, and not swayed by the changing tides of arbitral fashion.

The evidence is twofold: (1) clear admissions by Wallen in his arbitral opinions that his choice of appropriate decision-making criteria was made to enable him to further his goals of productive efficiency, industrial relations stability, and justice and equity, and (2) consistent patterns of reasoning in his awards that reveal a basic concern with these goals.

CLAIMS OF EXPLICIT MODIFICATIONS TO THE CONTRACT

On several occasions in his career, Wallen was confronted with claims or evidence presented by a party that the written agreement was explicitly modified or enlarged, either by some verbal agreement between the parties or by written addendum, letter, or memorandum. The standing that Wallen gave these claimed modifications influenced his analysis of the parties' intent in originally reaching an agreement. The implied or implicit modification of the agreement through past practice, that is the parties' own interpretation of the agreement through use, was also of great importance, but the issue here for the moment is the examination of the expressed agreement (written and oral) between the parties. Wallen's treatment of claims of two general types of supplementary agreements deserve special scrutiny: (1) the oral supplement or modification of the written agreement, and (2) the local alteration, whether written or oral, of the master or plantwide agreement.

The weight given to any claim of an oral supplement or modification depended first on the treatment given such supplements by the written agreement. For example, where the agreement specifically denied to the arbitrator the power to consider as binding any provisions not expressed in the agreement or a formal written supplement, Wallen refused to consider evidence of any verbal supplement. In one such case, he commented,

The promise relied on is not contained in such a formal, signed supplement. It is therefore, no more than a "gentlemen's agreement." Such an agreement is good so long as the gentlemen who made it remain gentlemen. While there is every reason in this case to believe that the negotiators will continue in their relations with each other as gentlemen, we as Arbitrators are bound by the clear, concise and unequivocal limitation placed on our powers. . . . [1]

Wallen similarly declined to lend force to disputed claims of binding oral agreements that would modify, nullify, or violate existing provisions of the written agreements that were reasonably clear.[2] He relied in these situations on the so-called parol evidence rule,[3] which he defined as "a basic principle of contract interpretation that a claim that a verbal agreement to vary the terms of a written contract exists cannot be employed to set aside the writing." He further stated that "any other holding would put the parties' solemn written engagements at the mercy of claims of parol variations."[4]

Parties before Wallen asserting the existence of disputed oral agreements not clearly at odds with existing contract language, but merely clarifying' or enlarging such language, faced less of an uphill battle. The side asserting the claim of a binding oral promise had the general responsibility for proving both the promise's existence and its applicability to the particular case at hand.[5] Once the threshold issue of the existence of an oral agreement was shown either by evidence and testimony or by the admission of both parties, however, the logic of the situation could create a presumption in favor of the moving party's claim of the content of the promise. For example, Wallen arbitrated a 1960 case involving an alleged oral agreement made during contract negotiations to preserve all existing past practices. The union claimed that the promise applied to all past practices. Management admitted the existence of a promise, but stated that it applied only to procedural issues and not to benefits. Wallen ruled that since the union had shown the past existence of the practice in question, as well as the existence of some sort of oral agreement, the union was favored by a "presumption in favor of the established way of doing things," and, absent management proof that the promise did not exclude that logically included, Wallen found for the union.[6]

As a general rule, he was exceedingly reluctant to uphold claims of local or shop agreements that were at odds with plant or company master agreements, even where the existence of such a local agreement was indisputable, as in the cases of written local agreements or corroborative testimony by both union and management. Where such local agreements were specifically excluded from arbitral coverage by the master agreement, Wallen simply refused to assert arbitral jurisdiction. Where the master agreement specifically stated that it superseded local agreements where there was conflict, he so ruled.[7] Even where the master agreement did not declare its own supremacy, he refused to uphold a conflicting local agreement, reasoning that a master agreement "cannot be changed except with the assent of all signers."[8] This stringent treatment, however, only applied to local agreements at odds with larger agreements. It did not apply to matters specifically left for local negotiations or ignored by the master agreement. In these situations, a written addendum could be considered controlling or an oral agreement could be established by the weight of evidence and testimony.

Only in those situations in which the master agreement specifically stated that it and all local agreements, taken as a whole, constituted the agreement between the parties did Wallen consider local agreements to be coequal with the master agreement. Here, if there was a direct and irreconcilable conflict between the two, Wallen often attempted to devise a workable merger by "looking to the practicalities of the situation rather than to the bare words of the two agreements." As a last resort, he would remand such cases to the parties for reconsideration and renegotiation, retaining jurisdiction if agreement could not be so attained.[9]

METHODS OF INTERPRETING THE WRITTEN WORD

In reaching decisions over the intent or meaning of the written agreement, Wallen relied on several basic procedures for interpreting the true meaning of written words and phrases. In many cases, the past practice of the parties, prior arbitration decisions, the history of contract negotiations, and considerations of fairness and logic provided the necessary clues to lead Wallen to a decision. In many situations, however, these factors were either absent or countervailing. In such situations, he was forced to rely on his own reasoning and interpretative powers to unravel the meaning of the agreement and apply it to the facts of the case at hand.

Wallen's first and most common procedure in the event of such disputed contract language was to examine the language in the context of the entire written agreement. If one of the asserted interpretations was logically supported by other contract provisions, and the other was not, then the former meaning was upheld. Similarly, if one version violated, diminished, or nullified other contract provisions, it had to fall before an interpretation that did not have this detrimental effect. Wallen once stated in such a case that "it is axiomatic in contract construction that as between alternative interpretations, that one should be chosen which gives effect to all parts of a clause over the one which negates part of the clause."[10] For example, in 1946 Wallen rejected a literal interpretation of a requirement that an employee be on the seniority list to bid for a posted job where the employee involved was a former bargaining unit member just returning to the unit from an abolished supervisory position. He stated that such a super-literal interpretation would defeat other agreement provisions clearly expressing the vested nature of seniority rights of such returning employees. Wallen declared that these other provisions indicated that the "on the list" requirement applied to employees never before on the list, not to individuals such as the unit returnee in question.[11] He concluded,

Such a technical construction of an agreement governing the relations between management and labor does not promote sound industrial relations, and is usually rejected by arbitrators when advanced by an employer. It should not be invoked by a company as against a union; by the same token, it should not be invoked by a union as against a company.[12]

Wallen also relied on the context of the written word in a case involving the discharge of probationary employees with no seniority. Inasmuch as the seniority clause of the contract mentioned the requirement of cause for discharge as a benefit of seniority, he logically inferred the absence of such a benefit for employees without seniority.[13] In at least one case, however, Wallen did rule in favor of an interpretation that tended to nullify other contract provisions. He did so because of what he considered to be the unequivocal clarity of the clause in dispute and because there was no way to dovetail neatly their interpretations. The provisions were so at odds that one had to be ruled predominant and one nullified.[14]

Wallen also sought to clarify the meaning of particular words and terms in dispute by reference to their usage elsewhere in the agreement. For example, in a 1956 case involving termination benefits for pilots, he ruled that a physical disability included mental and emotional disability inasmuch as the agreement elsewhere outlined physical examination standards for pilots, which included the requirement of no past history of mental disorder.[15] Wallen rejected any strictly mechanical application of such terms, however, refusing to rely on definitions found elsewhere in the agreement if he believed them to be illogical in the case at hand. For example, in 1958, he rejected a claim that the word *temporary* had to mean four weeks in a clause allowing supervisors to transfer into the bargaining unit with top seniority whenever there was temporarily no need for their services. The union claimed that such top seniority had to be forfeited after four weeks since the word *temporary* was clearly and specifically defined as not to exceed four weeks in another entirely unrelated contract provision. Wallen stated that "words must be interpreted with a view to the context in which they are employed," and reasoned that such a mechanical application of the defined term would defeat the broad purpose of the clause, which was to allow management to retain employees with supervisory skills.[16]

As a second rule of interpretation, Wallen examined the meaning of contractual silence, that is, the lack of clarifying language, on the specific issue in dispute. The situation in which clarifying language was sought but rejected in negotiations is dealt with later. Here, the concern is with the problem of silence on the issue where there was never an attempt at contractual clarification. Frequently, Wallen ruled that such contractual silence lent a presumption of validity to the status quo. In a case involving overtime bargaining unit work by foremen, he asked, "What is the meaning of silence by parties who could have been eloquent on the subject?" and answered that he believed the silence to be "the embodiment of a tacit understanding that the parties' past practice in the matter" would continue unchanged.[17] While failure of an agreement specifically to bestow rights or benefits on a grievant under some particular circumstances generally created a presumption that such rights or benefits did not exist, the failure of the agreement specifically to exclude those rights or benefits under the particular circumstances of the grievance, where other exclusions were mentioned in the contract, could similarly create a presumption in favor of requiring bestowal of the rights or benefits in question.[18]

As a final rule of interpretation, Wallen frequently asserted that the practical administration, the underlying purpose, or the main thrust of the clause in question created a strong presumption as to the meaning of the entire clause and of its disputed component parts.[19] In such cases, in addition to any evidence presented, he necessarily relied heavily on his own familiarity with the general nature of labor agreements, the usual problems of plant administration, the particular practices of the industry or plant in question, and the likely sophistication and writing ability of the drafters of the disputed agreements.[20]

THE EFFECT OF ARBITRAL CASE PRECEDENT

In a great many cases before him, Wallen heard claims by the parties that previous arbitrators had decided the issues, or had at least laid down relevant and controlling principles, or else that the issue had already been dealt with under other similar contracts and that there existed some sort of arbitral consensus on it. An example of a prior arbitral finding is the interpretation or principle that a particular clause does not ban subcontracting, as opposed to an award or remedy providing backpay to a specific person. The latter type is universally deemed final and binding by arbitrators and such a case is not reheard on its merits. Generally, a case is only reheard before another arbitrator if there is a claim of noncompliance with the particular award. In such a case, only the fulfillment or nonfulfillment of the award is examined, not the validity or merit of the original award. Wallen subscribed to this universal tenet, stating that to rule otherwise would "provide no stability at all in the day-to-day plant relationships."[21]

Throughout his career, Wallen was reluctant to overturn a principle established by a previous arbitrator under the same contract, even though he might have some disagreement with the finding. In a 1951 case, he stated that he "would be loathe, when passing on the same question under the identical contract language, to arrive at a different conclusion when there is any ground at all for arriving at the same conclusion, because of the unstabilizing effect of different interpretations on the parties' day-to-day administration of their agreement."[22] A decade later he similarly stated that

...even a reversal of a principle established in an earlier case is likely to be the rare and unusual occurrence, for a conscientious arbitrator must weigh very carefully the virtue of continuing stability in the administration of the Agreement as against any doubts he may have about the wisdom of a prior decision, his own or someone else's. He should reverse an established principle only on a showing of drastically altered circumstances or on a conviction of error so deep and profound as to overcome all other considerations.[23]

In 1967, he noted that "while previous arbitration awards do not constitute precedents binding upon this Board, generally such decisions should not be overturned unless a sound basis for reversal is shown." He upheld the previous arbitral finding in that case since it was not proven to be "clearly erroneous."[24]

Wallen's interest in stability was not so overriding that he would refuse to repudiate prior findings when he was convinced that the earlier decision was totally unjust or in error. In the 1951 case just cited, he also stated that "if he could find no justification for the prior decision in logic or equity, he would not abdicate to his predecessor that function of judgment for which he was engaged."[25] At other times, he found the overturning of precedent justified if he had a "clear and supported conviction that the earlier decision does not reasonably resolve the issue," or "on a showing of drastically altered circumstances or on a conviction of error so deep and profound as to overcome all other considerations."[26] In a much publicized 1967 case involving an airline's no-marriage rule for its stewardesses, Wallen declined to uphold the rule even though a number of previous arbitration boards had found it reasonable and had upheld it: "While it has been upheld in arbitration as reasonable in several prior cases, all these decisions were made in the context of a universal application of such a rule in the industry. Now times have changed and views have been altered by experience."[27]

As a side note, Wallen applied this policy of respecting prior awards unless they were in error or unjust in those few cases where he served as an appellate arbitrator, reviewing initial awards on appeal—a procedure provided for, for example, in the newspaper industry. Unlike a number of other arbitrators, Wallen refused to hear such a case de novo, limiting his review to an examination of whether the lower award was unreasonable in light of the evidence, regardless of how he would have ruled himself had he first heard the case.[28]

In general, Wallen upheld principles established in prior awards, even if he disagreed with them or questioned their justice, if there was clear evidence that the parties had in some positive manner assented to those principles. This assent could be shown, for example, if another arbitrator interpreted contract language in a certain manner and at contract renewal time, neither party had then attempted to alter that language.[29]

Finally, all of the cases that Wallen determined had precedential value involved prior decisions under the same or predecessor contract and involved the same parties. He virtually never ruled that previous decisions under different contracts, even where the language and situation were the same, were controlling or persuasive.

THE IMPORTANCE OF THE HISTORY OF CONTRACT NEGOTIATIONS

If the contract language applicable to a case before Wallen did not lend itself to a reasonably clear interpretation and application on its face and there was no finding relating to the matter by a prior arbitrator, he frequently sought clues to the parties' intent by examining the history of negotiations over the language. If the language itself expressed clearly and without ambiguity a particular meaning or purpose, Wallen applied his parol evidence rule and relied on that clear meaning, rejecting any assertions of what the parties had in mind when drafting the language. He thereupon declined to examine the history of negotiations.[30]

If the evidence and testimony concerning the parties' intent when drafting the language in question was in irreconcilable conflict, as was frequently the case, he turned elsewhere for clues to intent, such as examining the past practice of the parties when handling the matter, deciding what was most fair, determining the basic or underlying purpose of the clause, or interpreting the clause "within the framework of the realities of administration."[31] The issues explored in these cases are those in which some evidence of the parties' intent is discernible and uncontradicted. On occasion, however, the evidence of intent in negotiations was not in conflict, but did point to the *inapplicability* of contract language to the immediate case that one of the parties claimed was controlling. Depending on the nature of the problem and the wording of the grievance or stipulation, such inapplicability of language could either dispose of the issue or could simply require Wallen to search elsewhere for an arbitral solution. For example, he once found that the contract negotiators never had in mind a strike situation when drafting a clause denying holiday pay to anyone absent for any reason but illness immediately before or after the holiday. Wallen ruled that this prohibition was inapplicable to the issue on the basis of evidence of the negotiators' intent. He then proceeded to examine the issue of holiday pay for strikers by weighing the equities involved.[32]

More often, however, any intent clearly shown by the history of negotiations was likely to be dispositive of the issue arbitrated. This could be accomplished in several ways. As already noted, failure of the parties to negotiate a change in language interpreted by a previous arbitral decision was considered by Wallen to be an assent to that arbitral interpretation. He upheld this concept even where it was shown that one or both parties had attempted to alter the language in question, but had failed to reach an agreement on new language.[33]

Additionally, where it was shown through the history of contract negotiations that one party had tried and failed to gain specific language that would clearly determine the issue in its favor, Wallen generally ruled that the failure to gain that language meant a tacit acceptance of the status quo, whatever it may have been. While, in general, Wallen did not accept the denial in negotiations of specific language as a bar to the arbitrability of the issue,[34] especially in cases involving job security or bargaining unit integrity, he did rely on such evidence in dealing with the issues on their merits. For example, he once denied holiday pay to workers where the holiday fell on a weekend, even though the clause did not specify that the holiday had to fall on a workday for the workers to receive holiday pay. Wallen denied the claim because it was proven that the union had tried and failed in negotiations to gain language specifically providing for holiday pay in the event that the holiday fell on a weekend.[35] Wallen similarly ruled against management assertions of certain job transfer rights, against union claims of a ban on subcontracting, and against a management claim of freedom from responsibility for employees' tools stolen on the job.[36] In each of these cases, the party asserting a claimed right had tried to gain specific contract language guaranteeing that right and had failed.

An acceptance of the status quo through a failure to press one's desired language to contractual reality did not necessarily mean that one's claim was automatically lost in arbitration, however. The claim might be upheld if it could be shown that the right claimed did exist prior to negotiations and that the pressing for specific language was merely an attempt to clarify the situation. In such a case in 1962, Wallen declared that

Frequently when one party advances language in negotiations and later abandons that language in the final document the inference may fairly be drawn that the intent conveyed by those words was also abandoned. But this is not always so. Sometimes such language is proposed in order to remove any doubts about the clarity of the clause but if the language is objected to and is withdrawn to facilitate agreement, it does not automatically follow that the party withdrawing the proposal embraces the opposite interpretation. He may in fact withdraw the language, in order to clear an obstacle to agreement, either on a specific assurance that the language accepted means just what the proposer of the additional words intends or, more frequently, in the expectation that the words finally agreed on will be interpreted in the light of their inherent meaning after due consideration is given to all factors and not alone to the fact of abandonment of the clarifying language. In the latter case the parties in effect agree to take a chance on what the clause, minus the clarifying words, means.[37]

In this particular case, Wallen found that management had certain rights in the establishment of work starting times, even though it had tried and failed in negotiations to obtain specific language guaranteeing these rights. Similarly, in a 1954 case, he granted an award of backpay to workers who had lost the opportunity to work hours due to management's maladministration of the seniority rules, even though the union had tried and failed in negotiations to gain a clause requiring backpay in such cases. He ruled that while the right to mandatory backpay might have been lost, the original contract allowed such an award at the discretion of the arbitrator and this was not changed by the negotiations. He further declared that to rule otherwise would fly "in the face of reason and of well-nigh universal labor relations practice."[38]

A final limitation Wallen placed on a clause's construction in examining the history of negotiations was that if there was evidence that a clause was meant only to solve a specific problem or grant a specific benefit, he would construe the clause to be applicable only to that specific problem or benefit. For example, in a 1948 case, management showed, by a letter received from the union before negotiations, that the union was proposing language granting extra vacation benefits to employees who had worked a certain large number of hours, except for those employees who had already received their yearly vacation. While the final clause did not clearly express this latter limitation, Wallen read this limitation into the disputed clause solely on the basis of the letter, which shed light on the intent of the particular negotiation in question.[39]

THE EFFECTS OF PAST PRACTICE

Wallen also faced the task of having to evaluate and assess the validity of claims by the parties either that their interpretation of disputed contract language was supported by past practice or else that, absent any relevant contract language at all, the parties were constrained to perform in the same manner as they had consistently done in the past. The notion he dealt with here was that the agreement was predicated on an unwritten and unspoken consensus to continue in the future those benefits and obligations the parties had come to rely upon, but which had never become part of the written agreement. Wallen's treatment of claims of controlling past practices is expressed in his philosophy that

Established practices not sanctioned by specific contract language but not barred by it and arising out of the logic of the work relationship are invoked frequently by unions as working conditions intended to be preserved, not supplanted by, the Agreement. This is as it should be. The customary ways of doing things not negated by an Agreement's specific terms are subsumed. But Management, as well as unions, have a right to rely on this principle.[40]

Wallen also considered the closely related situation in which past practice was not totally controlling on future behavior, but it created a "presumption in favor of the established way of doing things,"[41] a presumption rebuttable by a showing of changed circumstances, business necessity, logic, or considerations of equity. In such cases, a finding supportive of the continuing of past practices depended upon several factors.

It was, of course, necessary that the written agreement did not in some way preclude the arbitrator from taking past practices and obligations into account.[42] A very limited arbitration clause, for example, could prevent the arbitrator from considering past practices except where they illuminated or clarified written provisions.[43]

Wallen also relied on a sort of parol evidence rule, consistently disallowing claims that past practice overruled written contract language or gave it a meaning different from that which was reasonably clear on its face. This was true not only in those situations in which one party had failed to assert a contractual right or option for a period of time and then attempted to assert it, but also in those situations in which the parties had both acted contrary to the letter of the agreement in concert, but at some later time one of these parties asserted the right to "pull the pin" and observe the letter of the law.[44] In such a circumstance, Wallen once wrote,

I have a full appreciation of past practice's role in the administration of labor agreements. I recognize the validity of its use to clarify ambiguities, to give substance to generalities, perhaps to create obligations to continue conditions of employment not covered by an agreement. But I draw the line at using past practice to modify or amend what is unambiguous in an agreement.[45]

Wallen did admit that a past practice could be cited to negate or repeal a clear contract provision if it could be shown that the parties consciously undertook to reform their contract, but proving such conscious intent would require either an admission by both sides of their intent to do so or else a written agreement modification.[46] Without such proof, about the best that a party before Wallen could realistically hope to gain from a claim of past practice contrary to clear written provisions was the prevention of any retroactive redress and the requirement that appropriate notice be given by the opposing party before it exercised any previously unasserted contractual rights.[47]

Another basic requirement that had to be met to validate any past practice claim was that the practice had to stem from some sort of mutual acceptance or tacit agreement by the parties. It could not be the result of past unilateral and coercive behavior. Wallen stated that such mutual assent required that the "repetitious acts of one party are known to and are free of taint of objection of the other," although there did not necessarily have to be a positive meeting of the minds. This agreement or acceptance could stem from a course of action undertaken by one party and reluctantly and silently acquiesced to by the other.[48] In one such case, Wallen wrote,

This case brings to mind the story of the chambermaid in a summer hotel who, on her first day on the job, entered Room 604 where she was promptly raped. Later, in describing her experience she said "After that, it was rape, rape, rape all summer long!"

We may safely conclude that in this case there was, after a bit, acquiescence. The same is true of the case at hand.[49]

Where there was evidence of the hint of resistance in the face of coercion, however, Wallen declined to rule that there existed the necessary mutual assent necessary for the practice to be controlling or presumptive. This evidence could be a showing that the past practice was in fact mixed, or else a showing that the party disputing the past practice tried to prevent its establishment. For example, if management or immediate supervision unsuccessfully tried to prevent machinists from exceeding maximum machine speed, tried unsuccessfully to police a rule limiting wash-up time to a short, fixed period, or were forced to offer overtime to all shiftmates or none at all to make up the work assigned to absentees, Wallen ruled that the mutuality required to make such practices binding was absent.[50]

Still another basic requirement for a controlling or presumptive past practice to exist was that the practice was not grossly inequitable or unjust. In an early case, Wallen wrote,

In determining the intent of parties to a contract, the meaning attached to the disputed language by the parties themselves in the past as shown by their actions is an important but not controlling factor. It may be qualified by a consideration of the circumstances under which these actions were taken. And it must be considered in the light of the reasonableness and equitableness of the results flowing from a given construction. An interpretation that would have an unreasonable or inequitable result is justified only where the evidence is overwhelming that the parties intended such a result.[51]

Much later, in 1960, Wallen again related the importance of reasonableness and equity, inquiring first which was the more reasonable and equitable interpretation of the disputed language and second what was the past practice of the parties. This point should not be overdrawn, however. If the interpretation attached to the clause in question in the past was clearly shown, and Wallen did not deem the interpretation unjust or inequitable, but simply less logical than the interpretation he would have drawn, then he upheld the parties' own past interpretation.[52]

A final factor affecting the importance of past practice either in illuminating language or standing as a benefit or obligation by itself was whether the practice was initiated by the same parties to the agreement as were currently in arbitration, or whether a predecessor union or management was involved. In the latter case, the party in arbitration could sometimes be relieved of an obligation or interpretation that otherwise would have been binding. Wherever the successor was aware of its predecessor's past practices and obligations, the successor was similarly bound. Where the interpretation or obligation arising out of a past practice was drastically different from that which one could reasonably impute from a reading of the contract, and this prior practice was never discussed with or mentioned to the new union or management, however, Wallen ruled that the interpretation or practice was not binding, both because one could not really say that there was ever any mutual agreement between the present parties and also on the bases of equity and elementary justice.[53]

CONSIDERATIONS OF EQUITY, LOGIC, AND REASONABLENESS

In a great number of Wallen's cases, considerations of equity, fairness, logic, reason, or practicality played a large role in his decisions.[54] As was true in dealing with past practice, negotiating history, and arbitral precedent, however, Wallen consistently refused to be swayed by arguments urging considerations of equity or reasonableness if the written agreement itself was clear on the point at issue. Wallen presented his position and its accompanying rationale unambiguously in a 1954 decision, stating that if language is clear, the arbitrator

…has no choice but to apply it to the facts at hand, no matter what [his] reservations about the fairness of the results or the morality of invoking this clause in the instant situation. In choosing as between alternative interpretations of an ambiguous provision, considerations of equity or reasonableness are factors. But if the provision is not ambiguous then it must be honored even in the face of distasteful results. Otherwise contracts would become not what the parties made them but what neutrals are personally disposed to make them.[55]

In a similar case, Wallen explained the danger he saw to the rule-making relationship if this limitation was not respected by the arbitrator:

Only where the language is reasonably susceptible to more than one interpretation may the arbitrator construe it by applying the tests of intent, reasonableness, past or prevailing practice or the like. There is a sound reason for this rule. If the clear language of an agreement is not given full faith and credit, then a contract is in danger of constant attack by one or the other of the parties by means of the specious claim that despite what the words say, the parties meant something else. *Thus the stability and order the contract was designed to achieve would be lost to the parties.*

Later in the case, Wallen warned the union that, although the result it sought in the immediate case was reasonable, this immediate "temptingly expedient" means of ignoring clear language was fraught with long-term dangers: "But to do so would be to set aside clear language of an agreement, thus making every section vulnerable to the claim that its words do not mean what they plainly say. Such a precedent can gain the union a temporary advantage in the issue at hand but at a cost of jeopardizing the agreement as a whole."[56]

Where there was ambiguity in the written agreement, however, Wallen found there to exist a presumption that the result of the agreement's language was intended to be equitable, reasonable, and practical. In a 1950 case, upon finding ambiguity in the language, he wrote, "In view of this ambiguity it becomes necessary to construe this Section in the light of the parties' intent. It may be presumed that they intended a result that is reasonable and equitable."[57]

Wallen frequently employed a reasonable man test to alternative contract constructions, either asking how a reasonable man would interpret the language fairly and logically,[58] or else attributing such reasonableness to the framers of the agreement, as he did in a case involving seniority rules: "As between these alternative meanings advanced by the parties, which as reasonable men dedicated to their joint purpose of working out fair rules governing seniority in layoffs and promotions, would they have been most likely to agree upon?"[59]

Wallen often asked which alternative meaning or solution would reasonable men have agreed upon if they had faced the issue in negotiations, always assuming that these reasonable men reached their agreements "acting in the context of facts," rather than on the basis of strict economic strength. In some cases, however, he did not use this rationale, but rather simply chose the "more logical and sensible alternative," justifying his position on grounds of common sense and equity.[60] These presumptions of logic, equity, or reasonableness were rebuttable by a crystal clear showing of a consistent past practice,[61] of an intended negotiation result, or of an applicable arbitral precedent, particularly if the different result or interpretation asserted was only based on different judgment or logic and did not create what Wallen considered to be a gross injustice to an affected party.

In those cases where the evidence of the negotiating history and past practices of the parties was in irreconcilable conflict, and especially where the evidence showed that the parties had never before dealt with or contemplated the problem at hand, considerations by Wallen of equity, reasonableness, and practicality led not simply to rebuttable presumptions, but actually became the fundamental sources for his arbitral decisions. In 1951, Wallen plainly stated that "in the absence of a clear-cut understanding of the parties on the point, the arbitrator is constrained to determine the intent of the agreement; that is, to find that construction of the agreement as written which yields the most logical, equitable and consistent result."[62]

Later in his career, Wallen more frequently asked, "of the possible alternative solutions to the arbitral problem, and assuming the parties to be reasonable and logical, 'which is the one they likely would have agreed on had they faced the dilemma subsequently revealed?'"[63] While he appears to have softened the description of his role in these situations over the years, going from determining what he thought was right to determining what he thought the parties believed was right, in practice the result appears identical, inasmuch as he always attributed the qualities of fairness and reasonableness to those whose intent he was interpreting. It is at least arguable that Wallen modified his rationale in response to the changing popular conception of the arbitrator's role as less of a problem solver and more of a judge.

THE ROLE OF LAW

As a general policy, Wallen believed that it was necessary for the arbitrator to read the collective bargaining agreement in the light of any applicable statutory law. In a case involving vacation benefits for returning World War II veterans, he was faced with the question of whether "in the disposition of the issue submitted must consideration be given to the meaning of the Selective Service Act or should consideration be confined only to the language of the written agreements?" In reaching a decision, he plainly stated his philosophy that "it is a settled principle of contract law that the contract must be interpreted in the light of existing applicable statutes" and that "the existing statutes and the settled law of the land at a time the contract is made becomes a part of it and must be read into it." Later, in his decision, he stated that "every contract, not expressly providing to the contrary, is presumed to have been made with reference to the then existing state of the law."[64]

At various times, Wallen expressed a willingness to read into contracts provisions of the Fair Labor Standards Act or Wage-Hour Law, the War Labor Disputes Act, and state workmen's compensation laws, as well as the National Labor Relations Act and the Civil Rights Act of 1964.[65] Wallen only declined to rule on matters of law that he considered unclear or unsettled[66] or in cases in which he believed an administrative agency was the more qualified and more appropriate forum, as when he declined to assert arbitral jurisdiction over issues more properly the province of the National Labor Relations Board.[67]

In none of the above-cited cases did there exist contract language clearly and directly contradictory to statutory law, forcing Wallen into an

either-or choice between the law and the agreement, although in most of
the cases, he did say that if the language was clearly at odds with statutory
law, his ruling would uphold the law and invalidate that portion of the
contract in conflict with the law. As it was, he simply interpreted what he
declared to be ambiguous language in a manner consistent with the
relevant statutes.

ISSUES OF PROOF AND EVIDENCE

While there are no unanimously or universally held arbitral precepts
for the requirements of proof, the vast majority of arbitrators would hold,
in fact if not in word, that the party in arbitration asserting a contract
violation has the primary responsibility for producing sufficient proof to
sustain its case. The lone exception to this rule is the issue of discharge or
discipline which, when contested, must be supported by proof of sufficient cause by the party who undertook the action, namely management.[68] Wallen agreed with this basic arrangement and placed the responsibility for proof accordingly when it was an issue. Where Wallen
significantly differed from many, if not most, arbitrators was in answering
the question of quantum of proof, or how much proof was required to be
supplied by the responsible party to gain a favorable judgment.

Most arbitrators have required that the standard or amount of proof
vary with the nature of the contractual violation claimed, ranging from
what is often called proof "by a preponderance of the evidence" for cases
involving the interpretation of contractual language and minor disciplinary actions, to the higher degree of proof "beyond a reasonable doubt"
in those discharge cases involving an alleged crime of moral turpitude,
such as theft or immorality, in which a guilty verdict might brand a person
as socially unacceptable or economically unemployable.[69] Wallen declined
to require that this higher degree of proof be shown in discharge cases,
even those involving charges of gambling, theft, or immorality, instead
requiring a fairly uniform lower standard of proof by what he termed a
"preponderance or fair weight of the evidence."[70]

There is, however, an inherent difficulty in attempting to quantify and
compare such subjective judgments or standards. While some arbitrators
might equate proof by a preponderance of the evidence with probability,
others would declare that this standard means "more than quantitative
probability, and requires at least sufficient evidence to remove the matter
from the realm of conjecture."[71] Wallen himself defined this standard in
1955 to be "sufficient to persuade one to a moral certainty," and further
stated that "this is something beyond mere suspicion — even strong
suspicion. It must rest on a modicum of tangible evidence."[72] He declared
in 1963 that "the possibility of other courses must be so remote as to strain
the credulity of a reasonable man."[73] As one can see from the above

statements, Wallen himself was not perfectly consistent in defining proof by a preponderance of the evidence. In some descriptions, his standard is more nearly that which a great many arbitrators would describe as clear and convincing proof, a somewhat higher degree of proof.[74]

Wallen, however, made it clear that his standard was less than the standard of proof beyond a reasonable doubt,[75] and this is what is important. He saw the utility of the higher standard of proof beyond a reasonable doubt in a criminal proceeding, but denied its applicability to an arbitration proceeding, because no one was "being deprived of life or liberty."[76] While Wallen stated that it was possible for there to be some crime of moral turpitude which would be so socially and economically damning as to call for the higher degree of proof,[77] a thorough examination of his awards discloses no instance in which he specifically required this highest degree of proof, even in cases of moral turpitude.

To justify discipline or discharge, Wallen had to be shown not only that the particular misconduct claimed was committed, but also that the particular individual disciplined was in fact the individual who committed the misdeed. For example, he once heard a case in which management had disciplined three workers for shoddy workmanship. It was clear that at least one of the three had to be guilty, although managment could not pin down precisely which of the three on the crew was guilty, and no one would admit guilt or implicate either of the other two. Wallen declared that sufficient proof must indicate the guilty individual, calling guilt inherently personal and stating that "the concept of group guilt is alien to our system of justice."[78]

As a final comment on Wallen's treatment of matters of proof and evidence, he also claimed for himself the power to draw whatever adverse inferences he deemed necessary from a refusal by a party to supply relevant information as evidence where it was apparent that the party possessed the information. He outlined his philosophy in an early case:

An arbitrator has no right to compel the production of documents by either side. He may, however, give such weight as he deems appropriate to the failure of a party to produce documents on demand. The degree of weight to be attached to such failure will depend upon the relevancy of the documents requested to the issues at hand. If the information withheld appears to be strongly pertinent the withholding of it may be vital in the making of a decision. If it is of doubtful relevancy, and merely represents an attempt by one party to rove through the files of another on the mere chance that its position may be generally strengthened thereby, then the failure to produce such records should be disregarded.[79]

Seventeen years later, he restated this thesis, adding that this situation was generally not a serious problem if arbitrators warned the parties of their intentions.[80]

In one case, he ruled that, while the failure of management to disclose all relevant evidence did not impair the validity of the evidence that it did present, he would still take this failure into consideration when determining the penalty that he would levy against two individuals charged with the falsification of records. Wallen said he did this to emphasize the special responsibility that management had in this case "to make available details underlying the specifics of a case."[81] This disclosure requirement did not apply to the individuals charged with misconduct, however, as the case involving the group charged with faulty workmanship demonstrates, since the requirement of such disclosure could be tantamount to requiring self-incrimination.

WALLEN AND HIS COLLEAGUES:
A COMPARISON OF DECISION-MAKING PROCEDURES

In comparing Wallen's views on the appropriate criteria and procedures for deciding a case with those of his contemporary arbitrators, based on such traditional frameworks of analysis as determining if the arbitrator is a strict constructionist or a loose or liberal constructionist, one is struck by some inconsistencies.[82] Although it is necessarily a subjective judgment, Wallen was no less strict a constructionist than the majority of his contemporaries when it came to respecting the written provisions of the agreement. The situation is somewhat different in his handling of other facets of the case.

In his attempts, for instance, to reconcile the bare language of the agreement to the situation at hand and determine the application that a reasonable man would impute from that language, without recourse to considerations of claimed contrary oral agreements, past practice, equity, negotiation history, or arbitral case precedent, Wallen was very much the strict "judge," and his results stand in contrast to those arbitrators known as loose or liberal constructionists. Arbitrator William Simkin, for example, generally considered a spokesman for the problem-solving or liberal constructionist school of arbitral thought, once stated that while "no arbitrator in his right mind wants to change the clear-cut terms of an agreement," of the over two thousand cases he handled, "not more than five per cent of the cases were issues concerning [matters] which the contract provided a clear and unmistakable answer."[83]

In cases involving the interpretation and application of the written provisions of the agreement, an examination of Wallen's awards reveals that he found a sufficiently clear and unmistakable answer in the contract language itself about 20 to 25 percent of the time, a figure four to five times greater than Simkin's. In these situations, Wallen went no further in his examination, issuing an award on the reasonable import of the written provisions and ignoring other parol evidence. In relying so heavily on the written document itself, he performed his decisionary role in a manner quite similar to the strict constructionist.[84]

Wallen's treatment of nonwritten indicia of intent, such as claims of past practices, precedent, clause history, and equity, does not lead one as easily or consistently to label him as either a strict or liberal constructionist in comparison to other arbitrators. Take, for example, Wallen's assessment of the importance of arbitral case precedents. It is difficult to measure accurately his views on this subject against those of others because there is such a disparity of arbitral opinion on the issue and great inconsistency among the few studies already done on the topic. Wallen gave strong credence to evidence of authoritative precedent established by prior rulings under the same or predecessor contract and involving the same parties, but relied very little on claims of any persuasive precedent established by the findings of other arbitrators in roughly the same situations but operating under different—even if similar—contracts with different parties before them. Wallen felt so strongly about refusing to be persuaded by findings in other plants with which he disagreed that he once issued a ruling under his General Motors-United Auto Workers umpireship involving holiday pay eligibility that was directly contrary to a ruling made several months before by Harry Shulman, the Ford Motors-UAW umpire, under a nearly identical contract but involving different participants. This contrary ruling directly cost Wallen his permanent umpireship, as he knew it would when he rendered the award.[85] Even in those cases where Wallen might have agreed with the logic used by other arbitrators in similar situations, and in fact decided his cases along similar lines, he still did not use these other findings to buttress his decisions, but instead relied on his own logic and analysis of the facts.

A thorough study of the uses of arbitral case precedent published in 1967 concluded that most arbitrators use precedent differently than did Wallen. The study found that most arbitrators are somewhat resistant to being *controlled* by precedent, even where cases were decided under the same contract, but that arbitrators are being increasingly *persuaded* by arbitral precedents, both where the cases involved the same contract and parties and where they did not.[86]

The reluctance of arbitrators to be controlled even by previous rulings under the same contract was substantiated by Richard Shore in his study of arbitrators' role perceptions. On the other hand, studies by Charles Doyle and William Baer indicate that arbitrators do tend to give very substantial weight to prior decisions involving the same parties and contract, even where they might disagree with those findings, especially if the parties have shown assent to the prior award by leaving the contract language in question unchanged during any intervening negotiations or renewals. Some arbitrators, such as Harry Shulman, have strongly advocated respect for precedent within the same enterprise and have cited reasons of stability similar to those given by Wallen. Many arbitration awards can be found upholding such precedent.[87]

About the most that one can conclude from examining these studies or published arbitration cases is that Wallen was willing to be controlled at least as much as the majority of arbitrators by previous decisions under the same contract. He refused to be so controlled only when he found the prior result clearly erroneous, outmoded, or unjust. He relied considerably less, however, than did most of his contemporaries on the persuasive precedent of similar decisions under different contracts. One cannot easily describe this approach of his as being that of either a strict or liberal constructionist.

Wallen's treatment of claims of controlling past practices, binding oral agreements, and revealing negotiating history is similarly difficult to label. In some instances, his behavior paralleled that of the very strict constructionist. This is especially true where the agreement might have appeared clear on its face, but where the parties had in fact jointly applied a contrary interpretation and had never formally modified the written agreement. Of these situations, arbitrator Harold W. Davey wrote,

A strict constructionist will incline always to the view that the contract governs when practice and the contract are in conflict, notwithstanding the duration and uniformity of the past practice in question. A liberal constructionist, on the other hand, may incline to the view that the parties themselves have determined the meaning of the language by uniform past practice and will conform his decision to the past practice, even though this involves some torturing of the contract's grammar or meaning.[88]

In such cases, Wallen upheld the literal, written agreement, although under some circumstances he might have required that the party reasserting the written agreement give adequate notice of its intention. Many other arbitrators would take a liberal constructionist stance and rule that the practice was controlling. As Richard P. McLaughlin found in his study of the role of past practices in arbitration, "Indeed, beginning from the time near the start of the publication of Labor Arbitration Reports, there has been a steady stream of cases recognizing the existence of a policy allowing the use of past practice even though the contract is seemingly clear and certain in its terms."[89]

Arbitrators Benjamin Aaron and Richard Mittenthal have urged such a use of past practice, as has Morris Stone, who wrote that "there are times, however, when past practice is so purposeful that arbitrators are compelled to conclude it was the practice, not the language of the contract, which expressed the agreement of the parties."[90] S. Lester Block has commented that "there is a growing body of both judicial and arbitral authority that permits clear past practice to override plain contractual language."[91]

Where the contract was not clear and unambiguous, however, Wallen acted very much like those arbitrators characterized as liberal constructionists. In speaking of arbitrators dealing with an unclear agreement, Harold Davey wrote,

> The strict constructionist would probably be persuaded by whatever evidence in the record tends to support an interpretation that will involve the least change or disruption. A liberal constructionist would tend to view such a case as an opportunity to enforce his personal views as to what makes "common sense" from an industrial relations standpoint. Or he will make his decision in terms of an interpretation that appears to satisfy the equities in the situation.[92]

Wallen was unwilling to rely on past practices or the intent expressed by the history of contract negotiations not only where these indicia of intent were unclear or contradictory, but also where they were clear but their results were considered by Wallen to be unreasonable, impractical, or unjust. This approach fits Davey's description of the liberal constructionist's behavior under such circumstances.

While there is strong evidence that most arbitrators contemporary with Wallen preferred to rely on past practice and negotiating history, rather than on the liberal considerations of practicality, equity, or reasonableness, and that this trend toward caution is increasing,[93] Wallen was not alone in his views. Harry Shulman advocated an appraisal by arbitrators of the practicality of their alternatives in deciding a case, as have many other arbitrators. Ralph Seward pointed to the profound danger of relying too heavily on the history of negotiations, particularly the danger of reading too much into abortive attempts to gain particular language during negotiations, since doing so could tend to discourage the parties from clarifying and perfecting their contractual instrument.[94] These appear to be minority viewpoints, however. The majority of arbitrators do not rely to the extent that Wallen did on their own judgment of what is best or right where the contract is unclear or silent on the issue.

Wallen's views on the inclusion of matters of public policy and statute law in decision making also differed from those of strict constructionists, who hold the written agreement supreme. While there appears to be general agreement among arbitrators of all persuasions that, when choosing among alternative interpretations of ambiguous language, an interpretation in conflict with applicable statutory law should fall before an interpretation not in conflict, there has been considerable debate over whether a clear contractual provision in direct conflict with the law should be enforced or denied by the arbitrator. The strict constructionist position that would respect the agreement and ignore the law has been represented by arbitrators such as Bernard Meltzer and Theodore J. St. Antoine. Other arbitrators would rule that the law was supreme, either as a general rule or under certain qualified circumstances.[95]

Wallen's views on the degree of proof required to establish guilt for an offense are not easily characterized as the views of either a liberal or strict constructionist, although in some sense arbitrators such as Wallen who were not exacting as to the degree of proof required for discipline were often termed tough on discipline cases and were aligned with the strict constructionist school of thought.[96]

Most arbitrators would have agreed with Wallen that proof by a preponderance of the evidence was a sufficient degree of proof for discipline cases not involving any charge of criminal activity, although a minority would have held that the economic consequences of discharge required proof to be beyond a reasonable doubt.[97] There has been no clear consensus among arbitrators as to what should be the appropriate quantum of proof for criminal offenses, however, especially those involving some sort of moral turpitude. Many arbitrators have advocated that proof beyond a reasonable doubt be required because an upholding of discharge or discipline in these cases "permanently brands an employee just as surely as a criminal conviction would."[98] The majority of arbitrators, if they were not in agreement with the requirement for proof beyond a reasonable doubt in cases involving criminal activity, at least tended to require a degree of proof greater than by a preponderance of the evidence, perhaps a degree approaching clear and convincing proof. Wallen resisted this tendency, as was previously discussed, although he indicated that for a particularly serious crime of moral turpitude, he would consider a higher degree of proof than he normally required.

As this discussion and comparison of Wallen's views indicates, his decision-making procedures and criteria were an apparently odd amalgam of strict and liberal constructionist thought, with few threads of consistency. When one analyzes these criteria and procedures in light of the goals he believed the arbitration process should further, however, a much more consistent and directed pattern emerges.

The goal of stability for a collective bargaining system that undertook reasoned rule making and problem solving was frequently mentioned by Wallen as a primary aim. Often, his strict constructionist approach was intended to support the stability of the parties' relationship. For example, by relying heavily on the written agreement and deciding a large percentage of his cases solely on what he considered a reasonable reading of the written document, he attempted to encourage the parties to use the negotiating process and codify the rules of their relationship. This encouragement was so important that he was loathe to consider meanings of the written language at variance with its reasonable meaning, even though, through their practices and behavior, the parties had consistently applied the less reasonable meaning, or even though there was evidence that the parties had orally agreed to modify their agreement. His heavy reliance on prior arbitral decisions under the same contract was also justified by Wallen as furthering the stability of bargaining and administration.

His pursuit of stability, however, did not exclude his consideration of individual justice, especially if these goals were not mutually exclusive. For example, he reserved the right to ignore arbitral precedent that he considered unjust or unworkable. Only if the written agreement was very clear and not contrary to law did he allow a plainly unjust or inequitable action to result from his interpretation of the contract.

Once Wallen had decided that the needs of stability did not dictate a decision (that is, that the language was not perfectly clear on its face or that a prior arbitral decision was controlling), he was relatively reluctant to decide a case solely on the basis of such traditional indicia of intent as past practice or negotiating history, if these indicia pointed to a result that he himself considered unreasonable, illogical, or unjust. Where the needs of stability were not in issue, Wallen became very much the liberal constructionist. Thus, he tended to reserve for himself (the critic could almost say for his own brand of justice) the large number of cases in which the solutions were not dictated by the needs of stability.

In the same light, Wallen set himself up as an interpreter of the applicability of statutory law to the parties' relationship, and refused to box himself in on disciplinary cases by rigidly requiring a very high degree of proof to establish guilt. Such a limitation potentially could hamper his discretion in deciding such cases and prevent him from considering stability and productivity, as he would by taking into account the effect of reinstatement on productivity, morale, or union-management relations. That limitation would require him to consider only the matter of individual justice. Since Wallen did not say that this was his reasoning in not requiring a very high degree of proof in disciplinary cases — a requirement that one might expect from an arbitrator who had spoken of the importance of justice for the individual — this justification is merely hypothesized at this point.

The fact that arbitrators leave a large number of issues to their own discretion, so that they might consider what is practical, equitable, logical, or reasonable, does not necessarily mean that they will be guided in their decisions by strong underlying principles. Their decisions may be based solely on caprice or convenience. How Wallen saw his role in decision making, what noncontractual rights and obligations he established for the parties, and how consistent these rights and obligations were with his stated goals are the subjects of Chapters V and VI.

Notes

1. The Murray Co. of Texas, Boston Gear Works Div. and United Steelworkers of Am., AFL-CIO, December 3, 1959, p. 6.

2. East Weymouth Wool Scouring Co. and Dep't of Woolen and Worsted Workers, Local 1715, AFL, November 7, 1946, p. 4.

3. Container Corp. of Am. and United Papermakers and Paperworkers, Local No. 68, April 12, 1967, p. 16.

4. Columbia Records Co. and United Elec., Radio, and Mach. Workers of Am. Local 237, May 13, 1963, p. 3.

5. Allegheny Ludlum Steel Corp., Brackenridge Works and United Steelworkers of Am., Local 1196, December 3, 1964, 43 LA 1043.

6. General Tire and Rubber Co. and United Rubber, Cork, Linoleum, and Plastic Workers of Am., Local No. 595, October 14, 1960, pp. 3–4.

7. Aluminum Co. of Am. and Aluminum Workers Int'l Union, Local 420, June 13, 1962, p. 3; Firestone Rubber and Latex Prod. Co. and United Rubber, Cork, Linoleum, and Plastic Workers of Am., CIO, Local No. 261, March 5, 1953, pp. 3–4.

8. East Weymouth Wool Scouring Co., November 7, 1946, p. 4.

9. Walworth Co. and United Steelworkers of Am., CIO, Local No. 2394, June 18, 1956, pp. 5 and 8.

10. The B. F. Goodrich Co. and United Rubber Workers of Am., Local No. 5, January 13, 1964, p. 9.

11. Walworth Co. and United Steelworkers of Am., Local 2394, CIO, October 25, 1946, 8 LA 255 at 257.

12. Id. at 257-58.

13. Connecticut Light and Power Co. and Int'l Bhd. of Elec. Workers, Local B-420, April 28, 1948, p. 5.

14. Gorton-Pew Fisheries Co., Ltd. and Int'l Longshoremen's Ass'n, Gloucester Seafood Workers' Union, Series 1572, Local 1, AFL, January 7, 1948, 9 LA 587 at 590.

15. Eastern Air Lines, Inc. and Air Line Pilots Ass'n Int'l, November 12, 1965, pp. 10–11.

16. Allis-Chalmers Mfg. Co. and Int'l Union of Elec., Radio, and Mach. Workers, CIO, Local No. 279, November 1, 1958, p. 2.

17. Allen Mfg. Co. and United Auto., Aircraft, and Agricultural Implement Workers of Am., AFL-CIO, Local 518, February 6, 1956, p. 4.

18. H. K. Porter Co. and United Elec., Radio, and Mach. Workers of Am., CIO, Local 252, October 30, 1946, p. 5; Aluminum Co. of Am., Massena Works and Aluminum Workers Int'l Union, Local No. 420, May 19, 1961, p. 4.

19. Aluminum Co. of Am., Lancaster Plant and Aluminum Workers Int'l Union, Local No. 415, April 16, 1963, pp. 2–3; Eastern Air Lines, Inc., November 12, 1965, p. 12; Aluminum Co. of Am., Lafayette Works and Aluminum Workers Int'l Union, Local No. 115, September 14, 1961, p. 2; The B. F. Goodrich Co., January 13, 1964, p. 8; Aluminum Co. of Am., Davenport Works and Aluminum Workers Int'l Union, Local No. 105, November 22, 1960, p. 2; Aluminum Co. of Am., Lafayette Works and Aluminum Workers Int'l Union, Local No. 115, September 14, 1961, p. 2.

20. Aluminum Co. of Am., Lafayette Works and Aluminum Workers Int'l Union, Local No. 115, September 1, 1961, p. 2; Aluminum Co. of Am., November 22, 1960; Aluminum Co. of Am., April 16, 1963, p. 3; B. F. Goodrich Co., January

13, 1964, p. 10; American Brass Co., Am. Metal Hose Branch and UAW-CIO, Local 1251, June 21, 1954, p. 6; General Elec. Co. and United Elec., Radio, and Mach. Workers of Am., CIO, March 3, 1948, 9 LA 757, p. 762; Connecticut Light and Power Co., April 28, 1948, p. 5; Eastern Air Lines, Inc., November 12, 1965, pp. 15–16.

21. The B. F. Goodrich Co. and United Rubber, Cork, Linoleum, and Plastic Workers of Am., Local No. 43, August 21, 1961, p. 4.

22. Gorton-Pew Fisheries Co. *et al.* and Int'l Longshoremen's Ass'n, Gloucester Seafood Workers' Union, Series 1572-1, AFL, March 8, 1951, 16 LA 365 at 368.

23. B. F. Goodrich Co., August 21, 1961, p. 5.

24. Trans World Airlines, Inc. and Int'l Ass'n of Mach., Dist. Lodge 142, February 17, 1967, p. 4.

25. Gorton-Pew Fisheries Co., 16 LA at 368.

26. General Elec. Co., 9 LA at 763; B. F. Goodrich Co., August 21, 1961, p. 5.

27. Southern Airways, Inc. and Air Line Stewards and Stewardesses Ass'n, September 14, 1966, 47 LA 1135 at 1141.

28. Atlanta Newspapers, Inc. and Atlanta Web Pressmen's Union, No. 10, February 1, 1963, 41 LA 400; Atlanta Newspapers, Inc. and Atlanta Paper Handlers' Union, Local 28, October 19, 1964, 43 LA 1094 at 1099.

29. Greenfield Tap and Die Corp. and Local 274, United Elec., Radio, and Mach. Workers of Am., CIO, August 24, 1949, 4 ALAA 68,667; The Goodyear Decatur Mills and Decatur Textile Workers, Local No. 88, United Textile Workers of Am., AFL, September 1, 1953; General Cable Corp. and Int'l Ass'n of Mach., Lodge 2101, Dist. No. 157, January 23, 1958; The B. F. Goodrich Co. and United Rubber Workers of Am., Local No. 281, April 6, 1964.

30. Chicago Pneumatic Tool Co. and Int'l Ass'n of Mach., Dist. Lodge No. 157, April 10, 1961, p. 2.

31. Nicholson File Co. and United Steelworkers of Am., CIO, Local 4408, January 19, 1951, p. 11; John B. Stetson Co., Mallory Hat Div. and United Hatters, Cap, and Millinery Workers Int'l Union, Locals Nos. 10, 11, and 12, Int'l Bhd. of Bookbinders, Local No. 108, March 21, 1957, p. 5; Raytheon Co. and Int'l Bhd. of Elec. Workers, October 28, 1964, 44 LA 295 at 297.

32. Aluminum Co. of Am., Cressona Plant and Aluminum Workers Int'l Union, Local No. 405, April 1, 1963, pp. 2–3.

33. Trans World Airlines, Inc., February 17, 1967, p. 4.

34. See pp. 41–43.

35. Standard Grocery Co. and Int'l Bhd. of Teamsters, Local 829, AFL, May 14, 1947, 7 LA 745.

36. Threadwell Tap and Die Co. and United Elec., Radio, and Mach. Workers of Am., Local No. 274, April 15, 1957; The Am. Brass Co., Metal Hose Div. and Int'l Union, United Auto., Aircraft and Agricultural Implement Workers of Am., AFL-CIO, Local 1078, March 11, 1948; Trans World Airlines, Inc., February 17, 1967.

37. The B. F. Goodrich Co. and United Rubber, Cork, Linoleum, and Plastic Workers of Am., Local No. 5, August 30, 1962, pp. 6–7.

38. Firestone Tire and Rubber Co. and United Rubber, Cork, Linoleum, and Plastic Workers of Am., CIO, Local No. 261, July 19, 1954, p. 6.

39. E. Frank Lewis Co. and United Textile Workers of Am., Local 187, AFL, January 31, 1948.

40. Fitchburg Paper Co. and United Papermakers and Paperworkers, Local Union No. 12, June 1, 1966, p. 9.

41. General Tire and Rubber Co. and United Rubber, Cork, Linoleum, and Plastic Workers of Am., Local No. 595, October 14, 1960, p. 4.

42. Aluminum Co. of Am., Massena Works and Aluminum Workers Int'l Union, Local 420, June 13, 1962.

43. See pp. 36–37 and p. 39.

44. Scott and Williams, Inc. and United Steelworkers of Am., AFL-CIO, October 11, 1956, p. 6; The Budd Co. and United Auto. Workers, Local 813, September 7, 1967, p. 4; Thomas Strahan Co. and United Wallpaper Craftsmen and Workers of North Am., February 8, 1955, p. 3; The B. F. Goodrich Co. and United Rubber Workers of Am., Local No. 5, January 13, 1964.

45. Sylvania Elec. Prod., Inc. and Int'l Union of Elec., Radio, and Mach. Workers and Its Affiliated Local No. 352, January 10, 1962, p. 8.

46. B. F. Goodrich Co., January 13, 1964, p. 7. See also his treatment of claims of oral modifications to the written agreement, pp. 56–57.

47. Sylvania Elec. Prod., Inc., January 10, 1962, p. 8; Firestone Tire and Rubber Co. and United Rubber, Cork, Linoleum, and Plastic Workers of Am., Local No. 336, May 18, 1959.

48. Fafnir Bearing Co. and United Auto. Workers, Local No. 133, February 6, 1964, p. 5; Pan-American World Airways, Inc. and Flight Engineers Int'l Ass'n, PAA Chapter, January 22, 1957, p. 7.

49. General Tire and Rubber Co. and United Rubber, Cork, Linoleum, and Plastic Workers of Am., Local No. 9, April 8, 1959, pp. 1–2.

50. Scott and Williams, Inc., October 11, 1956, p. 6; Firestone Tire and Rubber Co. and United Rubber, Cork, Linoleum, and Plastic Workers of Am., Local No. 336, December 8, 1960; Fafnir Bearing Co., February 6, 1964; Fafnir Bearing Co. and United Auto., Aircraft, and Agricultural Implement Workers of Am., Local No. 133, January 22, 1962; General Tire and Rubber Co. and United Rubber Workers of Am., Local No. 9, December 9, 1966.

51. Brown Co. and United Mine Workers of Am., Dist. 50, Local No. 12175, April 1, 1947, p. 9.

52. Aluminum Co. of Am., Davenport Works and Aluminum Workers Int'l Union, Local No. 105, December 19, 1960, p. 2; The B. F. Goodrich Co. and United Rubber Workers of Am., Local No. 281, April 6, 1964, p. 4.

53. Supreme Embossing Co. and Int'l Fur and Leather Workers Union, Local No. 21, CIO, November 11, 1947; J. I. Paulding, Inc. and United Auto. Workers, Local 899, December 6, 1965, p. 13; Oxford Paper Co. and United Papermakers and Paperworkers, Local 900, March 11, 1964, p. 7.

54. Aluminum Co. of Am., Cressona Works and Aluminum Workers Int'l Union, Local No. 405, April 1, 1963, p. 3; Trailways of New England, Inc. and Div. 1318, Amalgamated Transit Union, AFL-CIO, December 23, 1965, p. 2; Supreme Embossing Co., November 11, 1947, p. 5; Raytheon Co. and Int'l Bhd. of Elec. Workers, October 28, 1964, 44 LA 295 at 296; Scovill Mfg. Co. and United Auto. Workers, CIO, Local 1604, November 18, 1955, p. 2; E. Frank Louis Co., January 31, 1948, p. 5; Merrow Mach. Co. and Int'l Union of Elec. Workers, Local No. 249, November 8, 1961, p. 6.

55. The Stanley Works, Stanley Tools Div. and Int'l Ass'n of Mach., Hardware Lodge No. 1249, September 9, 1954, p. 5.

56. Providence Dyeing, Bleaching and Calendering Co. and Textile Workers Union of Am., CIO, March 6, 1952, pp. 3 and 5; see also Scott and Williams, Inc., October 11, 1956, p. 7; Raytheon Mfg. and Int'l Bhd. of Elec. Workers, AFL-CIO, Local No. 1505, July 1, 1957, p. 4; Union Hardware Co. and Int'l Union of Elec., Radio, and Mach. Workers, CIO, Local 247, March 16, 1954, p. 2.

57. Allen Mfg. Co. and Int'l Union of United Auto., Aircraft, and Agricultural Implement Workers of Am., CIO, Local No. 518, September 25, 1950, p. 4.

58. E. K. Porter Co. and United Elec., Radio, and Mach. Workers of Am., CIO, Local 252, October 30, 1946, p. 5.

59. Nicholson File Co. and United Steelworkers of Am., CIO, Local 4408, January 19, 1951, p. 11.

60. Eastern Air Lines and Air Line Pilots Ass'n, Int'l, June 10, 1966, p. 5; Draper Corp. and United Steelworkers of Am., February 7, 1967, pp. 5–6.

61. B. F. Goodrich Co., April 6, 1964, p. 4; Brown Co., April 1, 1947, p. 9.

62. Waterbury Farrel Foundry and Mach. Co. and United Steelworkers of Am., CIO, Local Union No. 3381, June 19, 1951, p. 10.

63. Southern Airways, Inc. and Air Line Pilots Ass'n, Int'l, September 4, 1963, p. 2.

64. Westinghouse Airbrake Co., Union Switch and Signal Co. and United Elec., Radio, and Mach. Workers of Am., Local 610, September 26, 1946, pp. 7 and 9.

65. East Weymouth Wool Scouring Co., November 7, 1946; General Foods Corp., Atlantic Gelatin Div. and Local 295, Int'l Fur and Leather Workers Union, April 13, 1950, 4 ALAA 68,672; American Tel. and Tel. Co., Long Lines Dep't and Am. Union of Tel. Workers, January 8, 1947; Fafnir Bearing Co. and United Auto., Aircraft, and Agricultural Implement Workers of Am., Local No. 133, November 28, 1955; Brown Bros. Co. and United Furniture Workers of Am., CIO, November 9, 1946; Trailways of New England, Inc., December 23, 1965; Southern Airways, Inc. and Air Line Stewards and Stewardesses Ass'n, September 14, 1966, 47 LA 1135.

66. Southern Airways, Inc. 47 LA at 1140.

67. See p. 46. Wallen was also hesitant to rule on unclear provisions of the Civil Rights Act of 1964. This is discussed in detail on pp. 134–36.

68. I. Hirst Enterprises, Inc. and Burlesque Artists Ass'n, December 1, 1954, 24 LA 44; Russel Smith, *Collective Bargaining and Labor Arbitration* (Indianapolis: Bobbs-Merrill, 1970), p. 393; Myron Gollub, *Discharge for Cause* (New York: New York State Department of Labor, 1948), p. 14; Orme Phelps, *Discipline and Discharge in the Unionized Firm* (Berkeley: University of California Press, 1959), p. 33.

69. For an example of the latter rationale, see The Kroger Co., Grand Rapids Branch and Int'l Bhd. of Teamsters, Local 406, November 28, 1955, R. Smith, arbitrator, 25 LA 906 at 908.

70. For examples, see Scott-Testers, Inc. and United Steelworkers of Am., Local 3904, CIO, January 24, 1949, p. 4; Curtiss-Wright Corp., Wright Aeronautical Div. and United Auto., Aircraft, and Agricultural Implement Workers of Am., CIO, Local No. 669, March 1, 1955, p. 4; Firestone Tire and Rubber Co. and United Rubber, Cork, Linoleum, and Plastic Workers of Am., Local No. 336, May 2, 1958, p. 3; Curtiss-Wright Corp., Wright Aeronautical Div. and United Auto. Workers, Local 669, November 23, 1964, p. 9; American-Standard, C. F. Church Div. and Int'l Ass'n of Mach., Lodge No. 2145, October 26, 1965, p. 8; The Bridgeport Gas Co. and United Mine Workers of Am., Local 12298, January 5, 1967, p. 8.

71. Smith, *Collective Bargaining and Labor Arbitration*, p. 398.

72. Curtiss-Wright Corp., March 1, 1955, p. 4.

73. Aluminum Co. of Am., Vancouver Works and Aluminum Workers Int'l Union, Local No. 300, April 16, 1963, p. 4.

74. Edgar Jones, "Problems of Proof in the Arbitration Process: Report of the

West Coast Tripartite Committee." In Dallas Jones (ed.), *Problems of Proof in Arbitration* (Washington, D.C.: BNA, 1967), p. 195.

75. Curtiss-Wright Corp., November 23, 1964, p. 9; American-Standard, October 26, 1965, p. 6; Curtiss-Wright Corp., March 1, 1955, p. 4; Ford Motor Co., Mound Road Plant and UAW, Local 228, June 7, 1956.

76. Curtiss-Wright Corp. and United Auto. Workers, Local No. 669, March 1963, p. 10.

77. American-Standard, October 26, 1965, p. 6; Curtiss-Wright Corp., November 23, 1964, p. 9.

78. The B. F. Goodrich Co. and United Rubber Workers of Am., Local 281, November 30, 1965, pp. 5–6.

79. American Tel. and Tel., January 8, 1947, p. 25.

80. Wallen, "Procedural Problems in the Conduct of Arbitration Hearings," p. 5.

81. General Elec. Co. and Int'l Union of Elec., Radio, and Mach. Workers, Local 255, April 11, 1968, p. 16.

82. Harold Davey, "The Arbitrator Views the Agreement," *Labor Law Journal* 12 (1961): 1161–76.

83. William Simkin, *Acceptability as a Factor in Arbitration Under an Existing Agreement* (Philadelphia: University of Pennsylvania Press, 1952), p. 40.

84. Davey, "The Arbitrator Views the Agreement," pp. 1164–66.

85. General Motors Corp., Pontiac Motor Div. and United Auto. Workers of Am., CIO, Local 653, August 25, 1948. A joint announcement about the end of the umpireship was made in 1948 by Wallen and T. A. Johnstone, assistant director of the UAW-CIO General Motors Department. It was also reported in *The New York Times*, May 4, 1962 (p. 18, col. 5). Mrs. Wallen, in an interview on December 6, 1973, indicated that her husband was aware of the probable impact of his award.

86. Bruce Hafen, "A Study of Labor Arbitration: The Values and the Risks of the Rule of Law," *Utah Law Review* 1967 (1967): 233–35.

87. Richard Shore, "Conceptions of the Arbitrator's Role," *Journal of Applied Psychology* 50 (1966): 175–76; Charles Doyle, "Precedent Values of Labor Arbitration Awards," *Personnel Journal* 42 (1963): 69; William Baer, "Precedent Value of Arbitration Awards," *Personnel Journal* 45 (1966): 484–86; Shulman, "Reason, Contract, and the Law in Labor Relations," pp. 1020–21; Union Pacific R. R. Co., Eastern Dist. and Bhd. of Locomotive Firemen and Enginemen, September 26, 1962, J. Seidenberg, chairman, 62–3 ARB 8946.

88. Davey, "The Arbitrator Views the Agreement," pp. 1164–65.

89. Richard McLaughlin, "Custom and Past Practice in Labor Arbitration," *Arbitration Journal* 18 (1963): 224–25.

90. Benjamin Aaron, "The Uses of the Past in Arbitration." In Jean T. McKelvey (ed.), *Arbitration Today* (Washington, D.C.: BNA, 1955); Richard Mittenthal, "Past Practice and the Administration of Collective Bargaining Agreements." In Spencer D. Pollard (ed.), *Arbitration and Public Policy* (Washington, D.C.: BNA, 1961); Morris Stone, *Labor-Management Contracts at Work* (New York: Harper and Row, 1961), p. 279.

91. S. Lester Block, "Customs and Usages as Factors in Arbitration Decisions," *New York University Fifteenth Annual Conference on Labor* (New York: New York University Press, 1962), p. 323.

92. Davey, "The Arbitrator Views the Agreement," p. 1169.

93. Hafen, p. 235.

94. Shulman, "Reason, Contract, and the Law in Labor Relations," p. 1018;

Ralph Seward, "Arbitration and the Functions of Management," *Industrial and Labor Relations Review* 16 (1963): 238.

95. Bernard Meltzer, "Ruminations about Ideology, Law, and Labor Arbitration," *University of Chicago Law Review* 34 (1967): 557; Theodore St. Antoine, Discussion of "The Role of Law in Arbitration." In Charles M. Rehmus (ed.), *Developments in American and Foreign Arbitration* (Washington, D.C.: BNA, 1968), p. 82; Robert Howlett, "The Arbitrator, the NLRB, and the Courts." In Dallas L. Jones (ed.), *The Arbitrator, the NLRB, and the Courts* (Washington, D. C.: BNA, 1967); Jean T. McKelvey, "Sex and the Single Arbitrator," *Industrial and Labor Relations Review* 24 (1971): 335–53; Archibald Cox, "The Place of Law in Labor Arbitration." In Jean T. McKelvey (ed.), *The Profession of Labor Arbitration* (Washington, D.C.: BNA, 1957); Richard Mittenthal, "The Role of Law in Arbitration"; Michael Sovern, "When Should Arbitrators Follow Federal Law?" In Gerald Somers (ed.), *Arbitration and the Expanding Role of Neutrals* (Washington, D.C.: BNA, 1970).

96. Davey, "The Arbitrator Views the Agreement," p. 1165.

97. Robert Gorske, "Burden of Proof in Grievance Arbitration," *Marquette Law Review* 43 (1959): 162; Benjamin Aaron, "Some Procedural Problems in Arbitration," *Vanderbilt Law Review* 10 (1957): 741. See also Maurice Benewitz, "Discharge, Arbitration, and the Quantum of Proof," *Arbitration Journal* 28 (1973): 95–104.

98. Aaron, "Some Procedural Problems in Arbitration," p. 742. See, as an example, General Refractories Co. and United Brick and Clay Workers of Am., Local 979, AFL, January 28, 1955, E. Hale, arbitrator, 24 LA 470 at 481-82.

Chapter V

Fundamental Rights
and Obligations:
Management

The purpose of this chapter and the following is twofold: first, to describe those basic rights and obligations of industrial life that Wallen accorded to the parties where the agreement was either silent or else spoke only in very general terms, and second, to determine to what extent these rights and obligations were predicated upon or in harmony with Wallen's goals of productivity and efficiency, stability of industrial relations and administration, and basic justice or equity, including the protection of the workers' investment in their jobs. Included in this examination are not only those situations in which the contract is totally silent with respect to the issue at hand, but also those in which the contract and accompanying evidence is ambiguous or contradictory. This ambiguity was resolved by Wallen on the basis of considerations of efficiency, stability, or justice.

In these chapters, the rights and obligations of management, unions, and individuals are examined, as well as the rights of the general public in those situations where they impinge upon the arbitral process. Management's rights and obligations in determining the mode of operation and the technology to be used; in handling job transfers, subcontracting, workrule making, and the promoting of personnel; and in administrative and record keeping responsibilities, safety, and discipline are considered. The union's representational and bargaining rights, its role in illegal work stoppages, and the relationship of the union to its individual members are also analyzed. The section dealing with the individual worker's rights and obligations covers the employee's grievance rights and duties; issues of discrimination based on race, age, or sex; and the extent of employee equity in a job, including employees with vocational handicaps. The public's stake in product, service, employee safety, and the enforcement of public policy is analyzed in the section concerning the public's rights in arbitration. The final portion of Chapter VI compares Wallen's views with those of other arbitrators and considers the effects of Wallen's goals and values on his substantive decision making.

Throughout these chapters, the delineation of an issue as a right or as an obligation is rather arbitrary, since the issue could be considered both. For example, the right of employees to be disciplined only for cause is, on the other side of the coin, the obligation of management to discipline only for cause. In such a case, it matters little whether one describes the issue as a right or as an obligation, so long as the underlying value considerations and judgments are explored fully.

DETERMINING AND SCHEDULING THE MIX OF PRODUCT, METHOD, JOBS, AND MEN

Perhaps the most fundamental function of industrial management is deciding what products the firm shall produce and in what manner this production will be accomplished. In not one of Wallen's cases was management's right to determine the product ever subject to challenge, but there were many cases concerning the manner of production. In 1948, he was required to decide a case involving a union challenge to management's right to introduce labor-saving machinery, that is, to automate. Neither the management's rights clause of the contract nor language claimed controlling by the union spoke directly to the issue. Wallen found for management, partly on the ground that some contract language might have contemplated or implied the right to introduce machinery, but more directly because explicit language would be required to prevent such introduction. He justified this presumption on the basis that

... the history of American industry is one of advancing technology which has increased general living standards, although admittedly it caused temporary dislocations in some cases. In the absence of such a specific prohibition, Management's right to determine the complement of the working force must be deemed to prevail.[1]

Wallen believed here that the long-term benefits of increased productivity outweighed any short-term effect on individual job security. Throughout his career, he justified technological innovation on these grounds, despite the sometimes adverse impact on individual job security, and tended to uphold management where it had eliminated jobs made obsolete or fictitious by technological innovation.[2]

In a similar vein, he justified, on grounds of efficiency, his refusal to overturn management decisions concerning proper manning requirements and the methods by which work was to be arranged or organized, even though those decisions might have caused a loss of jobs for some unit members. (This assumes that the agreement did not establish specific requirements or procedures for these decisions, which was usually the case.) On the arbitral treatment of this issue, Wallen wrote,

> My theory ... is this: the managerial art commands great respect in our society. The balancing of manpower and work is at its center. The so-called silent contract is silent on the status of past practices but usually contains a management clause recognizing that the attainment of the goal of management—efficiency—is to be restricted only to the extent necessary to enable fulfillment of the contract's commitments.[3]

Wallen determined that management possessed this right, even in situations in which the contract did not contain an explicit management's rights clause.[4] This right to balance manpower and work included two vital issues. The first was the right to determine which mix of *tasks* would be combined and organized to constitute a job or jobs. His view was that this determination was ordinarily a function that resided solely with management, unless clearly expressed restrictive language hampered the right. In one case, he wrote that "it is difficult to see how industry could operate in any other manner," and ruled that the broad interpretation sought by the union of language claimed to be relevant would "restrict productive ingenuity and stifle the introduction of improved methods."[5]

In a similar case, he ruled that management retained the right to "revise or redistribute the content of jobs so as to bring about greater operating efficiency, providing only that changes are motivated by bona fide business reasons." Wallen declined to hold that an employee's seniority rights acted as any sort of bar to this management right, stating that,

> At first blush there would appear to be an outright conflict between the acknowledged power of management to define the duties of a job and the seniority rights of the employees. But upon closer examination it becomes evident that the seniority rights conferred upon employees under this collective bargaining contract are not absolute and unqualified. Indeed, there is nothing in this Agreement which requires the Company to keep the content of a job "frozen" throughout the entire contract period, simply in order not to interfere to any extent with existing

seniority rights. And short of an express provision to that effect, we are not disposed to read one into the Agreement; *for, obviously, the net effect of such a provision would be to make it virtually impossible for the Company to achieve greater efficiency and productivity through the adoption of improved operating methods.*[6]

He believed that management could not have surrendered this basic right to alter job content "without sacrificing its ability to improve methods and reduce costs in an industry which is constantly undergoing technological change and which is highly competitive as well." Wallen then concluded that "where a job is redefined in good faith for legitimate business reasons, and the job as redefined is correctly evaluated, the mere fact that an employee's seniority is incidentally affected thereby does not deprive management of its basic right to determine the proper content of each job so as to run the plant at maximum efficiency."[7] This right to group and regroup tasks into jobs was also subject to the limitation of a fair day's work, that is, the relationship between output or effort to compensation which was fixed during wage negotiations.[8]

The second vital issue in the balancing of people and jobs was the determination of how *jobs* would be grouped or arranged. This issue itself can be subdivided into two problems. The first arises in that situation in which changed conditions or technology make it more feasible or efficient for management to alter the scale of its work operations by increasing or decreasing manning requirements or crew size. About this issue, Wallen once said, "Absent some limiting contract language, Management has the inherent right to man its operations with as many or as few people as its judgment dictates provided its decision does not impose on those working unreasonable work loads or exposure to undue hazards."[9]

Wallen consistently held in similar cases that changed technology, equipment, or machinery, changes in the organization of work, and the elimination by management of unnecessary duties or processes could each justify the alteration of manning requirements.[10] He believed that to rule otherwise would thwart management's pursuit of increased efficiency and productivity.

If none of these factors had changed, however, and management desired simply to escape from an onerous seniority arrangement, or a time study had shown an excess of employees on a crew and management tried to remedy the situation, Wallen did not see these type of changes as being justified, inasmuch as the work situation remedied or altered was the identical one over which the parties had struck a bargain during contract negotiations. He also felt that no better or more efficient technology was being introduced; excess baggage was simply being removed.[11] In such a situation, management, at best, was allowed to isolate the excess manpower and eliminate those excess or unnecessary duties for which that manpower was responsible and then cut back on manning requirements.

The second problem that often had to be considered in those cases involving the grouping or arrangement of jobs was the issue of management's right, in the absence of contractual restrictions, to transfer a job from one process or department to another. In one such case, he established as his touchstone the question, "was the transfer of the jobs involved made for bonafide operating reasons or was it made for the purpose of escaping from the consequences of seniority rules?" He found that the transfer in this case was "an improvement from the point of view of efficient operation and efficient supervision" and that management had "some latitude in shifting jobs as between departments provided it is done in the interests of efficiency and not merely to thwart the operation of the seniority rules."[12] This case involved a transfer of jobs from one department within the bargaining unit to another also within the unit, so the integrity of the bargaining unit was not a factor. A different situation is created when the jobs transferred are removed from the bargaining unit totally. Two early cases vividly demonstrate his balancing of the interests of efficient operation with those of individual job security and bargaining unit stability.

In the first, management had recently moved one of its divisions with which it had a collective agreement to a new location in close proximity to another of its divisions with which it had a different collective agreement. Management abolished the maintenance department of the division that had moved and allocated to the maintenance department of the other division *all* maintenance work for both divisions, justifying this move on grounds of efficiency. The division losing the work protested. Wallen here ruled that management possessed a "normal right to determine the occupational classifications into which the work force was to be divided." He found the change to be a reasonable procedure, since both divisions were now "logically and efficiently serviced by one maintenance shop." He also found no evidence of bad faith or evasion of the collective agreement inasmuch as the employees in the other division were also unionized.[13]

The second case involved an employer who desired to eliminate the positions and duties of six night watchmen from the bargaining unit, assigning their duties to plant guards, who were not unionized. The company argued for its freedom to "make such a transfer of duties in the interests of efficiency and economical production." The contract contained no explicit provision prohibiting the transfer of work to nonunit employees and did contain a typical management's rights clause. Wallen here saw no duplication of work or changed conditions, unlike the previous case in which the one division had moved, and vetoed the transfer, ruling that if anyone was to be laid off, it should in all fairness be the guards, since the watchmen had a greater claim in equity to the work due to their much longer service with the firm.[14] Wallen declared that

If wages is the heart of the labor agreement, job security may be considered its soul. Those eligible to share in the degree of job security the contract affords are those to whom the contract applies.

• • •

The transfer of work customarily performed by the employees in the bargaining unit to others outside the unit must therefore be regarded as an attack on the job security of the employees whom the agreement covers and therefore on one of the contract's basic purposes.

• • •

The management clause is designed to give management the freedom to conduct its affairs in the interest of efficient production, but this right may be exercised only within the framework of the limitations imposed by the contract. That clause cannot be utilized as carte blanche to defeat one of the basic aims of the contract.

If one of the purposes of the contract as a whole, and of the seniority provisions in particular, is to assure the bargaining unit employees a measure of job security then such security would be meaningless if the Company's view in this case were to prevail.[15]

Here, the threshold requirement of a bona fide showing of pursuit of efficiency was not met and the considerations of employee security and unit integrity had to prevail. In an article written years later, Wallen justified his decision on the grounds that the transfer was of identical duties and did not involve either changes in methods, organization, or the nature of the job, or the right of access to improved technology.[16] The only economies to be realized were those resulting from the payment of a lower wage. The lack of such a showing of efficiency gains appears to be the only real difference between this case and the previously discussed one, since in both, employees stood to lose their jobs and the scope of the unit's customary duties was to be narrowed by the transfer.

The question of the control of scheduling as a function of management, the determination of when goods should be produced, also arose before Wallen. Absent any strict guidance from the contract, Wallen again was strongly influenced by considerations of productive efficiency. In one such case, during a prolonged slack period, management sought to schedule its production on a week on–week off basis, producing at full capacity for a week and then shutting down for a week. This meant that those who ordinarily would have been on full layoff received some work they normally would not have, and those with high seniority who ordinarily would have had full-time work now worked only every other week. The contract language was not clear on this point, and management argued that *in any one week,* no peak force (junior) employees were at work while a normal force (senior) employee was on layoff and hence no violation occurred. The union argued that the spirit and intent of the seniority provisions, if not their letter, was destroyed by such an interpretation. Wallen in his decision stated that "in a close question of interpretation, the decision should be based not only on an analysis of the words employed but also on a realistic evaluation of the alternatives in terms of the day-to-day operations of the Company and the Union." About the union's claim, Wallen further stated that "the arbitrator sees no basis...[in the language] ...for a ruling that the parties intended such an extreme limitation on management's right to utilize its capacity efficiently."[17]

In several other cases, Wallen upheld the right of management, on grounds of efficiency, to alter work schedules.[18] In one, he not only upheld the right of management to shorten hours during a slack period, but also stated that this right was not subject to the contract's requirement that management meet and bargain with the union on "all matters pertaining to wages, rates of pay, *hours of employment* and other conditions of employment." He stated that here he was influenced not only by this right generally being solely management's, especially since there did exist a typical management's rights clause, but also due to "the fact that the bargaining requirement would appear to be least fruitful in a situation where lack of work compels the Company to reduce the hours."[19] Here, not only considerations of efficiency but also a conviction that bargaining would be futile under the circumstances led to his decision.

The issue of whether management could schedule involuntary or required overtime, absent any pertinent contract provisions, was another scheduling–rights issue that Wallen had to face. He consistently held that, in addition to the tradition of the industry (itself "reflecting the underlying conditions of technology"), the nature of the plant's operations and the relative productive efficiencies of voluntary or involuntary policies determined the issue.[20] Where the contract was silent with respect to such overtime and management could establish business necessity for the requirement, Wallen held that management had the right to require reasonable overtime.[21]

In summary, in numerous cases involving the issue of management's right to blend jobs and men, Wallen was influenced by his own concepts of efficiency and by the necessity for allowing management to pursue the goal of increased productivity. This conclusion is supported by the negligible impact that the *absence* of a formal management's rights clause or other contractual acknowledgment of efficiency had in many of these cases and by the fact that the arbitral issues with which he dealt here were sparked by changing technological conditions not even contemplated by those drafting the collective agreement.

SUBCONTRACTING

One aspect of the problem of matching men and jobs is that of subcontracting. Why should subcontracting, that is, the transfer of work to employees of some other employer, be any different from the transfer of work to management's own nonunit employees? Wallen never explicitly answered this question, although the implication that can be drawn is that Wallen saw that management was responsible for its entire corporate entity, including nonbargaining-unit sectors. To insure its survival, management had to be able to organize its entire corporate investment and manpower in the most efficient manner possible. Job and unit security were not irrelevant factors in such in-plant job transfer decisions; they were merely secondary to considerations of efficiency. Where the threshold showing of efficiency was made, security considerations had to be put aside. On the other hand, where subcontracting was involved, the party receiving the work was an outside firm whose own efficiency and long-run survival were irrelevant to the case. Only the size and importance to survival of the cost savings to the management doing the subcontracting and the impact on the job and bargaining unit security of its employees were important, with neither clearly receiving first priority. How Wallen balanced these considerations is reviewed here.

Wallen had an opportunity to explain his approach, which was consistent in all fundamental aspects throughout his career, in a 1966 article.[22] The effect of the importance that Wallen accorded to considerations of productive efficiency and job security are demonstrated in the following excerpts:

The long and the short of the matter is that the very essence of a collective agreement implies *some* limitation on the power to contract out work and that with the signing of a labor agreement, the right previously held is no longer absolute. At the same time, where the agreement is silent on the subject, such implied limitation as is inherent in the writing is a country mile from an outright prohibition. This represents the general thinking among arbitrators.

The concept that the labor agreement by implication represents a balance between the right of management to arrange for the conduct of the work of the enterprise and the right of the union and its members to receive the benefits of the labor standards created through collective bargaining stems from the logic of the productive process in a society which sets off rights against responsibilities.

• • •

The innate logic of the implied-obligations view of the collective agreement is that it reconciles this conflict by recognizing that society needs the benefits of management's productive radicalism but that it must not be employed to mask an attack on the security of the work force as a whole.

• • •

By signing an agreement which says nothing about subcontracting, the employer can be adjudged to have done no more than agree not to see the right in an unreasonable way to reduce the scope of the unit or thwart the agreement's stated terms.

• • •

This balance between rights and responsibilities in the matter of subcontracting is essential if the flexibility of our productive system is to be maintained and reconciled with the legitimate aspirations of workers and unions for security.[23]

The lack of a specific ban on subcontracting and even evidence of an unsuccessful attempt to gain such a ban during negotiations did not preclude the union from gaining a full hearing on its implied rights.[24] By the same token, the simple absence of a management's rights clause in the agreement did not impair the basic right of a firm to subcontract where it otherwise was permissible.[25]

In balancing considerations of efficiency with job security, the weight of each factor had to be determined. If there was no measurable cost savings to be realized, Wallen disallowed subcontracting if it had any adverse effect at all on job security.[26] Where the only cost savings realized by management was that gained through the payment of a lower wage rate, Wallen also disallowed the subcontracting if it had any adverse effect at all on the job security of unit members.[27] Here, no real efficiencies were being introduced, only economies. In one of these cases, Wallen also indicated that he believed that to allow such subcontracting would also be destabilizing to the relationship because it would frustrate one of the basic purposes of reaching a collective agreement, that being to fix the wage rate paid for the work in question.[28]

Efficiency considerations did receive considerable weight in Wallen's decisions where management showed that through subcontracting it could gain access to improved technology, machinery, equipment, work methods, or economies of scale, avoid making a costly capital investment that would be underutilized, contract for skills not available in its own plant, or avoid expensive training costs and excessive overtime.[29] In such cases, the impact on job security had to be very considerable to outweigh considerations of efficiency. Where, because of slack economic conditions a full-time position was no longer economically feasible and a mere shell of a job remained, Wallen held that the subcontracting of the job was not unreasonable, even though no improved technology considerations were present and the incumbent was to be laid off.[30]

Additionally, where it proved to be more economical or practical to subcontract an entire employment unit, for example the functions of an entire maintenance or service department, Wallen generally refused to cut off from the unit those particular jobs or tasks that would not be done by any improved work method or technology.[31]

Finally, where those employed were already working a full workweek and no one was on layoff, he frequently approved subcontracting needed by management to meet delivery dates or production deadlines, even if the outside party possessed no special technology, but just extra manpower, and even though this meant lost overtime opportunity for unit employees.[32]

It is not the intent here to demonstrate that Wallen relied on any consistent trade-off of cost savings with jobs lost to determine whether subcontracting should be allowed in a specific situation. It is doubtful that any such consistency existed. The size of the firm, its competitive position, and the necessity of the cost reduction to the firm's long-run survival all influenced the weight that any efficiency and cost considerations had on his decision. At the same time, the impact of job losses on the survival or integrity of the bargaining unit, the unit's size, the economic climate, and whether the firm was expanding or declining all influenced the relative weight that he attached to the number of jobs lost through the subcontracting. What is important, however, is that these considerations of efficiency and job security played an important part in Wallen's decision making over subcontracting issues, even though the written agreement itself was often silent about these criteria and their specific application and little, if any, evidence was presented of the parties' intent during negotiations.

RULE MAKING AND STANDARDS

Another important area of management activity was management's right to establish or change standards and rules of conduct. In several cases, the issue involved was the right of management to pursue efficiency by establishing or changing the standards of output required for a particular job. While in piece-rate industries procedures for output standards and compensation rate changes were generally spelled out explicitly in the written agreement, this was frequently not the case where employees were paid hourly. Here, the wage rate for a job was generally frozen for the life of the agreement and so, argued union advocates, was the output requirement. Generally, these cases involved standards being changed because the job itself was in some way changed or else standards that management claimed were unrealistically low were revised upward. Specific contractual provisions usually dealt with the problem of establishing standards and pay rates for totally new jobs. In these disputed cases, the union usually argued that any changes in output standards from those existing when the agreement was signed required its consent through negotiations. Wallen upheld the union's position in those few cases in which specific contract language mandated such negotiations[33] and also in at least one case in which the contract allowed both the union and management to submit disputes to arbitration when they disagreed.[34]

In the more general case, however, where the contract was silent and a job was altered, for example by providing the worker with more efficient machinery, Wallen held that management could increase the work load requirement if it could demonstrate that the previous output standard was so "excessively low in relation to the concept of a [fair] day's work."[35] Where there was no change in the nature of the job since the current contract had been signed, but management believed the standard to be unrealistically low, or, in the absence of a formal standard, the output of the incumbent to be insufficient, Wallen did allow management to boost work load requirements or establish definitive standards. Here, again, he required that management "sustain the burden of establishing that its new requirement does not cause the employees to exceed the bounds of a fair day's work.[36] While the previous standard, or the past average output in the absence of a formal standard, was presumed the correct measure of a fair day's work that must prevail in the absence of any contrary evidence, it was not immutable. Wallen outlined the grounds upon which management could justify change:

This it could attempt by time studies, by reference to prevailing performance standards on similar or related jobs in the plant. In short, in such a case the past level of production creates a presumption of adequacy in terms of a normal day's work, but this presumption is rebuttable by evidence tending to establish that it is below a commonly accepted standard of normality.[37]

Wallen's holding that management could pursue efficiency at least through the goal of a fair day's work where a job was discovered to be too easy is seemingly contradictory to his holding that management could not similarly pursue this goal by reducing existing crew sizes or manning requirements where they were found to be excessive. In both cases, the end object of management was to receive a fair day's work and employee windfalls in question had existed since the contract had been signed. While Wallen never explained the reason for this apparent inconsistency, it can be conjectured that in the cases concerning crew size reduction, the return to a fair day's work equilibrium would most likely involve layoffs or the potential loss of seniority benefits through transfer, while in those cases in which a plain increase in output standards was sought, there would not be these negative consequences. Perhaps Wallen was unwilling to ascribe to the parties' intent the former and more severe result without a clearer contractual mandate.

Management's right to establish standards of personal physical or mental ability, appearance, or marital status as employment requirements was another disputed subject. Wallen demonstrated his basic approach to this issue best in a case involving a no-marriage rule for airline stewardesses. He first made it clear that management could "indubitably establish *initial* employment standards and thus hire anyone it chooses."[38] Once a person had been hired (without fraudulent application) and thus acquired some seniority rights, however, termination of that person for a violation of these standards would be upheld only if the standards were proven to be reasonable. He so held consistently in cases where specific contract language gave management the right to establish reasonable standards, where such rights could reasonably be inferred from a management's rights clause, and also where the contract was totally silent on the subject. Reasonableness here meant in general that any employment prerequisite had to be shown to be a "continuing element" necessary to the ongoing performance of one's job at minimum acceptable standards in order to be applied to those already hired.[39] Wallen's specific means of evaluating the reasonableness of standards were essentially the same he used to determine the reasonableness of rules of conduct.

While employers were free to alter their standards for initial employment at any time and in any manner they chose, they could apply these tighter standards to employees already hired as a condition of their continued employment if and only if the nature of the job changed or the previous standards were manifestly in error.[40] Such a changed requirement or standard also had to pass the test of reasonableness, and for these incumbent employees the test of reasonableness meant in part that the previous standard under which they were hired and which they were required to maintain conclusively had to be proven insufficient to meet the minimum acceptable requirements of their present jobs before discharges could be effected for not meeting these newer and more stringent standards.[41]

In addition to reasonable standards for employment, there were many situations in which Wallen determined that management had the unilateral right to establish and to change reasonable rules or procedures of conduct, provided that the issue in question was not a condition of employment for which a collective bargaining obligation existed or a condition which was controlled by a clear and mutually accepted past practice.[42] This right to implement rules could originate from an explicit contractual grant or requirement to formulate rules, from the rights implied by the management's rights clause, or simply from the inherent right of management to direct its work force even in the absence of any management's rights clause.

When dealing with either rules or standards, the critical issue that had to be determined by Wallen was precisely what constituted reasonableness. He treated this matter as two issues: first, was the objective that the rule sought to attain sufficiently valid to justify jeopardizing employee seniority, their investment in their jobs, in the event of noncompliance and, second, was the conduct or condition sought by the rule or standard likely to contribute significantly to the attainment of that objective? He upheld as being valid objectives, for example, safety, regular attendance at the plant and at one's work station, a stable and predictable labor supply, the optimization of efficiency, the protection of confidential information, and customer satisfaction or sales promotion.[43] However laudable the objective, though, if the rule or standard could not be demonstrated to be effective in the attainment of the objective, he declined to rule it reasonable. He also denied the reasonableness of rules or standards that conflicted with other contractual provisions, especially where they mandated penalties for noncompliance that conflicted with the requirement of corrective discipline only for just cause.[44]

A final qualification that Wallen imposed on management in the implementation or alteration of rules otherwise found reasonable was that appropriate notice be given to those affected (and not just to the union) before the tool of discipline was utilized to secure compliance. His treatment of management's disciplinary powers is explored later in this chapter, and his generalized requirements discussed there apply to the particular instance of rules enforcement, unless exceptions are noted.

ADMINISTRATIVE RESPONSIBILITY AND DISCRETION

Wallen often had to deal with questions concerning management's rights in everyday administration and the direction of operations. For example, how much discretion should management and lower-level supervision be allowed in reacting to unusual or extraordinary circumstances where the contract specified the ordinary course of action? Should there be a differentiation between willful violations of the contract and good faith misinterpretations or misapplications? How binding or, conversely, how correctible were errors that jeopardized one's contractual rights? These are some of the issues discussed here. This discussion does not apply to errors committed, or unwarranted discretion exercised, in the disciplining of employees. Rather, it deals solely with administrative and operating procedures and attitudes affecting those procedures, such as the application of seniority provisions to transfers or layoffs, the role of supervisory opinion and the given facts of a case in promotion decisions, the correction of errors in compensation, problems in overtime assignments, call-in pay obligations, and the unauthorized assumption of authority by lower-level supervisors. In many cases, management did not flatly claim that at least a technical violation of the contract or an error did not occur, but instead contended either that the decision was reasonable in light of special circumstances or that the decision was within the province of managerial discretion, so long as no bad faith was shown to exist.

Controversy arose, for instance, when management either transferred employees away from jobs or refused to transfer them to jobs to which they seemed contractually entitled (that is, they met the seniority and ability requirements) on the grounds that the jobs would endanger the health or safety of either the employees or those around them. In one such case, Wallen declared that

I believe it fair to state that management has an obligation to avoid exposing employees to undue hazards to their health or safety and that this obligation creates a right, under the Management clause, to transfer an employee if his presence in a given occupation creates an undue hazard for himself or others. This obligation and right exist even where the employee denies that there is a hazard or asserts his willingness to undertake the risk.[45]

In another case, he ruled that management could similarly deny a requested transfer for the same reasons.[46] He was inclined to respect management's judgment if it was evident that the decision was made in good faith, on reasonably adequate evidence, and in an atmosphere that would not indicate any discriminatory purpose.[47] While Wallen believed that "prudence dictates error on the side of safety,"[48] he recognized that the solution was not transfer or termination simply because any risk existed:

What is required in such cases is an approach which recognizes that while there are always some risks in factory jobs, places must be found for people so handicapped (in line with the seniority provisions of the Agreement) in which the risk is relatively small even though not totally absent. And wherever possible, steps should be taken in the form of special safety measures to further reduce the risk in such cases.[49]

The rights of management to terminate employees where handicaps were of such magnitude as to impair efficiency or productive output were not an issue in these cases. The ability to perform the job was plain in each; the only question was management's right to protect health and safety, and hence protect itself from liability.

The appropriate role of managerial discretion also arose in some promotion decisions. Under most agreements, promotions were granted to the most senior qualified bidder; problems arose when management promoted a junior employee over a senior bidder whom it deemed unqualified. Under this type of clause, Wallen generally required that management, if challenged by a grievance, "establish in a clear and convincing manner the employee's non-qualification for the job."[50] This showing had to be made by concrete and detailed evidence, not simply through the general observations of supervisors;[51] the burden of proof was on management.

Under a somewhat different type of promotion clause, which required seniority to be the determining factor only where ability was equal or relatively equal among bidders, Wallen upheld managerial promotion actions that were shown to be "based on a belief stronger than impression but less strong than positive knowledge."[52] Here, while managerial discre-

tion was not completely unfettered, the burden was clearly on the union
or the grievant to demonstrate either the incorrectness of the decision or
the fact that pertinent evidence was ignored. Wallen, however, to insure
the individual equitable treatment, did require that management in this
situation clearly demonstrate the meaningfulness of the claimed superior
skills to the actual performance of the job in question. Thus, the promotion of a common laborer on the grounds of superior knowledge or
training would not fall within the true intent of such a clause, reasoned
Wallen, although superior physical fitness might be a factor on which the
promotion of a junior bidder could be successfully based.[53]

Wallen upheld the right of management under this type of clause to
rely on written ability tests provided that they were fairly and uniformly
administered, not given predominant influence in cases where other valid
evidence of ability existed, and could be shown to be reasonably related to
the actual job requirements.[54]

Another area in which there was both inadvertent error and intentional
but supposedly justified departure from the letter of the law of the
agreement's provisions was the distribution of overtime opportunity. The
typical overtime distribution clause generally required distribution of
available overtime "as equitably as practicable" or "as fairly as possible"
among a fixed group or classification of employees. The presumption
was, all other things being equal, that the person within the applicable
group with the least overtime opportunity to date was given first opportunity to do the work. Where an inadvertent error was made in the
assignment of such work, Wallen's general policy was to provide backpay
to those deprived of their proper opportunity if that opportunity was
irretrievably lost, that is, if the work had been given in error to someone
outside of the grievant's overtime distribution group.[55] If the error simply
involved giving the wrong person in the distribution group the work, and
hence the work was not lost to the group, the deprived low-hour person
was awarded the next available overtime job needed to equalize his or her
hours.[56]

Wallen held that the fact that the deprived employee knew of the error
as it was being made but did nothing to inform management did not
mitigate management's responsibility to make the correct assignment and
did not prevent the awarding of the above-described penalties.[57] He
justified his reasoning here not so much as a matter of equity, but rather as
a spur to management to fulfill its very basic responsibility as the adminis-
trator of the contract.

Where there was evidence that the violation was not just an inadvertent
error or an understandable failure in judgment, but rather a clear or
willful violation of the agreement or the latest of a persistent string of
negligent errors, Wallen required a monetary remedy (backpay) even if

the work had been assigned to someone else in the group and hence no hours were lost.[58]

In some situations, management argued that, as a matter of simple justice or equity, it had fulfilled its good-faith obligation to try to assign overtime hours in the manner required by the contract and had failed due to circumstances beyond its reasonable control. While the precise wording of the overtime clause in question was, of course, a major determinant of management's responsibility (and hence liability) in a given case, two decisions provide considerable insight into what Wallen believed to be a fair and proper exercise of discretion in diverging from the ordinary requirements.

In the first, the need for overtime did not become apparent until the last five minutes of the shift. The low-hour man at that time was working in a shop more than one thousand feet from the locus of the project requiring overtime when the opportunity became known to the supervisor on the spot. There was not sufficient time to find and inform the low-hour man before the shift end; rather than try, the foreman gave the work to a nearby employee. Wallen held that the foreman took the most reasonable course of action under the circumstances and held that it would be unfair to management to penalize it for conditions out of its control. The grievance was denied.[59]

In the second, a crew had been selected for some overtime welding work. While the crew was doing the work, it became apparent that the welder could not reach part of the equipment he was to weld because it was in a cramped place and he was very overweight. Rather than call in another welder or a welding assistant, a rigger on the crew was given the work. Wallen held that while management was required to plan its overtime requirements adequately in advance, it could not in all fairness be expected to plan in such detail as to foresee that the overweight welder could not reach his work. Wallen further held that it would have been unreasonable and inefficient to hold up the entire crew while waiting for a properly classified, low-hour replacement to arrive.[60]

Wallen refused, however, to uphold a claim by management that it could not be held responsible for the loss of overtime opportunity where some employees on an overtime job performed considerable clean-up work out of classification and without being so ordered. Although he found that management neither directed nor condoned the work being done in this manner, he held this to be an incorrect "assignment by default" of the work, creating the same liability as if the incorrect assignment had been made by a direct order. The deprived employees were compensated for the lost work opportunity.[61]

Wallen was also required to rule on similar claims of equitable mitigation in cases involving management's obligations to provide call-in pay to employees reporting for, but not receiving, work. The typical call-in pay provision in an agreement stated that employees reporting for work on their normal shifts who were not notified to stay home received some pay, frequently a half day's pay, if they were sent home due to the cancellation of the shift. The clause generally relieved management of this obligation if the cause of the shift cancellation and the nonnotification of the employees affected were beyond management's control. Wallen defined what he believed was the responsibility that management bore under this type of provision:

The call-in pay provision is a protective clause designed to shield employees from the expense and inconvenience of reporting for non-existent work. Its purpose is to spur Supervision into exercising the highest degree of diligence that can reasonably be expected in a given set of circumstances to determine whether or not work will be available for employees scheduled to report. In cases of doubt this clause, in view of its nature and purpose, should be strictly construed so that its protective purpose will be fulfilled.[62]

Where management mistakenly determined that work would be available or gambled on its availability and lost, such as in guessing whether needed machinery could be repaired before the start of a shift, Wallen held that it was obligated to provide call-in pay. Where management gambled on enough employees arriving through a snow storm and then sent the too few who arrived home after a time, Wallen held that the situation was not beyond management's control and ordered call-in pay. Where a mistake or a gamble was not really made, but a more serious development than could have reasonably been anticipated at the time of the decision developed, such as a second machine breaking down, he relieved management of its pay obligation. In cases of doubt, he resolved the case in favor of payment, inasmuch as the clauses were protective in nature. He also held that if management delegated the responsibility for notification to an agent, such as a telephone answering service or a radio station, it was responsible for providing call-in pay if the agent failed to notify the employees.[63]

In some situations in which management asserted that administrative, computational, or clerical errors had been made inadvertently, Wallen was often forced to weigh the potential injustice of depriving employees of their contractual rights against the need for some sort of administrative stability. This situation sometimes arose when management erred in making job assignments by seniority. While Wallen believed it proper to hold management accountable for the consequences of its errors and awarded backpay to those deprived of a superior job opportunity,[64] he declined, "in the interest of order and stability in the administration of the Agreement between the parties," to entertain any secondary or "chain reaction" grievances so resulting from the primary error of misassignment. Under some complicated seniority systems without built-in liability safeguards, for instance, a misassignment of Employee A might not only deprive that employee of rights to a better paying job, but also deprive Employee B who would have filled Employee A's old job when he or she moved up, and might even have deprived Employee C of some rights. Wallen would here award Employee A backpay for the primary error, but termed further liability for an administrative error to be impractical, unreasonable, and unfair.[65]

Similar considerations of stability governed Wallen's approach to claims of error involving the computation of the appropriate wage rates for various jobs. While errors of mathematical calculation, typing, or recording were correctable, providing such errors were clearly proven to be errors, he ruled that managerial errors in judgment (such as improper rating for speed or effort in a piece-rate time study) should not be correctable, but rather deemed final. He believed this to be necessary if there was to be any stability in the administration of a compensation system and if the agreed upon contract was to remain meaningful.[66]

The final issue to be explored concerning management's operating rights and discretion is the degree to which incorrect supervisory decisions or commitments are binding on higher management even though higher management would have decided the issue differently in the first place and wants to reverse the decision. Considerations of administrative stability and equity again weighed heavily here in Wallen's decisions. Where decisions or promises made by lower-level supervisors were clearly and customarily within their authority, such as whether an employee was entitled to call-in pay or whether poor work was due to carelessness or faulty raw materials, he ruled that if these decisions or commitments were already communicated to the employees involved, they could not be later reversed by either higher management, or by the supervisor. Wallen said that to allow higher management reversals of such decisions would have the same destabilizing effect on plant relations as would allowing union officials to overturn the settlements of grievances agreed to by stewards and committeemen. He considered commitments, promises, settlements, or decisions that exceeded the expressed or customary authority of supervisors, or those which conflicted with the terms of the agreement, however, to be totally reversible by top management, again alluding to the fact that to rule otherwise would harm the stability of the parties' relationship by eroding firm commitments previously made.[67]

In none of the above cases did Wallen allow a clear contractual provision to be ignored or suspended. In virtually every instance where the loss of real monetary rights was suffered by employees, and it was not of their own doing, Wallen ordered a monetary remedy, regardless of the reasonableness of management's actions. A partial exception to this policy was his refusal to consider secondary or chain reaction claims arising out of the misapplication of seniority provisions. In at least one other case, however, where employees suffered real losses of contractually guaranteed benefits through no fault of their own, Wallen ruled that the circumstances surrounding management's circumvention of the agreement were so unusual that the company was relieved of any obligation to compensate for these past losses. In this case, the company's business dropped off over 90 percent during the life of the collective agreement. To keep its supervisory force relatively intact, management assigned some bargaining unit work to supervisors, even though the contract banned this practice. While Wallen required that management cease and desist from this practice in the future, he declined to order backpay to those employees who had lost the work, stating that the management decision "while not proper, was understandable" in light of mitigating circumstances.[68] In this situation, his usual position that stability required a respect for clear contractual provisions regardless of circumstances at least partially gave way to equity considerations, although even here he required as part of his remedy that the contractual provisions henceforth be respected.

EMPLOYEE DISCIPLINE

Perhaps no part of the typical labor agreement allows for greater discretion in fewer words than the simple statement that discipline and discharge shall only be for just cause or just and sufficient cause. As already noted, Wallen read this requirement into the labor agreement even when it was not specifically stated. He presumed that the parties intended this requirement unless the agreement plainly stated otherwise.[69] Wallen held that, as an arbitrator, he had jurisdiction to examine not only the issue of whether the grieving party was guilty of the misconduct asserted, but also whether, in light of all relevant circumstances, the penalty levied was suitable to the offense committed. He specifically rejected the thesis that under the just cause requirement, management retained discretion about the appropriate penalty once misconduct was established and no bad faith or arbitrariness was apparent.[70] If, however, the written agreement specifically reserved such discretion of appropriate penalty for management alone, Wallen respected the agreement's clear terms, albeit reluctantly.

In all of the cases covered in this section, Wallen ruled in a consistent pattern, consistent across firms and industries and consistent over time, as to what specific procedures and requirements had to be met to fulfill the just cause criterion. In attributing the same general meaning to the intent of the term *just cause* in all instances, he did not do so after any intensive exploration of what the parties meant by this very general term or, if the term was not in the contract, what its absence meant; rather, he assumed that the term meant the same in all instances. What were the specific rights and obligations this clause accorded to management? What factors had to be considered by management and by the arbitrator in a discipline or discharge decision? What particular procedures were required? And finally, how much did Wallen's own values influence his answers to these questions and the interpretation that he attached to the parties' intent with respect to just cause?

Wallen was adamant that the power of discipline could not be used to punish or to exact retribution, but rather had to be used correctively to prevent repetitions of undesirable conduct. The discharge penalty could be invoked only where it was obvious that any lesser penalties would not be fruitful in bringing about desired changes. He justified this approach as one that would protect an "employee's rights in his job from capricious or mistaken actions of supervision" and "management's investment in the employee whom it has hired and trained at considerable cost."[71] Appropriate goals for corrective disciplinary action included the correcting of careless or unsafe work habits; the spurring on of employees to raise their efficiency or productive output up to acceptable levels, that is, to provide a fair day's work; and to prevent deliberate violations of the agreement's provisions, plant rules, or accepted norms of in-plant conduct, including suitable respect for supervisors.[72]

Wallen upheld the use of the ultimate penalty of discharge for the following purposes: (1) where it was necessary to remove a chronically or congenitally careless, immature, dangerous, or unsafe employee from the workplace; (2) where it was necessary to remove chronically inefficient, unable, or disinterested employees who did not or could not carry their own weight; (3) to remove employees who willfully and repeatedly violated rules or accepted norms of conduct or who could not accept authority; (4) to remove any employee who committed a single offense so repugnant to accepted norms as to be deemed incorrigible and unlikely to respond to lesser penalties; and (5) to remove employees whose continued employment would clearly bring disrepute to the firm that employed them and would jeopardize its relations with its customers or the public.[74]

In close cases, Wallen also, on occasion, gave some weight to the question of whether the employee was so unpopular or disliked by coworkers or supervisors that reinstatement would create havoc or lead to further disruptions or even resignations by other employees.[75]

Wallen was concerned with the means used in discipline as well as with the ends achieved. In employing the tools of discipline and discharge to meet approved goals, management was also required to follow certain procedures that Wallen believed would minimize injustices to affected individuals. He held it an improper use of disciplinary powers to discipline an entire crew or group of people where only one or some were guilty, but management could not narrow it down to precisely which person or persons were culpable. He asserted that guilt was inherently personal.[76] He refused to lend force to management's use of a shotgun approach to discipline where numerous employees violated the contract's no-strike provisions and were discharged. Here, he stated that

It is a fundamental premise of any modern system of penalties — whether for violations of the law or for violations of obligations under an employment relationship governed by a collective bargaining contract — that sanctions should vary in accordance with the degree of responsibility for the act involved. In a mass violation of the no-strike provision, such as the one that occurred here, there are inevitably differences in the degree of involvement.[77]

On the other hand, an individual could not be singled out or made an example of where several were equally guilty of an offense, unless evidence was presented establishing that the particular employee's extraordinary punishment was justified by a worse prior record.[78]

Also, when evaluating the means employed, Wallen abhorred the indiscriminate managerial use of the technique of gaining incriminating evidence against an employee by setting a trap (particularly for suspicion of only a first offense), rather than confronting and questioning the suspected employee and the union with whatever circumstantial evidence it already had, issuing a warning if appropriate, and reserving such traps only for cases where warnings proved insufficient. Wallen called this technique "a questionable device if the aim of the parties is to maintain good industrial relations and a wholesome atmosphere in the department" and a "step backward rather than a step in the direction of better industrial relations."[79] Wallen's pique concerning this technique was reflected not only in his admonitions to the managements concerned to refrain in the future from such methods but also in the remedies he found appropriate in the cases.

In one such case, where the trap was successful and the offense was one that threatened the health and safety of fellow employees (the employee had washed a toxic substance off hands in drinking water), Wallen accompanied a reluctant upholding of the discharge with a "sincere" recommendation that the company consider reinstating the employee without backpay in a different job where he could not endanger the health of others.[80] In another decision, where the evidence of guilt obtained through the trap was strong but not conclusive, Wallen required that guilt be established beyond a reasonable doubt for the offense, a standard clearly more stringent than he usually required. This, incidentally, was the only award in which he required this standard. Wallen ruled that the evidence did not meet this standard, ordered the employee's reinstatment, but without backpay and with the warning that the circumstances of the case provided suspicion with respect to the employee's conduct.[81]

Part of management's task of substantiating its use of discipline consisted not only of proving what an employee's conduct actually was, but also showing that such conduct was in fact contrary to the agreement, reasonable rules, or established and accepted plant norms. In many cases involving fighting, unauthorized work stoppages, theft, and the like, it was self-evident that the actions, if proven, were violations. In cases involving other offenses, the point was not so clear. Management was faced with the need to show the existence of accepted norms. For example, a company might have disciplined or discharged an employee for loafing or not providing a fair day's work. Here, Wallen required management to establish not only what the employee's actual output was, but also the fact that it was sufficiently abnormal to merit penalty. This management could accomplish only by quantifying what a fair day's work really was, either by demonstrating that accepted production standards did exist or by measuring the past average output of all employees doing that work. Unsubstantiated testimony by supervisors that output was low was by itself insufficient to uphold discipline.[82] Where the charge also included elements of willfulness, such as an assertion that low production was really a slowdown, quantified data demonstrating the low output also had to be accompanied by testimony of others witnessing willful acts, such as employees working at an excessively slow pace, loitering, or leaving their work stations.[83]

Once the guilt of an employee was firmly established in all aspects, there were many factors that Wallen then required be considered in the selection of appropriate discipline. First, the type of offense committed affected the magnitude of the penalty merited.[84] In some violations, the offense was considered so serious or repugnant by Wallen as to merit discharge regardless of any other circumstances or factors. Offenses which Wallen believed merited almost automatic discharge reflect Wallen's own values. Discharge was *almost* automatic for these types of very serious offenses because Wallen held that a completely automatic penalty policy "would sacrifice an occasional individual who merits an exception to the general rule." Wallen stated that "Even a court of law does not go that far in the exercise of its sentencing power. Against the community's stake in retribution is weighed the differential circumstances of individuals."[85]

Wallen often held that serious or dangerous safety violations merited discharge regardless of the circumstances, since continued employment of risky persons would endanger their coworkers' job investments or management's capital investment. Physical assault generally merited discharge for the same reasons and because, in Wallen's words, "in a civilized society, the security of the person is paramount."[86] The discharge of employees responsible for unprovoked work stoppages was also usually upheld, primarily because of the damage to stability that such conduct created. Wallen sustained the discharge of anyone clearly implicated in organized gambling, viewing such activity as "an intolerable evil that corrupts men and morale." Of such an offense, he stated, "Its harmful effects on production on the one hand and on the Union structure on the other, are too great to permit the practice to be condoned. Discharge, and not a lesser penalty, is in order for those clearly implicated."[87] Wallen also upheld discharge in "cases of bald theft of something of value" on the grounds that the losses from theft by employees imposes severe losses on industry and, through it, on society as a whole in the form of uneconomic costs which the consumer ultimately pays for."[88]

For lesser, more correctable offenses, Wallen required that lesser, graduated penalties be levied before a discharge could stand. These graduated penalties were to depend on the second factor that he considered, the employee's past record, with the penalties increasing in magnitude with successive violations.[89] Where an employee had a poor past disciplinary record, but successively stronger penalties were not imposed with each offense, Wallen hesitated suddenly to impose a harsh penalty, such as discharge. For example, one case involved a discharge for reporting to work in unfit condition and using obscene language toward a foreman, the sixth such offense committed by the employee in about five years. He considered this common thread of conduct and the fact that all of the incidents resulted simply in reprimands, except for a one-day suspension for the fourth offense. He said that

...management has not properly applied corrective discipline principles to these incidents. The proper application of these principles would have involved administering successively severer penalties for succeeding offenses in the expectation that these would impress on T_____ the need for changing his ways.[90]

While Wallen did not require that insufficiently disciplined past offenses be totally ignored, he did state that "they cannot fairly be given the weight they would have had if the participants had then received direct warning to avoid future misconduct."[91] The real key to his logic here is the obligation to which he held management to afford an employee the opportunity of self-correction. As he once stated of such a discharge, "By firing him without giving him the chance to correct his conduct under the impact of a penalty short of discharge, it in reality withheld from him the opportunity for self-correction that is implicit in its stated disciplinary policy and that would have been reasonable and proper in his case."[92]

Another reason for such a policy by management was that such consistent application of discipline was necessary to "avoid the taint of discrimination or the charge that it acts capriciously."[93]

An employee's past record had some effect on the magnitude of the penalty he or she received not only where past discipline was imposed, but also in the case of first offenses. An employee with a long-time record of discipline-free service received a slightly lesser penalty for a first offense than would a short-service employee with a similarly discipline-free record.[94]

This analysis shows the importance that Wallen accorded to an employee's past record when determining an appropriate penalty for an offense. Wallen, however, did not require management to impose only warnings or reprimands for all first offenses that were not so serious or repugnant as to merit discharge for a first offense. There were many offenses of intermediate seriousness that merited strong penalties for a first offense still short of discharge, such as a suspension.[95]

A third major factor that Wallen considered in his determination of the appropriate penalty was whether the offense was one that was tolerated without discipline by management in other instances. Similarly, even if the offense was not tolerated elsewhere, he asked whether other guilty employees were given less harsh discipline for their offenses on the basis of factors other than their past records.[96] In one such case, he said, "Reasonable equality of treatment for like offenses is a basic precept of industrial discipline. While the gradation of penalties is proper, such gradation should be based on the records of the offenders in their relations with the employer."[97]

In this case, Wallen denied the discharge of an employee whose guilt of larceny was beyond doubt (the employee had gone to jail) and whose conduct was clearly repugnant to Wallen on the basis that another employee also proven guilty had been reinstated. This second employee had been sentenced by a court to probation rather than jail. He held that this difference was irrelevant, that both employees violated the agreement to the same extent, and that, while neither employee really deserved to be reinstated, the "principle of equality of treatment" demanded reinstatement of the grievant.[98]

A fourth factor that had to be considered was whether employees had real knowledge that their actions were proscribed. This issue arose most frequently where a rule of conduct was newly instituted or where a lapsed or nonenforced rule was reinstated by management. Without exception, Wallen required in these situations that the employee had to have clear notice of the rule's existence before any disciplinary action could be undertaken for nonobservance. Employees were presumed to be aware of clear contract terms and long-standing rules. If the language of the contract or rules inadequately conveyed the parties' intent, however, and employees, without independent knowledge of the true intent, followed the expressed terms or the letter of the law, and hence violated the intent of the rule or provision, they were relieved of responsibility.[99]

A similar situation sometimes existed where it was asserted that employees did not realize the gravity of their offenses or believed that their actions fitted the relevant proscription. For example, Wallen had to review the discharge of an employee charged with theft. The employee had taken a piece of scrap brass that was later discovered in his lunch pail when he left the plant. The employee had not attempted to conceal the object. Wallen examined the question raised by "the indication that he may not have realized the grave view taken by management of such offenses." He ruled that "it is one thing to know the rules and penalties for their violations; but it is another matter entirely to interpret them in specific circumstances." Hence, he reinstated the employee.[100]

A fifth factor was whether employees were clearly and willfully responsible for their offenses or whether they were simply following the crowd and perhaps acting out of fear of peer pressure or violence if they desisted, such as might be the case in an illegal work stoppage.[101] Again, Wallen was reluctant to uphold blanket penalties or "shotgun" discipline for work stoppages in these instances.

In a few cases, Wallen also found an employee not fully responsible for his or her actions if the employee at the time of the offense was under a severe personal strain or pressure and the transgression was an outgrowth of tension. If the extraordinary conditions causing the strain had abated and a repeat violation was unlikely, he ordered a less severe penalty than would ordinarily have been the case.[102]

Sixth, the spontaneity of the act or the existence of provocations of considerable magnitude were sometimes mitigating factors in assessing penalties. For example, he converted to a suspension the discharge of a long-term employee who assaulted a fellow employee because he had verbally abused the grievant repeatedly and obscenely. Wallen especially was concerned that no member of management be responsible for such provocation if the penalty levied was to be upheld by that person. For example, he ruled that profane, loud, and abusive language used by supervisors toward employees invalidated any discipline given to employees if they responded in kind. In two cases, Wallen also reduced to suspensions the discharges of black employees who had physically assaulted their foremen where it was shown that the foremen had provoked the actions by the use of racial slurs. The question of provocation was also raised frequently in cases concerning illegal work stoppages and sometimes led Wallen to at least reduce penalties levied if hard evidence was presented of provocative, arbitrary actions by supervision or management.[103]

A final factor was managerial or supervisory negligence that could act to mitigate or rescind disciplinary penalties. Thus, a foreman's neglect to separate and correct orally two arguing employees before they resorted to fisticuffs was an important factor in Wallen's decision not to uphold the discharge penalty for fighting. He similarly reduced penalties for carelessness and poor workmanship where the foreman failed to exercise sufficiently close supervision, for abuse of leave privileges where the overseeing supervisor was too easy-going, and for working to rule where management neglected to clearly tell the employees involved that such actions would invite discipline.[104]

Notes

1. Gorton-Pew Fisheries Co., Ltd. and Gloucester Sea Food Workers Union, Series 1574-1, Int'l Longshoremen's Ass'n, AFL, August 23, 1948, 4 ALAA 68, 626 at 71,392.

2. Aluminum Co. of Am., Massena Plant and Aluminum Workers Int'l Union, Local 420, June 12, 1962.

3. Saul Wallen, "The Silent Contract vs. Express Provisions: The Arbitration of Local Working Conditions." In Mark L. Kahn (ed.), *Collective Bargaining and the Arbitrator's Role* (Washington, D.C.: BNA, 1962), p. 134.

4. Novelty Shawl Co., Inc. and Textile Workers of Am., Local 75, CIO, September 8, 1946, 4 LA 655.

5. Curtiss-Wright Corp., Electronics Div. and Int'l Ass'n of Mach., Aircraft Lodge 703, AFL, September 22, 1953, 22 LA 831 at 834.

6. Sylvania Elec. Prod., Inc. and United Elec., Radio, and Mach. Workers, AFL-CIO, Local No. 352, December 14, 1956, pp. 4–5 (emphasis added); for a similar holding, see Crouse-Hinds Co. and Int'l Bhd. of Elec. Workers, Local 2084, November 17, 1965, pp. 4–5.

7. Sylvania Elec. Prod., Inc., December 14, 1956, p. 6.

8. Saul Wallen, "The Arbitration of Work Assignment Disputes," *Industrial and Labor Relations Review* 16 (1963): 198. See also Firestone Tire and Rubber Co., Pottstown Plant and United Rubber Workers of Am., Local 336, August 25, 1964, p. 9.

9. Kaiser Aluminum Corp., Bristol Works and United Rubber, Cork, Linoleum, and Plastic Workers of Am., Local No. 339, March 30, 1962, p. 3.

10. Wallen, "The Silent Contract vs. Express Provisions," p. 131; Allegheny Ludlum Steel Corp., Brackenridge Works and United Steelworkers of Am., Local 1196, December 3, 1964, 43 LA 1043; Firestone Tire and Rubber Co., August 25, 1964.

11. Wallen, "The Silent Contract vs. Express Provisions"; Wallen, "The Arbitration of Work Assignment Disputes," pp. 195–96.

12. General Tire and Rubber Co., Akron Plant and United Rubber, Cork, Linoleum, and Plastic Workers of Am., CIO, Local No. 9, September 23, 1955, pp. 2–3.

13. William Whitman Co., Monomac Spinning Mill Div. and United Textile Workers of Am., Local 30, AFL, February 24, 1949, pp. 3–5.

14. New Britain Mach. Co. and United Elec., Radio, and Mach. Workers of Am., CIO, Local 207, April 7, 1947, pp. 5–7.

15. Ibid., p. 6.

16. Wallen, "The Arbitration of Work Assignment Disputes," p. 197.

17. William Whitman Co., Arlington Div. and United Textile Workers of Am., Local 1113, AFL, January 28, 1952, p. 10.

18. Aluminum Co. of Am., Vancouver Works and Aluminum Trades Council, AFL-CIO, November 6, 1961, p. 4; Armstrong Rubber Co. and United Rubber, Cork, Linoleum, and Plastic Workers of Am., Local No. 93, January 10, 1955, pp. 5–6.

19. Armstrong Rubber Co., January 10, 1955, pp. 2 and 6.

20. The General Tire and Rubber Co., Akron Plant and United Rubber Workers of Am., Local No. 9 (Kraft Shop), December 7, 1965, p. 5. See also American Brass Co. and UAW-CIO, Local 1251, June 21, 1954.

21. The Crescent Co., Inc. and United Steelworkers of Am., CIO, Local No. 4543, June 5, 1951, p. 5.

22. Saul Wallen, "How Issues of Subcontracting and Plant Removal Are Handled by Arbitrators," *Industrial and Labor Relations Review* 19 (1966): 265–72. See also Guerin Mills and Industrial Trades Union of Am., July 9, 1953; The Murray Co. of Texas, Boston Gear Works Div. and United Steelworkers of Am., AFL-CIO, December 3, 1959; Anaconda Am. Brass Co. and United Auto. Workers of America, Local No. 1078, November 28, 1961; Kaiser Aluminum and Chem. Corp., Bristol Plant and United Rubber Workers of Am., Local 339, September 20, 1965.

23. Ibid., pp. 266–67.

24. See pp. 41–43.

25. Hershey Chocolate Corp. and Bakery and Confectionery Workers Int'l Union of Am., Local 464, April 28, 1957, 28 LA 491 at 493.

26. Guerin Mills, July 9, 1953, p. 6.

27. Rice and Barton Corp. and United Steelworkers of Am., February 6, 1959; Anaconda Am. Brass Co., November 28, 1961; Simplex Wire and Cable Co. and Int'l Bhd. of Elec. Workers, Local No. 1262, November 11, 1962, 41 LA 237.

28. Simplex Wire and Cable Co., November 11, 1962, 41 LA at 240.

29. Hershey Chocolate Corp., April 28, 1957, 28 LA at 493; Chase Brass and Copper Co. and United Auto. Workers of Am., Local No. 1565, November 30, 1961, pp. 4–5; Kaiser Aluminum and Chem. Corp., September 20, 1965, pp. 8–9; The B. F. Goodrich Co., Clarksville Plant and United Rubber Workers of Am., Local No. 194, August 9, 1966, pp. 5–6; Trans World Airlines, Inc. and Int'l Ass'n of Mach., Dist. 142 (Dining Service Unit), February 24, 1966, pp. 9–10.

30. General Cable Corp. and Int'l Ass'n of Mach., Lodge No. 2101, April 5, 1960, pp. 2–3.

31. Firestone Tire and Rubber Co., Fall River Plant and United Rubber, Cork, Linoleum, and Plastic Workers of Am., Local No. 261, May 16, 1958, p. 4; Southwestern Bell Tel. Co. and Communication Workers of Am., Dist. 6, December 8, 1964.

32. Murray Co. of Texas, December 3, 1959, p. 3; Fafnir Bearing Co. and United Auto. Workers, Local No. 133, April 15, 1963.

33. Pacific Mills and Local 784, United Textile Workers of Am., AFL, November 2, 1948, 4 ALAA 68,630.

34. Merrimack Leather Co. and Int'l Fur and Leather Workers Union, Local 212, CIO, March 24, 1947.

35. Consolidated Thermoplastics Co., Turex Div. and United Steelworkers of Am., November 15, 1965, p. 4.

36. Sylvania Elec. Prod. Inc. and Int'l Union of Elec., Radio, and Mach. Workers of Am., CIO, Local 608, September 8, 1953, p. 7.

37. Ibid., pp. 7–8.

38. Southern Airways, Inc. and Air Line Stewards and Stewardesses Ass'n, September 14, 1966, 47 LA 1135 at 1141. He inferred the same point in Connecticut Tel. and Elec. Corp. and Int'l Union of Elec., Radio, and Mach. Workers, CIO, April 3, 1954, pp. 8–9.

39. Trans World Airlines, Inc. and Air Line Stewards and Stewardesses Ass'n (TWU), Local 550, March 29, 1967, p. 12.

40. Connecticut Tel. and Elec. Corp., April 3, 1954, p. 8.

41. Southern Airways, Inc., September 14, 1966, 47 LA at 1141; Connecticut Tel. and Elec. Corp., April 3, 1954, pp. 8–9.

42. For a situation in which the obligation did exist, see Goodyear Decatur Mills and Decatur Textile Workers, Local No. 88, United Textile Workers of Am., AFL, September 1, 1953, p. 4. See also pp. 64–67 for an examination of Wallen's treatment of past practice issues.

43. Southern Airways, Inc., September 14, 1966, 47 LA at 1139–1141; Aluminum Co. of Am., Cressona Plant and Aluminum Workers Int'l Union, Local 405, October 13, 1961, p. 2; Sylvania Elec. Prod., Inc. and Int'l Union of Elec., Radio, and Mach. Workers, Local No. 291, August 27, 1958, 32 LA 1025 at 1027; United States Steel Supply Co. and United Steelworkers of Am., Local 3746, CIO, September 19, 1949, p. 6; International Shoe Co., Lake Street Factory and United Shoe Workers of Am., Local 128-A, CIO, January 23, 1950, 14 LA 253 at 255; Trans World Airlines and Air Line Stewards and Stewardesses Ass'n, Int'l, June 4, 1962, p. 4; Sylvania Elec. Prod., Inc., August 27, 1958; Goodall-Sanford, Inc. and United Textile Workers of Am., Local 1802, January 23, 1952, p. 3; Beggs and Cobb, Inc. and Int'l Fur and Leather Workers Union, Local No. 21, December 10, 1954, pp. 1–2; Raytheon Mfg. Co. and Local 1505, Int'l Bhd. of Elec. Workers, AFL, October 16, 1956, 7 ALAA 70,182 at 75,466; Premier Worsted Mills, Bridgeton Div. and Textile Workers Union of Am., CIO, January 7, 1947, p. 3; American Airlines, Inc. and Transport Workers Union, Local 501, April 25, 1967, p. 4; Connecticut Tel. and Elec. Corp., April 3, 1954, pp. 8–9; Taft-Pierce Mfg. Co. and Int'l Ass'n of Mach., Dist. Lodge No. 64, December 2, 1959, p. 5; American Airlines, Inc. and Transport Workers Union of Am., March 4, 1964, p. 6; Trans World Airlines, Inc. and Air Line Stewards and Stewardesses Ass'n (TWU), Local 550, March 29, 1967, pp. 11–12.

44. Southern Airways, Inc., September 14, 1966; Connecticut Tel. and Elec. Corp., Inc., April 3, 1954; American Airlines, Inc., March 4, 1964; Sylvania Elec. Prod., Inc., August 27, 1958.

45. International Shoe Co., January 23, 1950, 14 LA at 255.

46. Aluminum Co. of Am., October 13, 1961.

47. International Shoe Co., January 23, 1950.

48. Aluminum Co. of America, October 13, 1961, p. 2.

49. Ibid., p. 3.

50. Walworth Co. and United Steelworkers of Am., CIO, Local 2394, June 18, 1956, p. 7.

51. Fafnir Bearing Co. and United Auto., Aircraft, and Agricultural Implement Workers of Am., Local 133, June 16, 1961, p. 3; Boston Edison Co. and Util. Workers of Am., Local No. 387, March 6, 1961, p. 4; Universal Welding Co. and Int'l Ass'n of Mach., Lodge 1605, December 27, 1955, pp. 5–6.

52. Bell Tel. Laboratories, Inc. and Communications Workers of Am., May 4, 1967, p. 10.

53. Anchor Mfg. Co. and Int'l Bhd. of Elec. Workers, Local No. 1621, July 18, 1963, pp. 4–5.

54. Scott Paper Co. and Pulp, Sulphite, and Paper Mill Workers Union, Local 1, June 21, 1965, p. 2.

55. Borden Chem. Co., PVC Div. and Int'l Chem. Workers Union, Local No. 553, May 29, 1959, pp. 2–3; The Firestone Tire and Rubber Co., Fall River Plant and United Rubber Workers of Am., Local 261, February 19, 1963, p. 2; Aluminum Co. of Am., Warrick Works and Aluminum Workers Int'l Union, Local 104, May 24, 1965, pp. 2–3.

56. General Tire and Rubber Co., Waco Plant and United Rubber, Cork, Linoleum, and Plastic Workers of Am., Local No. 312, April 26, 1960, pp. 2–3; Aluminum Co. of Am., May 24, 1965, p. 3.

57. Firestone Tire and Rubber Co., Fall River Plant and United Rubber, Cork, Linoleum, and Plastic Workers of Am., Local No. 261, December 11, 1958, pp. 2–3.

58. The General Tire and Rubber Co., Waco Plant and United Rubber, Cork, Linoleum, and Plastic Workers of Am., Local No. 312, December 14, 1962, p. 3; Aluminum Co. of Am., May 24, 1965, p. 3.

59. American Airlines, Inc. and Transport Workers Union of Am., August 8, 1968.

60. Aluminum Co. of Am., Lafayette Plant and Aluminum Workers Int'l Union, Local No. 115, July 5, 1963, p. 3.

61. The Firestone Tire and Rubber Co., Fall River Plant and United Rubber Workers of Am., Local 261, February 19, 1963, p. 2.

62. Ford Motor Co., Mound Road Plant and United Auto. Workers, Local 228, July 3, 1956, p. 2.

63. Ford Motor Co., Cleveland Engine and Foundry and United Auto. Workers, Local 1250, October 9, 1957, pp. 2–3; Sylvania Elec. Prod., Inc. and Int'l Union of Elec., Radio, and Mach. Workers, Local No. 291, December 18, 1960; Federal Paper Board Co., Inc. and IPPAU, Local 508, September 16, 1964, pp. 4–5.

64. Aluminum Co. of Am., Massena Works and Aluminum Workers Int'l Union, Local No. 420, August 9, 1960, p. 3.

65. Firestone Rubber and Latex Prod. Co., Fall River Plant and United Rubber, Cork, Linoleum, and Plastic Workers of Am., CIO, Local No. 261, March 5, 1953, p. 4.

66. The B. F. Goodrich Co. and United Rubber, Cork, Linoleum, and Plastic Workers of Am., CIO, November 15, 1951, p. 3. For an interesting case involving the problems of proof in this situation, see Ford Motor Co., Kansas City Assembly Plant and United Auto Workers, Local 249, March 22, 1956.

67. The B. F. Goodrich Co. and United Rubber, Cork, Linoleum, and Plastic Workers of Am., CIO, Local No. 5, October 24, 1952, p. 3; Ford Motor Co., Monroe Plant and United Auto. Workers, CIO, Local 723, February 24, 1956, p. 3; The Am. Brass Co., Metal Hose Div. and Int'l Union of United Auto., Aircraft, and Agricultural Implement Workers of Am., AFL-CIO, Local 1078, March 11, 1958; American Airlines Inc. and Transport Workers Union of Am., Int'l, May 9, 1963.

68. Hudson Worsted Co. and United Textile Workers of Am., AFL, April 19, 1954, p. 4.

69. See pp. 39–41.

70. Campbell Soup Co. and Int'l Ass'n of Mach., Delaware Valley Lodge 2031, February 27, 1967, p. 10.

71. General Tire and Rubber Co., Waco Plant and United Rubber, Cork, Linoleum, and Plastic Workers of Am., CIO, January 24, 1949, p. 5.

72. Firestone Tire and Rubber Co., Pottstown Plant and United Rubber, Cork, Linoleum, and Plastic Workers of Am., Local No. 336, June 6, 1958, pp. 4–5; Chicago Pneumatic Tool Co. and Int'l Ass'n of Mach., Dist. Lodge No. 157, Local Lodge No. 645, April 13, 1959, pp. 3–4; Beggs and Cobb, Inc. and Int'l Fur and Leather Workers Union, Local 22, September 16, 1953, pp. 2 and 22; Dragon Cement Co. and Int'l Bhd. of Teamsters, Local 340, November 5, 1963, p. 6; Clarostat Mfg. Co., Inc. and Int'l Union of Elec., Radio, and Mach. Workers, CIO, Local 242, August 13, 1954, pp. 5–6; Ford Motor Co. and United Auto. Workers, January 3, 1957, p. 2; FMC Corp., Ordnance Div. and Int'l Union United Auto., Aerospace, and Agricultural Implement Workers of Am., Local 348, October 11, 1967, p. 16; General Tire and Rubber Co., Waco Plant and United Rubber, Cork, Linoleum, and Plastic Workers of Am., CIO, January 24, 1949, p. 5; The B. F. Goodrich Co. and United Rubber Workers of Am., Local No. 5, May 21, 1962, p. 3; American Brass Co. and United Auto., Aircraft, and Agricultural Implement Workers of Am., Local 1078, June 24, 1959, p. 3.

73. American Textile Co., Inc. and Amalgamated Lace Operatives of Am., Branch A-6, Levers Auxiliary Section, March 7, 1956, p. 3; Campbell Soup Company, February 27, 1967, pp. 10–11; American Airlines, Inc. and Transport Workers Union of Am., May 7, 1964, p. 2; Beggs and Cobb, Inc., September 16, 1953; Fafnir Bearing Co. and United Auto., Aircraft, and Agricultural Implement Workers of Am., UAW-CIO, Local No. 133, November 28, 1955, p. 5; Brown and Sharpe Mfg. Co. and Am. Fed'n of Technical Eng'r, Local 119, AFL, July 24, 1954, p. 6; Clarostat Mfg. Co., Inc., August 13, 1954, p. 7; Shack's Clothing Co. and Amalgamated Clothing Workers Union, April 21, 1964; General Tire and Rubber Co., January 24, 1949, p. 5; American Airlines, Inc., May 7, 1964, p. 2.

74. Southern Bell Tel. and Tel. Co. and Communications Workers of Am., Local No. 3401, March 20, 1964, p. 7; The Bridgeport Gas Co. and United Mine Workers of Am., Local 12298, January 5, 1967.

75. Shack's Clothing Co., April 21, 1964, p. 6; Hogan Bros. and Leather Workers Int'l Union, Local No. 21, July 9, 1956, p. 2.

76. The B. F. Goodrich Co. and United Rubber Workers of Am., Local 281, November 30, 1965, p. 5.

77. FMC Corp., Ordnance Div., October 11, 1967, p. 16.

78. Ford Motor Co., Lincoln-Wayne Plant and United Auto. Workers, Local 900, August 14, 1956, p. 2.

79. N. H. Poore Co., and Int'l Fur and Leather Workers Union, CIO, Local No. 21, April 16, 1947, p. 4; Woonsocket Rayon, Inc. and Indus. Trades Union of Am., September 30, 1947, p. 7.

80. Woonsocket Rayon, Inc., September 30, 1947, pp. 7–8.

81. N. H. Poore Co., April 16, 1947, p. 6.

82. Ford Motor Co., January 3, 1957; Verza Tanning Co. and Int'l Fur and Leather Workers Union, Local 21, February 15, 1951.

83. Fabet Corp. and Gloucester Sea Food Workers Union, Series 1572-1, Longshoremen's Ass'n, June 23, 1959, p. 6.

84. General Tire and Rubber Co., Waco Plant, January 24, 1949, p. 5; American Brass Co., June 24, 1959, p. 3.

85. The B. F. Goodrich Co., Miami Plant and United Rubber, Cork, Linoleum, and Plastic Workers of Am., Local No. 318, August 21, 1962, p. 3; see also The B. F. Goodrich Co. and United Rubber, Cork, Linoleum, and Plastic Workers of Am., CIO, Local No. 5, April 7, 1952, p. 4.

86. B. F. Goodrich Co., April 7, 1952; see also J. Flynn and Sons, Inc. and Leather Workers Int'l Union of Am., Local No. 21, January 28, 1957, p. 4.

87. Curtiss-Wright Corp., Wright Aeronautical Div. and United Auto., Aircraft, and Agricultural Implement Workers of Am., CIO, Local No. 669, March 1, 1955, p. 4.

88. B. F. Goodrich Co., August 21, 1962, p. 2.

89. Beggs and Cobb, Inc. and Int'l Fur and Leather Workers Union, Local No. 22, CIO, May 22, 1947, p. 9; General Tire and Rubber Co., Waco Plant, January 24, 1949, p. 5; Ford Motor Co., August 14, 1956, p. 2.

90. The B. F. Goodrich Co. and United Rubber, Cork, Linoleum, and Plastic Workers of Am., CIO, Local No. 5, June 30, 1952, p. 2.

91. Worthington Pump and Mach. Corp. and United Elec., Radio, and Mach. Workers of Am., Local No. 259, October 1, 1947, pp. 6–7.

92. The Bassick Co. and Int'l Union of Elec., Radio, and Mach. Workers, Local No. 229, June 14, 1960, p. 5.

93. Beacon Tanning Co. and Leather Workers Int'l Union, Local No. 21, June 13, 1960, p. 3.

94. Jones and Lamson Mach. Co. and United Elec., Radio, and Mach. Workers of Am., Local 218, March 23, 1950, p. 6.

95. B. F. Goodrich Co., May 21, 1962.

96. Beggs and Cobb, Inc., May 22, 1947, p. 9; Ford Motor Co., Dallas Assembly Plant and United Auto. Workers, Local 870, March 5, 1956, p. 3.

97. Lewis-Shepard Co. and United Steelworkers of Am., May 25, 1964, p. 7.

98. Ibid., p. 8.

99. Beggs and Cobb, Inc., May 22, 1947, pp. 9–11; Goodall-Sanford, Inc. and United Textile Workers of Am., AFL, Local 1802, August 29, 1952; General Cable Corp. and United Elec., Radio, and Mach. Workers of Am., UE, Local 331, July 21, 1954; B. F. Goodrich Co., May 21, 1962, p. 3; see also pp. 64–67.

100. B. F. Goodrich Co., May 21, 1962, p. 3.

101. Trailways of New England, Inc. and Div. 1318, Amalgamated Transit Union, AFL-CIO, December 22, 1965, p. 13; FMC Corp., Ordnance Div., October 11, 1967, p. 17.

102. Continental Airlines and The Flight Hostesses, Air Line Pilots Ass'n, Int'l, December 13, 1966.

103. Jones and Lamson Mach. Co. and UE Local 218, October 4, 1966, p. 4; Kaiser Aluminum and Chem. Corp. and United Rubber, Cork, Linoleum, and Plastic Workers of Am., Local No. 339, November 25, 1959; Ford Motor Co., and St. Louis Plant and United Auto. Workers, Local 325, April 2, 1958; J. Flynn and Sons, Inc. and Leather Workers Int'l Union of Am., Local No. 21, January 28, 1957; Republic Steel Corp., Chicago Dist. and United Steelworkers of Am., Local No. 1033, December 26, 1967; John J. Riley Leather Co. and Leather Workers Int'l Union, Local No. 22, January 21, 1959; Creese and Cook Co. and Leather Workers Int'l Union, Local No. 21, February 24, 1956.

104. Jones and Lamson Mach. Co., October 4, 1966, p. 4; Murray Leather Co. and Leather Workers Int'l Union, Local No. 22, December 4, 1958; Boston and Lockport Block Co., and Int'l Ass'n of Mach., District Lodge 38, November 27, 1963; Trans World Airlines, Inc. and Int'l Ass'n of Mach., April 12, 1961.

Chapter VI

Fundamental Rights and Obligations: Unions, Employees, and the Public

THE UNION

In the discussion of management's right to transfer and subcontract work, it was established that Wallen did not allow such actions if they constituted overt attacks on the integrity or the continued existence of the bargaining unit involved. He, in fact, upheld managerial actions producing negative effects on the bargaining unit only where these actions were dictated by a clear business need to gain access to better methods or technology. He believed that the future of the firm, and hence the long-run survival of the bargaining unit, took precedence over the immediate survival of a portion of the bargaining unit. Mere managerial convenience or economy, on the other hand, did not.

Just as Wallen rebuffed overt managerial attacks threatening the union's existence, he also disallowed managerial attempts to avoid or ignore the union in matters with which the union had a proper concern. These were matters which were "usually the subject of collective bargaining, and especially the wages, hours and working conditions under which the employer will cause work to be done by his employees."[1] In many of the cases Wallen heard concerning the avoidance of bargaining obligations, management had instituted changes that the union maintained should have been bargained under some explicit contractual provision. There were also many cases, however, where, even though the contract did not so specify, he ordered that negotiations be undertaken, since the changes dealt with conditions that he believed were properly frozen for the duration of the agreement. For example, this was the case in a situation in which management attempted to secure not only what the parties had deemed to be a fair day's work from all employees, but also sought a greater work load. Here, Wallen ordered that negotiations were required.[2]

In some instances, the changes sought by management were within their traditional powers and hence not subject to negotiations, but the contract required that discussions or notice and conference be undertaken with the union before such changes were unilaterally implemented. Where management ignored or failed to fulfill completely such requirements — frequently with the assertion that such a violation was of no consequence, since management retained final authority and would not be dissuaded by any union arguments — Wallen did not hesitate to underline the importance of such requirements by awarding monetary remedies for any work opportunity lost to employees through such incorrectly implemented changes. The changes themselves were allowed to stand, however.[3] Wallen thought it important that the union should have the opportunity not only to try to convince management that a particular change was unwise, but also to present other alternative changes to which the union was amenable, which management might not have considered.[4]

In addition to its negotiating rights, the union also possessed extensive rights and obligations to represent individual employees or groups in the processing of grievances. In general, where the contract was silent or ambiguous on the issue, Wallen held that the union could press a grievance, even if the particularly affected individuals themselves chose not to do so. He stated that in such situations, the union was entitled to defend not only its own interests, but the interests of other employees whose present or future rights might be affected adversely if a managerial act violative of the agreement was to remain unchallenged. Only where the contract explicitly called for the participation of the affected individual in any grievance did Wallen hold that the union could not press the grievance on account of the individual's failure to participate.[5]

Wallen generally held that the right of the union, through the shop steward, to represent employees under the contract began only with the act of discipline or after management had affected a result the union assumed was violative of the agreement. Stewards and other union representatives did not have a right to represent employees when they were being counseled, cautioned, trained, or directed. When formal disciplinary action was to be undertaken, the affected employee's steward had a right to be present, absent any contractual prohibition, not for the purpose of negotiating the action, but rather to assure observance of the employee's procedural rights under the contract.[6] Wallen also held that stewards and other union officials had no protected rights to countermand management orders that they thought violated the agreement or to advise employees to ignore or refuse such orders.[7] Here, their representational role was limited to the filing of grievances.

Other aspects of the union's role as employee representative in negotiations and grievances include: (a) balancing the union officers' need for freedom of action (and freedom from influence) to effectively represent their members with management's need to assert its disciplinary and promotional powers over the union leaders in their capacity as employees; (b) the union's responsibility to process grievances promptly and without delaying tactics; and (c) the relation of the union to its individual members.

The Union Officer as an Employee

Sometimes, with little explicit contractual guidance, Wallen had to deal with the issue of the degree to which a union steward, committeeperson, or other representative or officer should be independent of any influence by management, while still receiving an income as an employee from management. In most of these cases, the union officials were either part-time union functionaries—the remainder of their time being spent on their regular job—or else were employees working as full-time representatives, while on some sort of leave of absence. What rights and obligations as employees accrued to these representatives? To what degree were they subject to management's disciplinary powers? How were promotion decisions properly determined?

In discipline cases, Wallen held that employees who were also stewards or officials were subject to ordinary plant rules while both working at their jobs and functioning in their representational status. Thus, for example, he held that a steward could be held subject to discipline for swearing at a foreman while pressing a grievance. He ruled that a steward had "every right, and even the obligation, to be as vigorous in his defense of the Union's and the worker's rights as he can be, but he is bound to exercise that vigor within the limits of normal conduct," and furthermore had "no license to ignore the rules of decent relations with fellow human beings."[8] To guarantee that the use of discipline in this situation would not inhibit the steward's proper functioning, Wallen established the following test: "Only if a Steward engages in actions that one would expect management to prevent if engaged in by its representatives will be deemed as exceeding the bounds of normal conduct."[9]

A steward or official could not be disciplined or denied rights for refusing illegitimate management orders not to perform proper representational functions. For example, Wallen ruled that a foreman could not require a committeeman to seek permission before consulting with "higher-ups" in the union about the disposition of a grievance, inasmuch as such consultation was a normal part of a committeeman's duties.[10] Management could, however, require that the committeeman give notice before leaving a work station and could impose discipline if it could prove that these rights were being abused to avoid work.

A steward or other union official functioning as an employee was subject to the same standards of behavior as were ordinary employees. Early in his career, Wallen established that while stewards and officials were not immune from ordinary shop rules and norms, "neither may they be held to a greater degree of responsibility than other employees."[11] This appears to be his general philosophy,[12] although in a much later case, he asserted that an employee's representational status "not only gives him no special privileges but actually imposes extra responsibilities," this responsibility being to act "as an example to the rank-and-file."[13] In this particular case, the employee's conduct would have merited discharge regardless of any representational status he held. Except for the special circumstance of illegal work stoppages, Wallen never handed down a decision in which a union steward or official was disciplined or discharged for conduct that would have merited a lesser penalty had the employee not held the representative position.

A special problem arose in several cases when an employee went on a long-term leave and, while remaining in the company's employ, worked full time for the union as a representative. Wallen ruled that the management should treat such an employee in the same manner as it would a union representative who was not in its employ. In other words, the employee should be totally immune from the management's disciplinary powers. In one such case, while the contract itself was silent on the matter, Wallen so ruled because he believed it to be "proper for such fulltime union representatives to be free from concern as to their personal status," and because he believed that such independence was "vital to the proper exercise of collective bargaining."[14] He stated,

We think it proper that decisions of men so placed should be made in an atmosphere not beclouded by concerns for their personal status vis-a-vis Management. The check on their actions is the knowledge that the Union members who respond to their directions, as well as the Union as an entity, will be held responsible if such directions are improper. If full-time Union representatives are irresponsible, they must be curbed or displaced not by Company action but by action growing out of the sense of responsibility of their organization. After all, their opposite numbers on Management's side may take actions of equally drastic import. They are held responsible only to their own organization — the Company — and not to the Union. We see no justice in holding the full-time Union representative responsible not only to his Union and its members but to the Company as well.[15]

A complicated problem arose for both management and for Wallen in evaluating the eligibility of stewards and officials for promotions. The problem was that they were often away from their jobs performing union duties. Should they then be ineligible for some positions? On the one hand, allowing such a person to be promoted to a critical job or position in essence would have required management to uneconomically promote two people to the one vacancy, since the union official would have need of a constant replacement. On the other hand, denial of the opportunity for advancement might be considered discriminatory and unjust to the otherwise qualified worker. It also might discourage those who were thinking about serving as union representatives. The relevance of public policy as voiced by the National Labor Relations Act was also a factor to be considered.

Wallen first ruled on this issue in a case involving the denial of a promotion to a steward. In answering the management assertion that the promotion of a person to a position for which he or she frequently would not be available was grossly inefficient and hence inequitable to management, Wallen stated that "all business management is a compromise between the *most* efficient method and the one that is practical under current circumstances" and that "in business life maximum efficiency is foregone in favor of optimal efficiency." Applying this logic to the particular case, he asserted that

Maximum efficiency might dictate the manning of each job in the plant by men who will work it eight hours a day. But collective bargaining and written agreements are public policy. And the desirability of a grievance procedure, staffed by intelligent management and union representatives, is not only of the essence of collective bargaining but is recognized as sound personnel administration as well. An important unit of that procedure is the Steward-Foreman level. To make the procedure work, so that the obligations of the law and the contract are met and the benefits of a well-functioning grievance procedure can be realized, it is necessary to sacrifice the efficiency inherent in having jobs filled by Stewards manned a full eight hours a day.[16]

Wallen specifically stated that his finding did not apply to full-time committeemen or officers whose eligibility for promotion might involve other considerations.[17] A short time later, however, in another case with the same parties, he did examine this issue with respect to full-time committeemen and ruled that "the contributions of these Union officials to a well-functioning grievance procedure and the conflict between that contribution and the goal of maximum efficiency differs not at all in concept from that discussed" in the previous case;[18] his ruling also differed not at all. This ruling and its underlying logic were seen in another such case involving a committeeman a number of years later.[19]

Work Stoppages and Grievance Handling

As noted, Wallen's views and values influenced the seriousness with which he approached various types of offenses and hence his decision on the appropriate penalty for committing them. This was especially true in the case of participation in or instigation of illegal walkouts or work stoppages. Wallen flatly declared that an employee engaging in a work stoppage was participating in "the most serious offense under the Agreement"[20] and that "such a person merits a measure of discipline as severe as any that can be administered for an offense at the industrial code."[21]

In several cases involving work stoppages, he explained the reasons behind his feelings. He admonished one union involved in an illegal walkout:

This International Union, like many others before it, was not handed the benefits embodied in its Agreement on a silver platter. Like most of the American Labor movement, it had to struggle for a foothold which made it possible to achieve what the current generation of unionists too often take for granted.

That struggle was first for recognition and later for an agreement to embody the benefits and concessions the local union now enjoys. The collective agreement became the bedrock on which the whole structure of benefits — wages, union security, vacations, and protections against arbitrary treatment — was built. This structure was created step by step and stone by stone.

The success of these efforts was made possible by the continued growth and prosperity of the employer. The growth of production and the enhancement of efficiency were the sources of the gains in wages and benefits for the men engaged in production. The collective agreement guarantees those benefits and at the same time protects the worker against arbitrary treatment.

In return for the concessions made to the union in collective bargaining the employer secures one concession that is basic to his security as well as to the security of the men in his employ. That is a pledge that during the term of the agreement (except in limited circumstances on which both parties have agreed) work will be continued without interruption by either strikes or lockouts so that the Company will continue to produce and the men to earn, to their mutual benefit.

Whoever on the union's side subverts this no-strike commitment by instigating, leading, condoning, or participating in a wildcat strike attacks the fundamental basis of collective bargaining. He defiles that which the union has set out to achieve —a fair agreement to cover the terms of employment. He dishonors the pledged word of his union leadership and despoils the efforts of those who preceded him in erecting the structure of industrial relations which has replaced the jungle warfare of an earlier day.[22]

Wallen considered that particular walkout to be "an attack on the job security of every man in this plant."[23] In another case, he reasoned that

The lesson to be drawn from this unfortunate case is that grievances, real or fancied, must be handled through the orderly procedures of the contract and not by "hitting the bricks." Not only management but Union members are entitled to rely on the contract negotiated for the parties' joint benefit as an instrument that promotes stability and order. That is its purpose. The grievance procedure may appear to take longer than it should but its end result is justice through reason. The wildcat strike can lead only to frustration.[24]

He also believed that the exposure of the union to the risk of a crippling damage suit (hence threatening the entire collective bargaining structure) could also result from an illegal work stoppage and that this was further justification for his stern treatment of such offenders.[25] The negative effects of the work stoppage on productivity and wages, the threat to job security, and ensuing instability were all factors behind Wallen's strong condemnation of illegal work stoppages.

There is one dramatic exception to Wallen's general position that union officials are neither more nor less responsible than other bargaining unit employees for observance of the agreement, shop rules, or ordinary norms of plant behavior. This occurs in the question of the union official's responsibilities in work stoppages.

Wallen, for the most part, held that, barring any extraneous considerations, instigators or leaders of illegal work stoppages were subject to discharge, even when it was the employee's initial offense. Wallen did not impose such a penalty only when it was proven that management in the past had failed either to discipline others for the same type of offense or to give notice that such disciplinary action would be taken in future instances. Where a past policy of discipline existed and was known to the employees and the union, discharge was upheld. Furthermore, even where previous walkouts had been tolerated, management had the inherent right to alter unilaterally this so-called past practice, provided adequate notice was given before disciplinary policies were enforced.[26]

All that has been discussed thus far applies to all employees, whether they be union officials or not. (As a practical matter, however, the natural leadership status of union stewards and officials made it much easier for them to lead a walkout than could regular rank-and-file employees.) But here the similarity of treatment ended. Wallen required union officials not only to refrain from leading or instigating illegal walkouts, but also to take positive preventive steps. Failure to do so subjected these individuals to special penalties. In speaking of these preventive steps, Wallen ruled that

These include the taking of positive, firm and decisive steps to make it plain to their followers that a violation of the no-strike pledge is forbidden. If a wildcat strike is threatened, they have the responsibility to make clear the union's position that it is illegal and improper. By their conduct, the union leaders must not only refrain from condoning the strike but also make plain their repudiation of it and make manifest their attempts to end it. They should be held responsible for maintaining a firm position against a violation of the no-strike pledge not only in their own councils but in a public way, so that the rank and file will know, by means of all media of communication, that such a stoppage is destructive of the agreement and of the rights and interest of all concerned.[27]

Where the union officials concerned were working at the time of a walkout, Wallen made it very clear that this positive duty to repudiate the stoppage included not only verbal exhortation, but also staying on the job to act as examples.[28] Any excuse that they left to convince those already off the job to return was given little weight.

Wallen did hold, however, that the failure of union officials to take these positive preventive steps deserved a penalty of lesser magnitude than that given for active leadership or instigation of the walkout. Generally, a substantial suspension was ordered instead of discharge in cases of what Wallen termed "negative leadership."[29]

The prevention of illegal work stoppages was not the only obligation Wallen required of union leaders in grievance handling. He also required that grievances be processed promptly and conscientiously, and, where such was not the case, he denied the full remedies generally granted when a grievance was found to have merit. For example, where there was evidence that the union neglected or delayed a grievance for an inordinate amount of time, confident of retroactive adjustment to the date of filing, Wallen was willing to order a less than full remedy when upholding the grievance, subtracting those benefits that accrued during the time of delay.[30] In one particularly interesting case, the contract contained no no-strike provision and arbitration of grievances was voluntary. During the course of the grievance, the union went out on strike, although the company was willing to arbitrate. Finally, both parties agreed to arbitration. Although Wallen found the grievance to have merit and the strike to be legal, he reduced the retroactive award to a degree sufficient to compensate for the union-caused delay, because it was "injurious to the interests of all concerned if strikes are called where alternative remedies exist" and because a full award would "condone that lack of restraint."[31]

Wallen, in some instances, similarly reduced or denied retroactive redress where there was evidence that the union condoned a violation for a substantial period of time. Thus, where work was assigned to the wrong classification or to nonunit personnel for a long time and the union was aware of the situation, the grievance was upheld and the misassignment corrected. The award did not, however, impose any monetary liability on management for depriving those entitled to the work.[32]

The Union and Its Members

While it is relatively rare that problems concerning a union's treatment of its members arise in arbitration, the issue nevertheless sometimes comes up. One such instance occurred in 1947 — in a case involving management's obligation to discharge an employee pursuant to the terms of a maintenance-of-membership clause requiring employees who were union members to remain members in good standing for the life of the agreement. An employee had been expelled by the union leadership for failing to respect a legal picket line. The employee was willing to pay his dues and retain his membership in the union. While this case has little importance today (shortly after his ruling, the Taft-Hartley amendments to the National Labor Relations Act allowed termination in such cases only for the failure to tender dues and fees), it is nevertheless very revealing of Wallen's own values and their effect on his decision making.

The union claimed that it alone should be the one to determine the good standing of a member, while management argued that, in reviewing the case, the arbitrator should ascertain whether the union's determination was fair and reasonable before upholding the employee's termination from his job. Wallen ruled that the union's discipline of a member in such a situation was subject to arbitral scrutiny only on very limited grounds and could be overturned only if one of the following circumstances existed: (1) if the discipline was for a refusal to violate law or public policy; (2) if it was for a refusal to violate the parties' collective agreement; and (3) if the disciplinary action was administered in a manner not in accordance with the constitution and bylaws of the union.[33]

The reasonableness or fairness of the union's judgment or the adequacy of the union's bylaws and constitution to provide fair procedures were issues that Wallen believed should not be reviewed. Wallen stated that the appropriateness of refusing to allow a union to coerce an employee to violate the law or public policy was obvious. To allow the union to coerce employees to violate the agreement "would be to tolerate the undermining of the social interest by discouraging the faithful observance of labor agreements." Finally, he stated that "the community will intervene if the procedures followed in determining the conflict between the individual and the organization have not been fair," although he assumed this test would be met if the union did not exceed its constitutional authority.[34]

In explaining his refusal to examine the issue any further, Wallen spoke of the importance of intra-union discipline to the stability of the parties' relationship:

The maintenance of intra-union discipline is necessary to the development of sound, stable unions capable of playing a wholesome role in the field of industry. The very power, the abuse of which is alleged today, may be the means by which an employer is assured stable relations and freedom from unrestrained contract violation tomorrow. It may be the buffer between the employer and power-hungry Union factions willing to use any weapon, including employer harassment, in their struggle to win control from a more temperate and far-sighted leadership. The power of discipline is an inevitable counterpart of democracy; and healthy, disciplined democracy in trade unions is essential to our political and economic well-being.[35]

Wallen believed that to push his inquiry further would undermine this power of discipline and hence potentially damage the stability of the relationship between the parties.[36]

A second, very different case decided by Wallen concerning the union's relations with its members involved the administrative responsibilities that a union may have toward its members. In this one, a long-time bargaining unit member withdrew from the union and the unit, and took a supervisory position. A few months later, this employee's supervisory position was abolished and he sought to reenter the unit with his former seniority status of nearly forty-four years' accumulated seniority. The contract did not provide for the retention of seniority in such cases and the union held that the employee had relinquished all rights and had to return with no seniority status. While Wallen agreed that where the contract was silent, management did not have the unrestricted right to place supervisors in the bargaining unit with their accumulated seniority and thus jeopardize unit workers' security, he nevertheless upheld the retention of seniority in this particular case. This he did not only because to fail to do so would be "harsh and unfair," but, also, and primarily, because the union in administering the membership withdrawal cards did not adequately notify the employee that his seniority would be lost if he ever returned to the unit. He held that "the Union is under a strong moral obligation to give the man involved adequate warning of the significance of his request" in such a situation.[37]

A final case decided by Wallen involving union officer-membership relations dealt with the degree of finality attached to grievance settlements reached by union officials where these settlements were subsequently repudiated by the membership. Wallen first examined whether the agreement and the union's constitution provided union officials with final authority for settlement and whether such an arrangement was democratic. He ruled that the agreement and constitution appeared to allow officers to reach final and binding settlements and further justified his decision on the grounds of practical necessity:

A local union could scarcely function otherwise. If the officers and representatives of the group cannot act in a binding way without first calling on the whole body for a vote, they cannot act effectively at all and the alternative is a local union in continuous session to act on all matters. Neither the union, nor its members nor the company could function thus. They can function only on the basis of *representative* democracy which is what the constitution and the contract are based on.[38]

THE EMPLOYEE

Wallen's values and goals also influenced his arbitral decision making in cases involving the rights and obligations of the individual employee. His values were especially apparent in cases involving the individual employee's right to pursue grievances, individual job security rights— especially in the case of handicapped employees — and charges of discrimination.

Employee Rights and Obligations in Grievance Processing

Wallen's treatment of employees who refused on their own to work or to obey orders of management was to a considerable degree affected by the value that he placed on the maintenance of stable, reasoned problem solving and on the continuity of production. In one case involving an individual's refusal to follow orders of management and perform work in a specified manner, Wallen disclosed his feelings about the importance of continued production:

If there is one cardinal rule in industrial relations, it is that employees have an obligation to obey orders of management which do not present a patent danger to their health or safety, even if they honestly believe such orders contravene their rights under the collective agreement, and to pursue their protest of the order through the grievance procedure. This must be so because the basic aim of the enterprise is production, which is the source of jobs, wages and profits. The collective agreement is designed to assure that this aim is achieved within the framework of agreed-upon standards of wages and conditions and with due regard for the just rights of each party. But the goal — production — cannot be deferred pending a resolution of all the conflicts which may arise about the effectuation of these rights.[39]

In a similar case, he stated that lost production due to work refusals harmed not only the employee and management, but also fellow employees whose income and production may depend on the output of the one refusing work in an integrated process.[40] Because of these factors, Wallen consistently held that proven work or order refusals met the just-cause criterion for discipline with only a few very specific exceptions.

The first such exception was that employees could refuse any order or work which would subject them to undue hazard or to undue peril or jeopardy to health or personal safety.[41] Wallen did not hold that there had to be a clear and real safety or health hazard to justify such a refusal. A refusal resulting from a real fear or honest belief of such a safety threat, even if that fear or belief was later shown to be incorrect, could be excused if the refusal was a reasonable conclusion reached by employees at the time on the basis of their information and knowledge. His test here was whether, at the time of any refusal, "there was sufficient doubt about the degree of hazard present to have justified action geared to safety as the first consideration."[42] Where it was apparent that the primary reason for a refusal of an order or work was not safety, but rather personal pique or animosity toward supervision, a refusal was still upheld as justified if a real and considerable hazard did truly exist, even though under other circumstances employees might have been willing to subject themselves to the hazard.[43]

The second exception to the requirement that all orders of management be followed, one that Wallen seemed to progressively abandon throughout his career, was that the order must be reasonable or at least not flagrantly violative of the agreement. For example, in 1949 Wallen rescinded the discipline given an employee who had refused an order that both parties, the employee and his supervisor, knew violated a provision of the agreement. This was not the case of an order being given in good faith based on at least the semblance of a reasonable interpretation of the agreement. Where supervisory bad faith was not so manifest, Wallen refused to countenance refusals regardless of whose interpretation of the agreement was ultimately shown to be correct. In another case of that period, Wallen asked if the order was unreasonable or "beyond the borders of propriety," holding that if it were, a refusal was warranted. In a similar one that arose toward the middle of his career in 1956, Wallen held that a "manifestly unjust" condition or result could be valid grounds for the refusal of an order. At the end of his career, however, only refusals based on the existence of a safety or health hazard appeared to be held justifiable.[44]

Where Wallen had determined that a refusal of an order or work was indeed not justified, the question of assessing an appropriate penalty arose. Here, again, his values and goals appear to have had a strong influence on his deliberations. One case, illustrative of his approach and the influence of the values he held, involved an employee who had walked off his job in the middle of a shift after a disagreement with his foreman over which tasks he was to perform. The employee refused repeated orders to return to his job and was finally told that he would be deemed a voluntary quit by the company; this also had no effect. At the hearing,

Wallen found the employee totally unrepentant, convinced that he was justified in his actions, and willing to so act again if faced with the same situation. Wallen stated that such a bullheaded employee who showed "no signs of having learned from the experience" would be a destabilizing influence in the plant. He further considered the fact that the employee had little equity or investment in his job (less than two years seniority) and that the job disrupted was a "vital plant operation" necessary for continued production. Considering these factors, he upheld the termination.[45] In virtually all of these cases dealing with unjustified work refusals, stability, production, and employee investment in their jobs were some of the factors considered in determining the appropriate penalty, although he did not necessarily cite them in as candid and clear a manner as in this case.

Job Security and Seniority Rights: The Individual's Job Investment

A worker's investment in a job, an investment that grows with the passage of time, is to some degree contractually recognized in the principle of seniority. Wallen respected and even protected this investment to various degrees in cases before him where the contract was not explicit.

As previously noted, Wallen refused to rule a dispute not arbitrable on the grounds that the grievant was no longer an employee in those situations where the employee had hastily quit out of anger or frustration.[46] He required that clear intent be shown for a quit to be held voluntary and hence binding, especially in the case of long-term employees. He was also willing to go one step further: in a few cases before him an employee had voluntarily (and not in a moment of anger) terminated employment, but later sought reemployment with a restoration of his previous seniority standing rather than as a new employee. In one such case, the employees involved had resigned during a legal strike because they needed income and other employers in the area had refused them employment unless they had formally tendered their resignations with the company they were striking. After the strike was settled, these employees were rehired by their original employer, but the union sought that they be hired as new employees with no seniority standing. Wallen termed such a formality unfair, ruled the employees' actions "a temporary expedient" rather than true resignations, and upheld the restoration of their previous seniority standing.[47]

In a second case, an employee had resigned to enter the priesthood, but soon returned to his employment and sought his previous seniority standing. Wallen admitted that "there is no question in my mind that under a literal application of the contract, M____ forfeited his seniority." He held, however, that he could "see no point that would be served" by the refusal of seniority "under the exceptional and peculiar circumstances of the case."[48] In restoring the employee's seniority standing, Wallen stated that

The Company advanced no reason, other than its technical position under the agreement, for its refusal to restore his seniority; M_____'s departure was not an act of caprice or irresponsibility. He left out of high motives and returned only after he found himself unable to meet the great responsibilities required by a life devoted solely to religion. It would hardly be just if his worthy purpose, now defeated, was to cause him the loss of his employment standing. The restoration of his seniority will therefore be ordered.[49]

Wallen took pains, however, to point out that this was "an exceptional and unusual case" and that in any future cases, he would allow management to rely on the literal requirements of the agreement.[50]

Wallen in many other ways was reluctant to uphold an employee's loss of acquired seniority rights unless such loss was explicitly required by the agreement's terms. In a case discussed earlier concerning the return of a supervisor to the bargaining unit,[51] although Wallen thought that the employee's loss of seniority would be unfair, he primarily upheld the restoration of seniority because of the union's previous failure to inform adequately the employee that he risked losing his seniority by leaving the unit. Ten years later, Wallen heard a similar case involving the seniority rights of exsupervisors, but one in which there was no such failure by the union. Here, Wallen disclosed the true extent of his feeling that a loss of accumulated seniority would be unfair, stating that "While a man who makes such a move relinquishes most of the protections of the collective bargaining agreement, in all equity, one link — the right to seniority retention — should not be deemed severed unless clearly required by the Agreement's terms. I find no such clear requirement here."[52]

Another threat to employees' seniority rights sometimes occurred when management restructured its work setup and transferred jobs out of one department into another, perhaps even abolishing one department and distributing its jobs among other departments. In this situation, valuable departmental seniority rights could be lost to those employees transferred if management decided that the seniority of such transferred employees should reside in the departments to which they moved. Wallen was called on to rule on this problem many times. In one instance, he explained his approach where the contract was silent on the issue, as was often the case. Wallen held that, despite administrative inconvenience and some inefficiency, employees so transferred should be able to exercise their layoff and other seniority rights in the seniority unit that existed when the agreement was signed, unless there was a clear showing that "some overriding consideration of efficiency after the move made the retention of the old seniority unit improper or unworkable." While it was not guaranteed that seniority rights of employees were frozen for the life of the agreement, Wallen held that any patent impairment of these rights had to be justified by a similar or greater impairment of efficiency.[53] Again, his decision in cases where the contract did not treat the issue explicitly was based on two value considerations that he thought important: efficiency and the individual's job investment.

Wallen was not willing to go so far, however, as to read into the agreement implied or inherent seniority rights that logically would have been expressed in writing had they been intended. For example, the union once argued that management should be prohibited from hiring new employees in one department of the plant when employees who could perform the jobs were on layoff in other departments also in the bargaining unit. The contract's provisions clearly established departmental seniority rights. Laid-off employees had priority over new applicants for openings in their own departments. In addition, there was a transfer clause that pledged management to seek to transfer employees to openings in other departments before laying them off. Wallen held that the rights sought by the union might well have been based on sound policy, but he thought it would be an abuse of his powers to find an implied obligation which was so conspicuous by its absence in the contract.[54]

This policy is not inconsistent with the policy in those cases in which Wallen held that employees retained contractually clear seniority rights, even though the contract did not guarantee their continuance through various changes in employment status. It was one thing to deprive an employee of rights previously held which had never been contested and quite another thing to create rights nowhere explicit in the agreement. Wallen very carefully respected this distinction.

As noted in the discussion on arbitrability, Wallen held that the requirement of just cause in discipline and discharge cases was an inherent employee right created with the birth of any labor agreement, whether the right was expressed in writing or not and unless it was explicitly limited or excluded.[55] Wallen also considered an employee's length of service — an individual's investment or equity in a job — to be one of several legitimate factors that should be taken into account by management, and by the arbitrator in review of management, when assessing the appropriate penalty for a proven infraction.[56] What, on the one hand, may be considered an obligation of management can also, on the other, be considered an employee's right.

Two cases, one decided early and one late in his career, demonstrate the consideration that Wallen gave to the individual's equity in a job when determining if discharge is merited. In the first, an employee with 13 years of service was found to have falsified his production count to gain undeserved payment, an offense for which Wallen ordinarily held the discharge penalty as appropriate. The employee had worked for a long time "in a hotbed of petty conspiracy." Nearly all his fellow workers exaggerated their output and he had resisted the temptation for a long period. Wallen ruled in this case that the employee's "advanced years and long service," previously unblemished, when viewed in the light of his surroundings, justified an exception to the general rule of discharge for the offense. Instead, he substituted suspension.[57]

The second case involved an employee with 15 years of service who was found sleeping on the job. Wallen noted that the employee was "a 'hard luck' type, not likely at his age and with his health record, to find other employment easily," and also not a "major thorn in anyone's side." Here, Wallen ruled that the employee had a considerable investment in his job not only because of his long service, but even more so due to his "health and hapless condition." As a result, Wallen converted the discharge to a penalty layoff, stating that "justice should be tempered with mercy in appropriate cases and this appears to be one such."[58]

Vocational Handicaps

Wallen's position on the investment an individual has in a job is best demonstrated in those cases involving the attempted discharge of employees who in some manner were vocationally handicapped or otherwise unable to perform adequately their duties. Often, here, the employee plainly could not fulfill the obligation to perform a fair day's work or attend work regularly. To force management to retain such personnel clearly collided with the value and respect that Wallen held for productivity and efficiency.

Wallen often wrote of the considerations that entered his mind when reviewing the proposed terminations of such handicapped employees. In a 1953 decision involving two alcoholics fired for poor attendance and work, Wallen observed that management had been extremely tolerant and forbearing in the past, but noted,

On the other hand, the arbitrator is stirred by the fact that S_____ has nearly a lifetime of service with this Company. To separate a man with so many years of service one must be convinced beyond all doubt that some less drastic step will not serve to cause him to change his habits. Likewise M_____ has undisputed talents as a workman which it would be a shame to lose if there is a lingering doubt about his ability to rehabilitate himself. The arbitrator does not mean to imply that long service men can never be discharged, but he does say that discharges in such cases should be invoked only after a full conviction that all hope is gone.[59]

In a 1958 case involving an employee subject to incapacitating asthma attacks, he wrote,

While the Company should not be expected to continue in its employ indefinitely a man whose health prevents him from discharging the duties of his job, it is reasonable to require it to "string along" with a long-service man so handicapped if there is a reasonable expectation that his situation will improve.[60]

He further explained and demonstrated his approach in a 1966 case involving an alcoholic employee whose problems were compounded by a sick wife:

In view of the circumstances I am reluctant to uphold the discharge of a man with 34 years of service and a satisfactory work record, except for his attendance record in the last few years, where there is a reasonable basis to expect that with skilled professional help he may again be a dependable employee. It is my conviction that the problem involved here can be handled in a manner that will avert a real tragedy at best or leave the conscience of the Company perfectly clear at worst, and without damage to the goal of production.[61]

All this did not mean, however, that Wallen was willing to require the continued employment of employees hopelessly or chronically unable to ever regain their former level of productivity:

An inability to work steadily, even if due to illness which the employee cannot help, if chronic and sustained, may constitute cause for discharge. The logic is simple. If an employee is unable to render in a consistent way that function of service for which he was engaged, he is unable to fulfill his obligation in a relationship which is reciprocal.

That inability can be cause for discharge even though the element of misconduct for which discipline, in the sense of suspension or discharge, is ordinarily levied is absent. It is not enough to say that a man cannot help being ill. The employer cannot help it either. At some point an employee whose health frustrates his ability to fulfill his duties to a reasonable extent ceases to be an employee solely because he cannot render the service that the term implies.[62]

• • •

On the other hand, even a generous policy must have limits. Management cannot be expected to carry hopeless cases on the dim chance that a miracle might occur. Its interests in efficient operations must be balanced against its humanitarian concern for individuals.

• • •

But the touchstone for consideration of such cases, it seems to us, is whether at a given time the prospects for rehabilitation have brightened or whether they remain the same as they had been. If the Company's enlightened policy is to be meaningful, it should be not unwilling to accept the possible inconvenience which may be involved in giving a man whose prospects for rehabilitation had improved another opportunity, provided there are grounds for believing that his situation has in fact changed for the better.[63]

Wallen also was not as willing to extend to employees the extra chance at rehabilitation where these employees had not developed a long-term investment in their jobs. In one case involving a frequently ill employee without such equity in his job, Wallen upheld his termination, writing,

I would have been inclined in his case to resolve all doubts in his benefit had he been a long-service employee with a generally good record whose attendance record had latterly gone sour. But that is not true in his case. He has two years seniority. He has developed no equity in his job of such a magnitude as to cause him to merit another chance to salvage it.[64]

As one can gather from these quotes, the standard that Wallen applied in deciding if the individual's job equity outweighed any temporary shortcomings in efficiency or productivity was very nebulous and un-quantified. As he once wrote, "One can only decide these cases by as careful an appraisal of the possibilities as can be mustered. And often this becomes a matter of feel."[65]

Basically, where there was a chance, a possibility, a fifty-fifty chance, or the situation was not yet hopeless, the employee was not terminated. On the other hand, if the situation or condition was chronic, showed no improvement, and no evidence indicated a possibility for such improve-ment, termination was upheld even where the employee had many years of service. Needless to say, where employees were undergoing some sort of therapy for their problem or condition, even if results had not yet been shown, Wallen, as a rule, deferred termination until after such therapy proved unsuccessful. Only where therapy and recovery were completed and the employee could still not work at minimum standards was dis-charge upheld.[66]

In most of these cases, if the productive ability of employees was severely impaired, Wallen ordered them placed on sick leaves of absence or layoff status, rather than keeping them on jobs they could not perform adequately. He did not require, however, that employees return to 100 percent of their previous fitness or all-around efficiency before allowing them to be recalled to some work, but instead required that a reasonable compromise be reached. For example, in some cases, Wallen held that if supervision could formulate a mix of tasks that the employee could perform adequately and efficiently, reinstatement under these conditions would be effected. Whether this was possible in each case depended both on the type and severity of the handicap and on the current degree of recovery, as well as the nature of the work and the organizational setup. The availability of work in general was also a significant factor. Wallen generally ruled that handicapped, only partially efficient employees could exercise their seniority rights to displace other similarly handicap-ped employees, but could not displace junior employees with no hand-icaps working at full efficiency.[67]

Wallen's concern with insuring safety and the wide discretion he al-lowed management pursuing or insuring safety were examined earlier. In the same vein, Wallen did not ignore considerations of safety when determining the fate of handicapped employees. The mere existence of some minor safety hazard, however, did not act as a bar to reinstatement.

For example, Wallen refused to uphold the termination of a diabetic employee who created "at most a slight extra hazard." Wallen here stated that

For if despite his condition a worker can function well as an employee, without undue hazard to himself or his fellows and without creating an excessive liability for his employer, then his ailment cannot be deemed to affect the employment relationship. Nearly all humans suffer from ailments or infirmities and many of these may be potentially hazardous. The question is to what degree? The effect of the ailment on the worker's employment status depends upon the degree of hazard thus created.[68]

Wallen believed than an undue hazard to the employee's health did exist in a case involving an employee who suffered from chronic and incurable muscle strains and who risked permanent disability by continuing to work — a risk the employee, incidentally, wanted to take.[69] Similarly, he declined to return to work a lineman who suffered from a spine condition and seizures, for whom a fall of any kind would mean permanent incapacitation. Although he refused to return this employee to work, Wallen also held that he should not be terminated, but rather placed on layoff status until either the employee agreed to a needed corrective operation that he had been avoiding or his layoff rights expired.[70]

Wallen found an excessive hazard to fellow employees in two cases involving mentally ill workers who had assaulted their fellow workers, but again he declined to terminate permanently their employment inasmuch as in each case the employee had committed himself to a mental institution for a period of time and was progressing toward normalcy under medical supervision at the time of the hearing. In both cases, Wallen placed the employees in a medical leave of absence status.[71]

Wallen even went so far as to consider the danger to handicapped employees of not returning to their jobs, as well as the danger of the job itself, in evaluating these types of cases. For example, he had to rule on an employee's right to reinstatement to a position as plant railroad conductor, where the employee had been terminated after suffering a serious heart attack. In the time between the grievant's termination and the arbitration hearing, he had taken temporary employment in the only job he could find, that of a laborer on a road gang. Wallen analyzed the medical evidence that demonstrated conclusively more than just a minimal risk to the employee in resuming his former job, and answered the company's contention that this evidence automatically justified termination:

That line of reasoning would provide a comfortable rule for disposing of such cases were it not for the possibility that a rejection of a man's claim to his prior job might confront him with alternatives which could be equally deleterious in their potential for harm to his physical condition. In C_____'s case, for example, a rejection of his grievance might conceivably impel continuance of his present employment which is considerably more strenuous than the job he seeks. Or it might consign him to a standard of living considerably lower than that which he previously enjoyed, with all of the effects that the consequent worry and deprivation might have on his condition.[72]

Here, Wallen found the employee's investment in his job to be relatively greater than otherwise would be the case, due to the dearth of suitable alternative employment opportunities and the relative safety of his original job. He held this factor to be sufficient to outweigh any risks to management. Reinstatement was ordered.

Discrimination and Improper Differential Treatment

In a few relatively rare situations, Wallen was required to decide charges than an employee was being discriminated against or being treated improperly in a differential manner on the basis of the employee's sex, race, or age. In some situations, statutory law or the contract was asserted as a specific bar to such treatment and, in other cases, the result was simply complained of as being unjust or inequitable.

Wallen saw a relatively limited role for the arbitrator in correcting racial discrimination. As he once stated in a speech on the topic,

First, it is plain that arbitration as a process can at this point in time play a useful role in dealing with minority problems in industrial relations only to a limited extent. It can be a useful tool for resolving the rights of minority individuals under existing contracts. Properly administered and developed, and given greater confidence of minority unionists in the support and good will of the union officialdom, it can be the preferred choice for pursuing claims of discrimination over recourse to human rights commissions or complaints to other government agencies or the courts.

But too often the complaints of minority people in the collective bargaining scene are directed against the union as well as the employer. Moreover, arbitration is usually a means of enforcing rights under a contract. Minority problems in industrial relations, on the other hand, often arise out of demands either for reforms in those contracts for the benefit of the minority group or for transfer of a greater share of union power to minority hands. Arbitration, given the present balance of forces, does not seem well adapted to that assignment at this point in time.[73]

Very few cases involving assertions of racial discrimination reached Wallen in the years before passage of the Civil Rights Act of 1964. Wallen at least considered factors such as overt supervisory mistreatment and racial slurring to be mitigating factors where they provoked misconduct among minority group employees. After passage of the Civil Rights Act, Wallen held that if discrimination was not specifically banned under the contract involved, it was nevertheless subsumed under the law and would be considered by him. In evaluating the discriminatory content of managerial actions, Wallen further indicated that he was willing to look deeper into the issue than simply to see if the treatment was superficially even-handed and in accordance with the fixed rules and policies in effect. For example, in a case involving the disciplining of a black employee totally new to the factory environment, Wallen wrote,

Here one feels that the rules were applied with a certain mechanical equality and without the sensitivity that shows a true comprehension of the problem of absorbing minority people, especially those without prior factory experience, into the industrial mainstream. *If we were faced here with the penalty of discharge, we might be impelled to give this fact more weight.* [74]

Since the penalty involved was not discharge, but rather a short suspension, the employee's grievance was denied, but Wallen was nevertheless on record for at least considering the possible injustice of management's not instituting some sort of affirmative action in this type of situation.

Many more cases reached Wallen, both before and after passage of the Civil Rights Act, involving charges of sexual discrimination. In many cases, the discrimination complained of was codified in the agreement in the form of dual wage rates, dual seniority systems, the listing of various jobs as male or female, or contractual standards or rules applicable to only one sex. In the years before passage of the Civil Rights Act, Wallen upheld such provisions where the contract was clear, including several cases in which their application resulted in reverse discrimination, with male employees being deprived of job opportunities solely because of their sex. While upholding these clear and at the time lawful provisions, Wallen did sometimes point out their inefficiencies and injustices, but he ruled that only the parties could change the agreement. [75] Where the contract was silent, Wallen generally refused to uphold rules that flatly disqualified people or stereotypes based on traditional sex roles. Thus, for example, he refused to disqualify women as a class from bidding on traditional men's jobs involving heavy physical labor, instead "judging each case on the capacities of the female involved." [76]

Wallen worked as an active arbitrator for only a few years after the Civil Rights Act became effective (from 1966 to 1968) and hesitated to deem long-standing provisions or rules that treated sexes differentially as being violative of the law, unless the point in question was very obvious or else had been already dealt with precisely by the federal Equal Employment Opportunity Commission. He generally suggested that complainants take unsettled matters to the federal agency, declining to rule on the legal matter in arbitration. For example, he refused to pass on whether an airline's no-marriage rule for stewardesses violated the law, stating that such rules carry a presumption of validity until specifically found unlawful by an administrative agency or court. In this case, however, he held that the rule was unreasonable and ordered it rescinded, making the legal issue moot.[77]

Wallen similarly applied and upheld state laws limiting the amount of such physical labor as lifting that women could perform, and, because of such laws, he ruled women ineligible for jobs exceeding the legal limitations. He did not consider the issue or possibility that such state statutes were in potential conflict with the federal statute.[78] Wallen left active arbitration before any real consensus was reached by the EEOC and the courts that such statutes did in fact conflict with the federal law. In at least one case, he also upheld the validity of a state statute limiting the hours that female employees could work.[79]

Issues of unjust differential treatment based on age were the rarest form of discrimination with which Wallen had to deal. The issues were at the time not those of statutory law, but rather of fairness in the administration of agreement provisions. Wallen generally held that differential treatment based solely on age could not be upheld in cases dealing with the application of contractual provisions. Thus, for example, in a 1958 case involving the promotion of a junior employee and the bypassing of a much senior, 67 year old employee due to retire in a few months, Wallen ruled that management's decision "was weighted heavily by a consideration which should have been ignored." He ruled that since seniority and ability were the contractual standards for promotion, "the imminence of a man's retirement and his chronological age should not weigh against his promotion unless his age is directly related to the man's ability to do the job."[80] Wallen held that this right totally outweighed any inconvenience or inefficiencies resulting from the need to find and promote a replacement in a few months, and directed the promotion of the elderly employee.

THE PUBLIC

In some instances, Wallen was asked, or else took it upon himself, to weigh the consequences to the public of the arbitral alternatives from which he had to choose. This situation of course occurred fairly frequently indirectly in those cases involving statutory law or public policy, in whose enforcement the public presumably had a stake. In a few cases, the public's stake was much more direct, especially in those having consequences potentially affecting the public safety.

Thus, for example, in three separate cases, Wallen upheld the discharges of bus drivers as safety risks to the travelling public and passengers. This he did despite the fact that in one case the transgression committed and poor judgment shown would have not merited discharge had not the lives of passengers been in the balance; in another the driver had rendered 25 years of good service; and, in a third, the offense committed was not one stipulated in the contract as being grounds for discharge.[81] In the last case, Wallen held that the company's obligation to provide safe transportation, pursuant to Interstate Commerce Commission rules, overrode the contract's limited discharge clause.

The consideration of public safety rights became even more difficult for Wallen in those cases involving airline pilots. These employees had a high investment in their jobs in terms of years of training and the relative nontransferability of their skills.[82] Because of the very high safety stakes involved in the flying of passenger planes, however, Wallen nevertheless held that airline discharges for safety considerations were not reviewable by him in the sense that ordinary discharges were, but rather that he could only consider whether management's decision in the matter was discriminatory, arbitrary, malicious, capricious, or palpably in error in light of the evidence. The question of judgment was left to management and with it resided the right to err considerably in favor of safety when in doubt.[83] The practical result of such a policy was basically to place the burden of proof in these discharge cases on the union or the employee to prove that management's decision was in error, rather than on management to clearly justify its action, as was ordinarily the case. It was in these cases that Wallen most directly considered and was influenced by the public's rights.

In at least one other type of case, Wallen found that the general public had at least an indirect interest in the outcome. This arose when employees desired to expose themselves to danger and possibly incapacitating injury on the job. Wallen allowed management to prohibit such exposure to limit its own liability. He, however, also went one step further in some cases and stated that the employee owed an obligation to the community, as well as to the employer, to avoid risks, because the community would be required to bear the costs of supporting such employees if they were in fact injured or incapacitated. Wallen upheld discipline in this type of case as justified, partly to impress upon the individual the importance of this obligation. For example, he so ruled in a case involving an employee who repeatedly risked his eyesight needlessly.[84]

GENERAL SUMMARY AND ANALYSIS OF WALLEN'S CONCEPTS OF FUNDAMENTAL RIGHTS AND OBLIGATIONS

The positive ends that Wallen saw in management's good-faith pursuit of efficiency manifested themselves in the wide latitude he gave management to introduce changes in machinery and methods; to determine, alter, and schedule the groupings of tasks, jobs, and employees; to subcontract work; and to establish rules and standards. He was also influenced by efficiency or productivity in determining the appropriate penalty for different types of misconduct, including work refusals and illegal strikes. Wallen thought it necessary to preserve, protect, and promote the stability of the parties' reasoned relationship, and he brought these considerations to bear in cases involving administrative errors, the handling of promotion and disciplinary matters involving union officials, and the review of intra-union discipline.

His respect for the individual's growing investment in a job and for the need for simple justice and equity in treatment showed itself in his handling of disciplinary matters, his protection of seniority rights, and in his treatment of workers whose efficiency or attendance was unsatisfactory due to disability or illness. Where justice demanded that the public's direct stake in an arbitral outcome be considered, he introduced this factor into his deliberation.

While it is beyond the scope of this study to determine if a great many, or a majority, of other arbitrators have decided the types of cases discussed here on the basis of values they personally held important, it is worthwhile to examine briefly the results reached by other arbitrators and compare them with Wallen's decisions to see if considerations of efficiency, stability, and justice (whether personal values of the arbitrator or merely the derived product of the parties' intent) have influenced them.

In the majority of cases examined where the contract was silent or ambiguous, other arbitrators have ascribed to the parties roughly the same rights, obligations, and discretion as did Wallen. These findings are based on a review of published studies of particular aspects of arbitration rather than on a case-by-case analysis, except in those areas where studies have not been undertaken.

Studies dealing with management's right to determine job content and how jobs should be grouped and matched with employees invariably point to the relatively free hand accorded management as long as bona fide efficiency considerations govern its actions. In a study of management's right to determine and alter job content, Milton Rubin concluded that this right was generally unfettered by arbitrators where the contract was silent and where efficiency considerations could be shown. Wallen himself determined that arbitrators generally allow management to become more efficient in response to changed technology by altering the work setup, including the transfer of jobs or work both inside and outside the bargaining unit. James Gross also determined that arbitrators by and large allowed management to transfer work out of unit in cases of dramatically changed technology and where great efficiencies could be gained, although they did so with greater reluctance than would be the case in the subcontracting of work to outside employers and with greater reluctance than Wallen's study indicated. Philip Harris made a similar finding that altered technology and potential efficiencies generally weighed heavily in arbitral decisions involving the transfer of work to supervisory personnel. A study by Lloyd Bailer found that arbitrators frequently upheld the right of management to effect out-of-classification work assignments where efficiency and productivity savings were possible. Both Wallen, in another study, and Frank Elkouri concluded that where specific contractual prohibitions were absent, management had considerable leeway in altering manning requirements and crew sizes to pursue efficiency.[85]

The topic of arbitral treatment of subcontracting matters has been extensively explored, and studies such as those by G. Allan Dash, Jr., Donald Crawford, Marcia Greenbaum, James Gross, and Wallen all reached the general conclusion that most arbitrators weighed the benefit of the managerial pursuit of efficiency and better technology versus the potential damage to job security and bargaining unit integrity.[86]

Orme Phelps conducted an extensive study of the arbitral treatment of discipline and discharge matters, confirming his belief that "the rulings of arbitrators have produced a definite pattern, consisting of proper grounds for disciplinary action, required procedures, and acceptable penalties."[87] His study frequently demonstrated that these widely held precepts are also based to varying degrees on considerations of efficiency, stability, and the demands of justice.[88] Phelp's conclusions about the general arbitral approach to management's rule-making powers and obligations also conformed closely to the approach followed by Wallen.

Other studies of the disciplinary process done by Robert Fisher, John Leonard, Morrison Handsaker, Harold Davey, and Harry Platt reveal a general consensus on matters of procedure, penalty, and mitigating factors. They also show a fairly considerable preoccupation by arbitrators with matters of justice, the individual's job investment, and management's efficiency needs when evaluating disciplinary actions.[89]

While fewer studies have examined the arbitral treatment of union rights and obligations, some studies do exist. For example, the rights of the union steward in representational and disciplinary matters were examined by Byron Yaffe, and several considerations not specifically included in the agreement, such as the effect on collective bargaining relations, are shown in general to be important to arbitrators in this type of case.[90]

A concern with the public's rights in safety matters is shown to be widespread among arbitrators where the public could be affected by the decision, according to a study conducted by Alfred Blumrosen. The mixed treatment given by arbitrators to charges of discrimination is discussed in studies by Harry Seligson and Jean McKelvey.[91]

These studies did not deal with the individual worker's job investment and the effect of justice or mercy considerations. An analysis of published arbitration cases handling ill and disabled employees, however, demonstrates that many of Wallen's concerns, especially the effect on productivity, safety, equity in a job held by long-service personnel, and the unlikelihood of employees gaining employment elsewhere, were also weighed in varying degrees by most other arbitrators. The majority of arbitrators, however, gave greater weight to short-run efficiency than did Wallen.[92]

There is no discussion in these studies about the role of personal values in arbitration. Thus, for example, while most arbitrators have considered efficiency and job security when reviewing subcontracting decisions, it is not clear whether they did so on the basis of their own values, deciding what is relevant and important, or whether they did so based on their reading of the parties' intent as voiced in the contract's preamble, management rights clause, or recognition clause, or in past practice.

Wallen's decisions were not drastically out of line with those of the majority of his contemporaries. Other arbitrators also took into account efficiency, stability, and justice, for whatever reasons. Whether they, like Wallen, were willing to declare that these considerations were relevant to the case, worthy of evaluation as ends in themselves, and values that any reasonable person would accept (and not just manifestations of the parties' intent) are questions that can be answered only by analyzing the career caseloads of other arbitrators. It appears that here there would be a very wide disparity among arbitrators, at least if the written assertions by arbitrators of how they reach decisions are to be believed. Furthermore, some other arbitrators appear to rely on value judgments, but their judgments are vastly different from Wallen's. For example, Paul Prasow and Edward Peters advocated that management should have a free hand to pursue efficiency not as a social good on its own, or as a guarantee of the future of the firm as a source of goods and jobs, as Wallen advocated, but rather as a means of justly protecting the large capital investment of the stockholders, an aspect of equity not considered, or at least not relied on, by Wallen. Here, while the result was the same, the value considerations varied greatly.[93]

Notes

1. Taller and Cooper, Inc. and Amalgamated Mach., Instrument, and Metal Workers, Local No. 475, UERMWA, Issue No. 2, January 12, 1950, p. 4.

2. Merrimack Leather Co. and Int'l Fur and Leather Workers Union, Local 212, CIO, March 24, 1947.

3. Firestone Tire and Rubber Co. and United Rubber, Cork, Linoleum, and Plastic Workers of Am., Local No. 261, May 16, 1958, p. 6; Pacific Mills and Local 784, United Textile Workers of Am., AFL, November 2, 1948, 4 ALAA 68,630 at 71,405.

4. Firestone Tire and Rubber Co., May 16, 1958, p. 5.

5. BLH Electronics and Int'l Ass'n of Mach., Dist. 38, Lodge No. 1836, June 5, 1968, p. 8.

6. The B. F. Goodrich Co., Oaks Plant and United Rubber Workers of Am., Local 281, February 24, 1967, p. 3.

7. The B. F. Goodrich Co. and United Rubber, Cork, Linoleum, and Plastic Workers of Am., CIO, Local No. 5, January 23, 1953, p. 2.

8. Boston Edison Co. and Util. Workers Union of Am., CIO, Local No. 369, May 19, 1953, p. 5.

9. Ibid., p. 6.

10. The B. F. Goodrich Co. and United Rubber, Cork, Linoleum, and Plastic Workers of Am., Local No. 5, July 28, 1954.

11. Goodall-Sanford, Inc. and United Textile Workers of Am., AFL, Local 1802, August 29, 1952, p. 4.

12. Ekco Housewares Co., Adams Plastics Div. and Int'l Jewelry Workers Union, Local 75, July 22, 1965, 46 LA 246.

13. Curtiss-Wright Corp., Wright Aeronautical Div. and United Auto. Workers of Am., Local No. 669, June 5, 1962, p. 3.

14. The B. F. Goodrich Co. and United Rubber, Cork, Linoleum, and Plastic Workers of Am., CIO, November 15, 1951, pp. 5 and 7.

15. Ibid., pp. 5 and 6.

16. Curtiss-Wright Corp. and United Auto., Aircraft, and Agricultural Implement Workers of Am., AFL-CIO, Local No. 669, April 6, 1956, p. 4.

17. Ibid., p. 5.

18. Curtiss-Wright Corp. and United Auto., Aircraft, and Agricultural Implement Workers of Am., AFL-CIO, Local No. 669, July 3, 1956, pp. 3–4.

19. The Fafnir Bearing Co. and Int'l Union, United Auto., Aircraft, and Agricultural Implement Workers of Am., Local No. 133, September 15, 1960.

20. Firestone Tire and Rubber Co. and United Rubber Workers of Am., Local No. 261, October 15, 1962, p. 5.

21. Aluminum Co. of Am., Warrick Works and Aluminum Workers Int'l Union, Local 104, December 18, 1963, p. 8.

22. Ibid., pp. 7–8. For the same admonition, see Trailways of New England, Inc. and Div. 1318, Amalgamated Transit Union, AFL-CIO, December 22, 1965, pp. 10–11.

23. Ibid., p. 9.

24. Borden Chem. Co. and Int'l Chem. Workers Union, Local No. 553, December 9, 1959, p. 8.

25. Creese and Cook Leather Co. and Leather Workers Int'l Union of Am., Local 21, October 27, 1964, p. 9.

26. Sylvania Elec. Prod., Inc. and Local 608, Int'l Union of Elec., Radio, and Mach. Workers, CIO, May 8, 1954, 7 ALAA 69,848 at 74,565; Mack Trucks, Inc. and United Auto Workers, Local No. 171, January 3, 1964, pp. 20–21; Borden Chem. Co., December 9, 1959, p. 7; FMC Corp., Ordnance Div., October 11, 1967, p. 18; Worthington Pump and Mach. Corp. and United Elec., Radio, and Mach. Workers of America, Local No. 259, October 1, 1947, p. 6; Firestone Tire and Rubber Co., Pottstown Plant and United Rubber Workers of Am., Local No. 336, September 9, 1966, p. 12.

27. Aluminum Co. of Am., December 18, 1963, pp. 9–10.

28. Worthington Pump and Mach. Corp., October 1, 1947, p. 7.

29. Aluminum Co. of Am., December 18, 1963, p. 12.

30. William Whitman Co., Arlington Mills and United Textile Workers of Am., Local No. 113, AFL, July 15, 1947.

31. Cities Transp. Co., Inc. and Int'l Bhd. of Teamsters, AFL, Local No. 633, April 17, 1947, p. 6.

32. Ford Motor Co., Dallas Assembly Plant and United Auto. Workers, Local 870, October 3, 1957; Firestone Tire and Rubber Co., Fall River Plant, and United Rubber Workers of Am., Local No. 261, January 4, 1958.

33. American Tel. and Tel. Co., Long Lines Dep't and Am. Union of Tel. Workers, January 8, 1947, pp. 4–5.

34. Ibid., pp. 6–7.

35. Ibid., p. 7.

36. Ibid., p. 8.

37. H. K. Barnes Leather Co. and Int'l Fur and Leather Workers Union, Local No. 21, CIO, August 7, 1947, p. 3.

38. General Insulated Wire Works, Inc. and Int'l Bhd. of Elec. Workers, Local 1242, September 18, 1961, 38 LA 522 at 523.

39. Aluminum Co. of Am., Warrick Works and Aluminum Workers Int'l Union, Local No. 104, December 19, 1963, p. 2.

40. Merit Mfg., Inc. and United Rubber, Cork, Linoleum, and Plastic Workers of Am., CIO, Local 442, July 31, 1953, p. 3.

41. The B. F. Goodrich Co. and United Rubber, Cork, Linoleum, and Plastic Workers of Am., CIO, Local No. 5, September 25, 1952, p. 3; Merit Mfg., Inc., July 31, 1953, p. 3; American Cyanamid Co., Plastics and Resins Div. and Int'l Chem. Workers Union, Local No. 436, February 2, 1965, p. 4.

42. Ford Motor Co., Cleveland Stamping Plant and United Auto. Workers, Local 420, October 1, 1956, p. 2.

43. B. F. Goodrich Co., September 25, 1952.

44. General Tire and Rubber Co., Waco Div. and United Rubber, Cork, Linoleum, and Plastic Workers of Am., Local 312, CIO, February 9, 1949; B. F. Goodrich Co., September 25, 1952, p. 3; General Tire and Rubber Co. and United Rubber, Cork, Linoleum, and Plastic Workers of America, Local No. 9, November 2, 1956, p. 3; American Cyanamid Co., February 2, 1965, p. 4; Aluminum Co. of Am., December 19, 1963, p. 2.

45. General Tire and Rubber Co., November 2, 1956, p. 3.

46. See p. 45.

47. Boston Record Am., Advertiser Div., The Hearst Corp. and Am. Fed'n of News Writers, Reporters, and Editorial Workers Union No. 21432, February 7, 1968, p. 8; Sylvania Elec. Prod. Inc., Huntington Plant and Int'l Union of Elec., Radio, and Mach. Workers, CIO, Local No. 608, October 3, 1953, p. 3.

48. Witch City Tanning Co. and Int'l Fur and Leather Workers Union, Local 21, July 25, 1949, p. 1.

49. Ibid., p. 2.

50. Ibid.

51. See p. 124.

52. Shahmoon Indus., Inc. and United Steelworkers of Am., AFL-CIO, January 23, 1959, p. 6.

53. General Tire and Rubber Co. and United Rubber, Cork, Linoleum, and Plastics Workers of America, Local No. 9, April 27, 1956, p. 3.

54. Allis Chalmers Mfg. Co. and Int'l Union of Elec. Workers, Local No. 279, February 8, 1960, pp. 4–6.

55. See pp. 39–41 and p. 102.

56. See p. 107.

57. Beggs and Cobb, Inc. and Int'l Fur and Leather Workers Union, Local 22, September 8, 1952.

58. The General Tire and Rubber Co. and United Rubber Workers of Am., Local 9, January 28, 1963, pp. 1–2.

59. Beggs and Cobb, Inc. and Int'l Fur and Leather Workers Union, Local 22, January 30, 1953, p. 2.

60. Curtiss-Wright Corp. and United Auto., Aircraft, and Agricultural Implement Workers of Am., Local No. 669, March 5, 1958, p. 3.

61. United States Envelope Co. and Fed. Labor Union No. 20681, AFL-CIO, February 9, 1966, p. 5.

62. The B. F. Goodrich Co. and United Rubber, Cork, Linoleum, and Plastic Workers of Am., Local No. 5, March 22, 1962, p. 4.

63. American Airlines, Inc. and Transp. Workers Union of Am., January 20, 1964, p. 10.

64. Beebe Rubber Co. and United Rubber, Cork, Linoleum, and Plastic Workers of Am., Local No. 570, March 30, 1960, p. 6.

65. The B. F. Goodrich Co. and United Rubber Workers of Am., Local No. 43, December 19, 1963, p. 2.

66. The B. F. Goodrich Co. and United Rubber, Cork, Linoleum, and Plastic Workers of Am., CIO, Local No. 5, June 23, 1953; Universal Tanning Co. and Int'l Fur and Leather Workers Union, Local 21, October 9, 1953; Phalo Plastics and United Steelworkers of Am., Local No. 6306, November 5, 1963; Aluminum Co. of Am., Chillicothe Plant and Aluminum Workers Int'l Union, Local 110, November 16, 1964, p. 6; Procter and Gamble Mfg. Co. and Procter and Gamble Employees' Ass'n of Quincy, November 10, 1965, p. 12.

67. Eastern Air Lines, Inc. and Int'l Ass'n of Mach., Dist. 100, May 5, 1964, pp. 10–11. For an example of a situation in which such reinstatement was *not* found justified, see Eastern Airlines, Inc. and Int'l Ass'n of Mach., Dist. 100, September 12, 1963, p. 4.

68. Barre Wool Combing Co. and Textile Workers Union of Am., Central Mass. Joint Board, CIO, September 6, 1949, 15 LA 257 at 261.

69. Procter and Gamble Mfg. Co., November 10, 1965.

70. Lynn Gas and Elec. Co. and United Gas, Coke, and Chem. Workers of Am., CIO, Local 497, September 28, 1955, p. 4.

71. Borg-Warner Corp., Warner Gear Div. and United Auto. Workers of Am., Local 287, June 12, 1967; The B. F. Goodrich Co., Miami Plant and United Rubber Workers of Am., Local 318, April 5, 1965.

72. U.S. Steel Corp., Fairless Works and United Steelworkers of Am., Local Union No. 4889, April 3, 1962, 38 LA 395 at 398.

73. Saul Wallen, "Lessons from Arbitration in Dealing with Minority Problems," a paper presented at The Collective Bargaining Forum — 1969, Waldorf Astoria Hotel, New York, N.Y., May 12, 1969, pp. 9–10, personal files.

74. Texaco, Inc. and Oil, Chem., and Atomic Workers Int'l Union, January 16, 1969, p. 14.

75. General Motors Corp., Frigidaire Div. and Int'l Union of Elec., Radio, and Mach. Workers, AFL-CIO, Local 801, December 30, 1960; Sylvania Elec. Prod., Inc. and Int'l Union of Elec. Workers, Local No. 352, June 22, 1962; The B. F. Goodrich Co. and United Rubber, Cork, Linoleum, and Plastic Workers of Am., Local No. 5, April 12, 1954.

76. General Cable Corp. and Int'l Ass'n of Mach., Lodge No. 157, Local Lodge No. 2101, April 16, 1959, p. 2; see also Curtiss-Wright Corp., Wright Aeronautical Div. and United Auto. Workers, Local 669, June 27, 1963.

77. Southern Airways, Inc. and Air Line Stewards and Stewardesses Ass'n, September 14, 1966, 47 LA 1135.

78. The General Tire and Rubber Co. and United Rubber Workers of Am., Local No. 9, April 15, 1965.

79. Scott Paper Co. and United Papermakers and Paperworkers, Local 431, August 22, 1966.

80. Ford Motor Co., Kansas City Assembly Plant and United Auto. Workers, Local 249, March 3, 1958, p. 2.

81. Central Greyhound Lines and Amalgamated Transit Union, Div. 1313, May 24, 1966, p. 12; Southern Greyhound Lines and Amalgamated Transit Union, April 17, 1968, p. 28; Trailways of New England, Inc. and Div. 1318, Amalgamated Ass'n of Street, Elec. Ry., and Motor Coach Employees of Am., April 18, 1962, pp. 4–5.

82. Continental Air Lines, Inc. and Air Line Pilots Ass'n, Int'l, October 21, 1966.

83. National Airlines and The Airline Pilots Ass'n, Int'l, August 1, 1950, pp. 46–47; Trans World Airlines and Air Line Stewards and Stewardesses Ass'n, Int'l, June 4, 1962, p. 4; Continental Air Lines, Inc., October 21, 1966, pp. 19–20.

84. Union Carbide Corp., Linde Div. (Newark Comb. Plant) and Int'l Bhd. of Teamsters, July 31, 1967, p. 5.

85. Milton Rubin, "The Right of Management to Split Jobs and Assign Work to Other Jobs," *Industrial and Labor Relations Review* 16 (1963): 205–20; Saul Wallen, "The Arbitration of Work Assignment Disputes," *Industrial and Labor Relations Review* 16 (1963): 193–99; James Gross, "Value Judgements in the Decisions of Labor Arbitrators"; Philip Harris, "Labor Arbitration and Technological Innovation," *Labor Law Journal* 17 (1966): 664–70 (Harris examined 324 arbitration awards dating back to 1942); Lloyd Bailer, "The Right to Assign Employees in One Job Classification to Jobs in Another Classification," *Industrial and Labor Relations Review* 16 (1963): 200–204; Saul Wallen, "The Silent Contract vs. Express Provisions"; Frank Elkouri, *How Arbitration Works* (Washington, D.C.: BNA, 1952), p. 237.

86. G. Allan Dash, Jr., "The Arbitration of Subcontracting Disputes," *Industrial and Labor Relations Review* 16 (1963): 208–14 (Dash examined 64 arbitration decisions published between 1947 and 1959); Donald Crawford, "The Arbitration of Disputes Over Subcontracting." In Jean T. McKelvey (ed.), *Challenges to Arbitration* (Washington, D.C.: BNA, 1960), p. 51 (Crawford examined the 64 subcontracting decisions assembled by Dash and drew some different conclusions); Marcia Greenbaum, "The Arbitration of Subcontracting Disputes: An Addendum," *Industrial and Labor Relations Review* 16 (1963): 221–34 (Greenbaum examined approximately 50 cases published between 1959, when the Dash study ended, and 1962); Saul Wallen, "How Issues of Subcontracting and Plant Removal Are Handled by Arbitrators," *Industrial and Labor Relations Review* 19 (1966): 265–72.

87. Orme Phelps, *Discipline and Discharge in the Unionized Firm* (Berkeley: University of California Press, 1959), p. vii (Phelps analyzed approximately 90 discipline cases published between 1944 and 1953 and several dozen unpublished awards of the same period).

88. Ibid., pp. 46, 49, 52, 61–67.

89. Robert Fisher, "Arbitration of Discharges for Marginal Reasons," *Monthly Labor Review* 91 (1968): 1–5 (Fisher analyzed approximately 35 cases published between 1946 and 1966 dealing with discharges for behavior having no direct relationship with their employment); John Leonard, "Discipline for Off-the-Job Activities," *Monthly Labor Review* 91 (1968): 5–11 (Leonard analyzed 92 arbitration cases decided between 1946 and 1967); Morrison Handsaker, "Arbitration of

Discipline Cases," *Personnel Journal* 46 (1967): 153–56; Harold Davey, "The Arbitrator Speaks on Discharge and Discipline," *Arbitration Journal* 17 (1962): 97–104 (Davey's impressions of general arbitral approaches to discipline and discharge); Harry Platt, "The Arbitration Process in the Settlement of Labor Disputes," *Journal of the American Judicature Society* 31 (1947): 57–60 (Platt's observations on the arbitration process).

90. Byron Yaffe, "The Protected Rights of the Union Steward," *Industrial and Labor Relations Review* 23 (1970): 483–99 (Yaffe examined approximately 26 arbitration decisions dealing with this issue).

91. Alfred Blumrosen, "Public Policy Considerations in Labor Arbitration Cases," *Rutgers Law Review* 14 (1960): 217–63; Harry Seligson, "Minority Group Employees, Discipline and the Arbitrator," *Labor Law Journal* 19 (1968): 544–54; Jean T. McKelvey, "Sex and the Single Arbitrator," *Industrial and Labor Relations Review* 24 (1971): 335–53 (McKelvey analyzed several dozen cases published since 1964 dealing with alleged sex discrimination in employment).

92. Celanese Corp. of Am., 9 LA 143; Whitin Mach. Works, 10 LA 707; Dandy Mattress Corp., 12 LA 34; Aspinook Corp., 15 LA 593; American Brass Co., 20 LA 266; Aluminum Co. of Am., 21 LA 617; Calorizing Co., 23 LA 268; Management Services, Inc., 26 LA 505; Royal Typewriter Co., 27 LA 107; Foundry Equip. Co., 28 LA 333; General Elec. Co., 32 LA 637; Central Soya Co., 34 LA 307; Joyce-Cridland Co., 35 LA 133; McLean Trucking Co., 36 LA 1307; Labor Standards Ass'n, 38 LA 1049; Interwoven Stocking Co., 39 LA 918; Federal Bearing Co., 41 LA 788; Western Elec. Co., 42 LA 1316; Kurtz Bros., Inc., 43 LA 678; U.S. Plywood Corp., 46 LA 436; Westinghouse Elec. Corp., 47 LA 464; Gries Reproducer Corp., 47 LA 747; Kelsey-Hayes Co., December 14, 1972, Robert Howlett, arbitrator, *Daily Labor Report*, No. 29, February 12, 1973, p. A–6.

93. Paul Prasow and Edward Peters, "New Perspectives on Management's Reserved Rights," *Labor Law Journal* 18 (1967): 3–14.

Chapter VII

Attempts to Influence the Parties' Behavior in the Future: Remedies

The degree to which Wallen relied on personal values to reach arbitral decisions where the written agreement provided no clear answer has been explored. But to what extent did he attempt to influence the parties to conduct their affairs now and in the future in a manner he considered proper or reasonable? The answer lies in the degree to which he was willing to (a) order the parties to perform in a specific manner in the future, (b) use his remedy powers in a punitive rather than a strictly remedial fashion where violations occurred, (c) offer suggestions of appropriate solutions which he felt he was not empowered to order, and, (d) where he had a continuing relationship with the parties, imply, warn of, or threaten some future action on his part if the parties did not comply with these suggestions.

"Appropriate" arbitral conduct, as viewed by both strict and liberal constructionist arbitrators, was discussed in Chapter I. Both groups have firm views on the use of remedy powers as well. The strict constructionist contends that arbitrators should simply redress past violations of the agreement, solving only the precise and limited issue placed before them.[1] Such redress is to be strictly remedial in nature and in no way make-up opportunity for the grievant. In this situation, the liberal constructionist does not follow the strict constructionist's credo that the complaining party must clearly establish a permanent monetary loss to be awarded a monetary sum as a remedy. For the liberal constructionist, the plain act of violating the agreement can itself be the basis for a monetary award, rather than a simple declaration that a violation has occurred.[9]

Wallen's use of remedy powers was a strange amalgam of strict and liberal constructionist philosophy. While he avoided such creative remedies as the assessment of damages or the issuance of injunctions against illegal strikes, he did attempt, in some instances, to solve those larger problems between the parties where he saw the immediate grievance as only part of the difficulty. He formulated detailed principles or procedures clarifying ambiguous or skimpy provisions. He developed innovative problem-solving remedies requiring the parties to undertake various courses of action. On occasion, he used his remedy powers in a punitive, as well as a remedial, manner. The exact manner in which he approached each of these situations is the topic of this chapter.

Examined here are not Wallen's views on the *legal* limits to which arbitrators can go in using their remedy powers, but rather those limits which he believed were practical or appropriate to the situation. In several instances, he refused to order a requested remedy, even though he believed or knew that the remedy would be judicially upheld if appealed, simply on the grounds that he thought the remedy was not a proper or suitable one for an arbitrator to assess. Such was the case where a party requested damages for a violation of the contract's no-strike provisions.[10] On the other hand, in some instances, he did order remedies which very well might not have withstood a judicial appeal because he believed that particular remedy to be truly necessary to solve the problem at hand.

It is sometimes asserted that arbitrators can properly perform more in a liberal constructionist manner, insofar as remedy powers go, in those situations in which they are acting in a permanent, as opposed to an ad hoc, capacity.[11] Over half of Wallen's cases were decided under permanent umpireships, but this study shows that there is no apparent difference between Wallen's use of remedy powers in both situations.

PROBLEM-SOLVING REMEDIES: THE ESTABLISHMENT OF PRINCIPLES AND PROCEDURES

In one of his decisions as a permanent umpire, Wallen declared that his function was "not only to provide answers in specific cases but also to develop principles and approaches to guide the parties when they discuss future grievances and make their friendly settlement easier." He further stated that "it is to be hoped that the parties will regard his decisions not punitive. Generally, strict constructionists limit their range of remedies to those specifically provided for in the agreement or to those so universally employed that they could be reasonably imputed as being intended by the parties, such as backpay in the event of a wrongful discharge or layoff. Pure strict constructionists avoid so-called creative remedies.[2]

Where the agreement is silent or unclear as to the appropriate remedy for a found violation, they may even consider it sufficient simply to declare that a violation occurred and let the parties decide the appropriate remedy, if any. Only if specifically asked to do so will they devise or legislate remedies of their own.[3] Further, strict constructionists in no way attempt to dictate the future conduct of the parties.[4] While even the strictest sometimes cannot resist offering suggestions as to what the parties should do in the future, these suggestions are confined to the dicta of the opinion, and it is left to the parties to determine the effect that these suggestions will actually have on their future conduct. Only where the submission specifically requests a set of standards or procedures for future conduct will this type of arbitrator attempt to dictate the parties' future behavior, although even here some strict constructionists might declare such a grievance premature or conjectural, requiring that a live violation be asserted before a ruling on the specific issue could be rendered.[5]

At the other end of the arbitral spectrum is the so-called liberal constructionist. These arbitrators tend to be problem solvers who are more likely to attack, and offer solutions to, larger problems of which they believe the immediate grievance to be symptomatic. They are less hesitant to offer suggestions as to how the parties could operate in a more effective or appropriate manner. They consider it within their proper province to order the parties to comply with the agreement, or their version or illumination of it, in the future.[6] Liberal constructionists are much more likely to introduce creative remedies as a means of redress, even though it might be apparent that the parties never specifically contemplated the remedy ordered. They might, for example, reinstate an employee who was discharged for alcoholism, on the condition that the employee enter a rehabilitation program, rather than simply either reinstate the employee or uphold the discharge. The touchstone for the liberal constructionist here is not whether the contract with any clarity intended such a remedy, but rather whether any injunction or prohibition against such a creative remedy was included in the contract.[7] Similarly, liberal constructionists are willing to wield their remedy powers in a quasi-punitive manner, especially where a history of repeated or willful violations is evident, in order to encourage future compliance with the agreement.[8] For example, where overtime was repeatedly misassigned, but not irretrievably lost, to an employee, this arbitrator might order backpay rather than a simple alone in terms of the specific case, but also in terms of their broader principles to be applied for the duration of their contract."[12] Wallen expounded such principles not only when he was a permanent umpire or chairman, but also when he served as an ad hoc arbitrator; he not only used such principles to explain his decisions, hoping that they would receive future application, but also ordered their application as part of his remedies where he believed that such a procedure was needed. Some critics, however, point out that the arbitrator can only hope that such an order is obeyed by the parties, that such an order is actually "more shadow than substance."[13]

In some situations, Wallen was essentially asked to legislate either solutions to problems or clear-cut, specific applications of very ambiguous language. The parties, as part of the submission, issue, or grievance, requested that Wallen determine and define procedures to be followed. For example, under one of his permanent umpireships, the parties asked that he clarify the conditions under which the union's time study engineer should have access to the plant, a problem that Wallen solved with a seven-step procedure.[14] In another case, under an airline system board, the parties asked if the airline's weight standards for employees and the airline's rules for administering these standards were reasonable. Wallen found the weight standards to be reasonable, but ordered that "the steps set forth below shall be taken to standardize the conditions under which the rule is to be applied," an order accompanied by a specific, standardized five-step procedure for applying the weight standards.[15] In a third case, where he served in an ad hoc capacity, the submission, in addition to grieving a particular employee's promotion denial, asked if the company's promotion procedures fulfilled the agreement's requirements. Wallen accompanied his denial of the particular grievance with a four-step procedure to be followed henceforth by management in selecting personnel for promotion.[16]

In several instances, however, Wallen chose to create generalized rules even where the submission or issue was limited to a particular asserted violation and did not request any generalized rules of application. To illustrate this point, under various permanent arbitration positions, Wallen ordered the following: (1) In response to a single grievance of improper overtime assignment, he established a code of six specific principles for management to follow henceforth in distributing overtime. (2) As part of the remedy for a grievance over reprimands issued employees for refusing to work an extended work schedule, he established a three-point procedure for management to follow when scheduling workers. (3) In response to a complaint that a piece rate was too low, but where Wallen discovered that the real trouble was a capricious supervisor whose willingness to grant rate variances for faulty raw materials varied with his moods, he ordered a quantified system to be implemented to determine when variances should be allowed.[17]

Wallen similarly established procedures to solve problems of assigning involuntary overtime, of determining an employee's bumping rights, and of allowing employees to bid for job vacancies.[18] The principles he established were not only the basis for solving the immediate grievance, but also were designated in the remedy as the future procedure to be followed.

Wallen acted similarly when serving in an ad hoc capacity. For example, in one case, the union brought to arbitration a claim that management constantly allowed nonunit personnel to perform bargaining unit work. Management admitted that such violations had occurred and claimed that it had attempted to prevent them; neither party could clarify exactly the frequency or magnitude of the violations. Wallen here established a procedure to be followed in the future, requiring: (1) a detailed union report to management of any observed violations, (2) management warnings to the guilty nonunit personnel, (3) monetary penalties against management if any particular nonunit employee did such work after having received two warnings, (4) reports by management to the union of all action taken, and (5) management advising its nonunit personnel and its supervisors of the terms of the award.[19]

In a second ad hoc case, which also involved some mediation, he remedied a work assignment grievance that he termed "symptomatic of a malaise in the department arising out of a shortage of manpower and a lack of adequate supervision" with a five-step procedure for making all future work assignments, including the one grieved.[20]

These examples are not intended to mislead the reader into assuming that Wallen always took it upon himself to legislate specific requirements where the agreement was silent, ambiguous, or contradictory on an issue likely to be recurring frequently in the future. In some instances, he simply found either a violation or nonviolation of the agreement and remanded the issue to the parties, while he retained jurisdiction. Often he established some general guiding principles and ordered that the parties negotiate the remaining particulars within this framework. In some cases, he simply declared that he had inadequate information on which to base a decision and ordered the parties to further explore the issue, for example to jointly time-study a job.[21] In other cases, he found the grievance to be unfounded, hypothetical, or premature, but also ordered the parties to negotiate a mutually satisfactory solution to the problem.[22] In yet some other instances, he had sufficient information to reach a decision that a contract violation had occurred, but not sufficient information with which to fix a remedy. Here, he ordered that the parties themselves negotiate the appropriate penalty or extent of liability.[23]

The most interesting of these cases, however, were those in which he reached a partial decision, outlining the general approach that should be taken in solving the problem and followed in the future, and remanding the case to the parties to reach a settlement as to what should be the specific practice or procedure. In the majority of these cases, Wallen was serving as a permanent arbitrator.

For example, while serving as a permanent impartial chairman, he ruled that a particular past practice for wash-up time was not binding on the parties and ordered that the parties negotiate an appropriate future allowance in consideration of his observations which he stated "may be of aid to them in resolving that question."[24] In a second case, involving correct job assignment procedures, it became apparent to Wallen that the parties simply had not had the present contingency in mind when they negotiated the agreement. Here, he considered it appropriate "to remand this case to the parties for reconsideration in light of the general criteria set forth above," retaining jurisdiction if the parties could not successfully negotiate the remaining particulars of the procedure to be henceforth utilized within 30 days.[25]

The important factor in all of these cases is that Wallen was not afraid, either as a permanent or an ad hoc arbitrator, to order the parties either to perform in some particular manner in the future or at least reach a negotiated decision themselves. In the latter instance, he would often set down guidelines for the parties and he always retained jurisdiction in the event they could not reach a negotiated decision. This approach clearly is not the one encompassed in the strict constructionist theory of arbitration, which applies the agreement to claims of past violations and leaves the parties to their own devices to determine their future mode of operation.

PROBLEM-SOLVING REMEDIES: ORDERS FOR SPECIFIC FUTURE PERFORMANCE

In addition to ordering that the parties follow set principles and procedures in the future when dealing with any recurrence of the issue precipitating a grievance, Wallen also, on occasion, ordered that the parties, as part of the remedy for the instant grievance, undertake a specific activity. Cases in which Wallen ordered the parties to find facts or negotiate a solution or remedy fall within this category, but there the orders were a part of the hearing process, over which the arbitrator undeniably had the right of control. The orders explored here are those defining future, posthearing conduct; they go far beyond simple orders calling for the payment of compensation for past violations, or orders specifically designed to prevent a recurrence of a problem arising in the immediate grievance. These orders require specific conduct in the future from management, from the union, and often from individual employees.

For example, in one instance where he was a permanent arbitrator, Wallen upheld management's contention that it could discharge a number of women who were hired only as temporary workers. As a matter of equity, however, he required the company to employ as many of these women as possible to fill permanent position vacancies and further required that the women to be discharged should be placed on a preferential hiring list for any future vacancies.[26] On several occasions, he also ordered management to instruct its nonunit employees to either undertake or refrain from some action. For example, he ordered management to instruct its supervisors not to molest or annoy the grievant in any way and to confine its communication with him to the giving of necessary orders. He ordered management to instruct its nonunit or supervisory personnel to refrain from performing bargaining unit work. He also instructed management to transfer a reinstated employee due to the strained relations between the employee and his coworkers and supervisors, and ordered management to restructure tasks into a job that a recovering handicapped employee could perform. In an ad hoc case, although he found no violation of the agreement, he ordered management to review and reassess all vacation requests as a show of good faith.[27]

In innumerable instances throughout his career, both as an ad hoc and as a permanent arbitrator, Wallen required individual employees, and in some cases the union as well, to perform certain undertakings as a condition of the employee's reinstatement. Here, Wallen was not satisfied simply to order reinstatement and let the employees fare for themselves. In the less complex of these cases, Wallen required that the employee meet production standards, maintain perfect attendance or a record free from discipline for a fixed probation period, or request a job transfer.[28] Where Wallen was serving in a permanent capacity, he bound himself to not review any future discharge for a recurrence of such offenses by the employee or else required the union to pledge not to press a grievance in the event of a future recurrence.[29] Occasionally, as a condition of reinstatement, he required the employee to provide management with a signed, but undated, letter of resignation to be used by management at its option if trouble recurred.[30] In one ad hoc case, he conditioned reinstatement on the employee's tendering of a formal apology to management in the presence of the union officials.[31]

In a number of decisions, however, these requirements that the employee, with or without the aid of the union, had to adhere to were much more detailed and far-reaching. This was particularly true in those cases involving reinstatement after discharge for financial irresponsibility, alcoholism, or some physical or mental ailment. Thus, for example, in some cases involving debt-ridden employees, he established very detailed debt-reduction regimens, calling for a systematized listing of all debts, a fixed reduction per week, written notice to all creditors, union supervision of the process, and automatic discharge for noncompliance. In one award, where he determined that backpay was warranted, he even required that the backpay be allocated toward repayment of the outstanding debts.[32]

Similarly detailed self-corrective measures for reinstated alcoholics were sometimes ordered by Wallen. Here, he ordered the grievant, subject to automatic termination for noncompliance, to contact a particular rehabilitative agency, such as a family service agency (even providing the precise address or the appropriate person to contact), to follow the program prescribed by the agency for a fixed period of time, and to maintain a certain level of attendance and performance at work. The union was sometimes required to aid or accompany the employees in making contact, to monitor their progress, or to refrain from appealing their discharges in the event of the employees' noncompliance.[33]

Wallen had a strong concern for protecting the individual's job investment where the employee was injured or ill, as well as a strong concern for safety. These concerns were evident in some of the innovative remedies he ordered. The most simple remedy was to condition any return to work upon full recovery or upon the employee's agreement to undergo corrective surgery if it was necessary. In some instances, however, he did allow the employee's return to work where doubt existed in his mind that the employee had fully recovered, but also ordered that special protective measures be undertaken, as well as the periodic inspection of the employee's condition by supervision and by the company's medical staff. In one case, he conditioned the reinstatement of a formerly mentally ill employee on certification of his well-being by a jointly selected psychiatrist and the requirement that the union arrange for the employee's continued treatment at a community mental health center.[34]

In all the cases summarized here, Wallen did not act within the constraints of the strict constructionist model of arbitration, but rather attempted to order the specific future behavior of the parties and prevent recurrences of the actions or conditions precipitating the grievances before him. In virtually all of these situations, his goal was to provide guidance or expertise to a party in need of such aid who was not willfully violating the agreement or causing the difficulty. The following section will examine Wallen's use of his remedy powers in a different situation, where such good faith by one of the parties could not be assumed and where violations were repeated or willful.

PENALTY AND "LESSON" REMEDIES

In the ordinary course of events, Wallen held that monetary remedies should be remedial in nature, that is, the employee should be made whole, receiving compensation for a clearly proven and irretrievably lost financial benefit rightfully due under the agreement's terms. Even where a violation or a denial of a monetary right of some magnitude was apparent, he was reluctant to order a monetary remedy unless the moving party could "supply details and support specific claims with concrete evidence" of exactly who was deprived of the right and of the magnitude of the loss, which had to at least be reasonably bracketed if precise specification was impossible or impractical.[35] Where an employee's monetary right was not irretrievably lost but merely temporarily misplaced, as in the situation of misassignment of overtime opportunity to the wrong employee within the grievant's overtime distribution group,[36] Wallen did not generally order a monetary award, but rather ordered a later make-up opportunity.

While in the case of irretrievably lost rights due to incorrect layoff, discipline, or for some other reason all monetary benefits of the lost compensation could be claimed, including not only the wage rate applicable to the lost work, but also any automatic progressions that would have accrued to the affected employee, such as predictable overtime compensation, holiday pay, and sick pay or insurance benefits, employers were also allowed the right to have the damages against them mitigated.[37] Thus, for example, any such award could be reduced by the amount of backpay liability that accrued due to union or employee delay in the handling of the grievance, any wages received by employees for work at other jobs during the period of their improper denial of work opportunity, and any nonreturnable unemployment compensation received by employees during this period.[38] Wallen also refused union and employee requests to require management's payment of interest on delayed compensation as part of the award.[39]

Where management intentionally violated the agreement, however, Wallen in several instances, both as an ad hoc and as a permanent arbitrator, included as part of the award a monetary penalty that was not mere compensation for an irretrievably lost right or benefit. Such was the case where management intentionally or persistently misassigned overtime opportunity within an overtime group. Regardless of the fact that the opportunity for overtime was not permanently lost to the employee, Wallen's policy here was to award backpay as a clear penalty.[40] He also used this approach in other situations, including those cases in which supervisors consistently performed small bits of bargaining unit work. One case involved the latest of several such violations by a foreman, each violation involving only a few minutes' work, and a very lax attitude by management toward the violations. The work done by the foreman was

not work that would have required an employee to be called in to perform it, resulting in a half day's call-in pay, but rather a few minutes' work belonging to an employee who was elsewhere in the plant. Wallen here declined to dismiss the violation as de minimus and awarded the deprived employee four hours' pay, stating that he hoped that this increased penalty "will serve as a reminder to foremen that they do their employer no good by ignoring the prohibition against foremen working."[41] Also, in what might be considered a penalty award, Wallen in a very few cases upheld an employee's discharge, but ordered severance pay or the unusual remedy of discharge with backpay where management had contributed to, or at least not taken adequate steps to prevent, the employee's condition that justified discharge.[42]

In other instances, while not levying an orthodox penalty against management, Wallen sought to teach management a lesson by including in the award what might be considered a negative penalty, that is, the reduction of a penalty given an employee found guilty of some offense where management had also acted improperly, even if management's actions had not precisely violated the agreement. Such a reduction of the penalty levied frequently created a backpay liability for management.

Wallen justified this type of remedy not only because management's actions may have in some way mitigated the blame or guilt of the employee, but because his actions were intended as plain lessons to prod management into improving some aspect of its functioning. Thus, he reduced penalties to various employees at least partially to induce management and supervisors to treat grievances less casually, to not harbor resentments against those who file grievances, to endeavor to find alternative employment opportunities for reclassified employees, to determine the full nature of objections to orders before making such orders final, to maintain a basic attitude of respect for all persons under one's supervision, and to refrain from "seeking to magnify into a 'cause celebre' a number of on the job irritations which are in the nature of business."[43] Whether his assignment was of a permanent or an ad hoc nature did not matter, since he ruled accordingly in both instances.

THE USE OF NONBINDING SUGGESTIONS, ADMONITIONS, AND IMPLIED THREATS

Wallen also attempted to bring about change in aspects of the parties' behavior that he considered inappropriate or incorrect (but which he believed he had no grant of authority to change) by offering gratuitous suggestions on how to improve or correct the matter and, in some cases, by strongly hinting that in the future he would consider invoking a penalty or remedy if the problem had not improved. These admonitions

or threats were obviously made only in those situations where he had some sort of permanent relationship with the parties and could conceivably carry out these threats; he frequently offered suggestions totally free from threat in both ad hoc and permanent arbitration situations.

The examples are very numerous and varied. As a permanent chairman or umpire, he advised parties to (1) institute the practice of reducing all local agreements to writing; (2) increase the sensitivity of supervisors toward in-plant racial problems; (3) refrain from embarrassing employees by publicly reprimanding or disciplining them; (4) split up their too-large seniority groups; (5) reexamine and review the content of, and rates for, several job classifications; (6) change over to a better method of output recording, which he detailed; (7) modify the method of job counseling used; (8) set up a training program for employees in order to eliminate one employee's monopoly of a job's very great overtime opportunity; (9) modify the schedule pooling method used to eliminate excessive overtime and undertime; (10) modify outmoded job standards; and (11) consider reinstating a discharged steward on the condition that he forever be barred from union office.[44]

While serving as an ad hoc arbitrator, he advised the parties to (1) modify the labor agreement to allow the arbitrator to evaluate the propriety of the penalty in addition to the issue of plain guilt or innocence in disciplinary grievances; (2) modify an agreement provision requiring full backpay anytime the arbitrator ordered a reinstatement; (3) change the distribution of job duties in a department; (4) establish and review at quarterly intervals records of machine-hour production in a department to reveal workload increases; and (5) review and systematize the procedures for grievance handling.[45]

In dealing with parties for whom he was a permanent arbitrator, Wallen added teeth to such suggestions occasionally by warning the parties that if the situation at hand deteriorated further, or if current contract violations creating no monetary losses continued, he would take some sort of appropriate action himself in the future. For example, in one case he warned management, whom he upheld in the immediate grievance, to investigate and correct certain allegations which he stated were "well known to the parties and which need no repeating here,"[46] allegations which it was obvious from the case concerned an aspect of the department supervisor's behavior and which had been alleged in at least one previous case. Wallen warned management that

These allegations becloud every supervisory action and complicate the ascertainment of the facts of cases in dispute. If such conditions exist, it is incumbent upon Management to move promptly to eliminate them. If it fails to do so, it imperils its position in the handling of disciplinary cases in this department.[47]

In a second case, he upheld management's discharge of a shop steward who had engaged in a fight with a foreman and who was struck over the head by a nonunit employee who was also discharged for fighting. There were allegations that management planned in the near future to reinstate the nonunit employee, who was "pro-management." Wallen warned management not to reinstate the nonunit employee, stating that if it did so, it would raise serious doubts in his mind of management's good faith, the very clear inference being that these questions could becloud future management disciplinary actions.[48]

The future action that Wallen threatened was much more explicit in cases of repeated overtime assignment violations. He plainly stated, for instance, that "if the Company repeatedly seeks to escape the responsibility imposed by [the Agreement] to give available hours to the low man, it may be necessary to induce it to cease by awarding back pay."[49] A similar situation arose in a case in which the foreman had a habit of doing small bits of unit work in violation of the agreement, while the proper employees were on smoke breaks. Although there was no real deprivation of work or pay, and hence no liability in the immediate grievance, Wallen warned management that if it tolerated a continuing of these violations in the future, it "courts back pay awards as the only means of securing compliance."[50]

Unions and employees also occasionally received such warnings to undertake or refrain from undertaking some future course of action. Thus, where he ordered management to compensate an employee deprived of a promotion opportunity due to an error made in the recording of his seniority, he at the same time told the union to refrain from filing grievances claiming secondary or chain reaction deprivations of seniority rights emanating from the primary error. He indicated that he would reject any such claims if they were presented.[51] In another case, while rescinding all penalties levied against employees who had refused to perform duties not mentioned in their descriptions, but traditionally performed by them, Wallen admonished the employees and the union that they were "technically but not morally or practically correct" and stated that in any future cases, he would consider the practice to be binding upon the parties, the immediate hearing constituting appropriate notice that the practice was binding.[52] In numerous cases, he also warned employees that their reinstatements provided them with a last chance and that repetition of their errors or misconduct would not be excused in the future.[53] Again, Wallen chose to try to prevent future contract violations, as well as remedy the misdeeds and mistakes committed.

SUMMARY OF WALLEN'S USE OF REMEDY POWERS

Wallen, for the most part, was a liberal constructionist in the use of remedy powers, although, he might better be described as an activist rather than as a radical. For example, he flatly declined to use some of the truly novel or radical remedies potentially available, such as the assessment of monetary damages. While he did institute penalty remedies, he did so in a very circumspect manner. He levied penalties only where clear agreement terms were repeatedly ignored and violated, where compliance could not be obtained by lesser means, and, incidentally, where lack of respect for the agreement's terms necessarily posed a threat to the long-term stability of the parties' relationship. In the vast majority of cases, he succeeded in correcting the situation through a simple warning or threat to use such a remedy in the future, rather than by actually levying such a penalty.

Wallen was by no means reluctant, however, to act as an activist problem solver or consultant in attacking the immediate problems before him and in furthering efficiency, justice, and stability when these values were not in direct conflict with the terms of the parties' agreements. This reveals two points about Wallen. First, he had great confidence in his own problem-solving expertise, considering himself to be at least as expert, if not more expert, than the parties themselves. Second, he did not believe that the imposition of such detailed and complete solutions by him, rather than allowing the parties to devise a solution, would damage or retard the ability of the parties to bargain collectively. Perhaps he recognized that the parties already had opportunities to reach a solution by themselves, both during contract negotiations and in the earlier steps of the grievance process, and that the most valuable contribution he could now offer was technical expertise. He did remand cases to the parties for their consideration of a precise solution where it was evident to him that their bargaining resources had not been exhausted or that their expertise far exceeded his own. It is also probable that in many of these cases he realized that the parties, for political reasons, could not formulate the remedies he imposed, but that they would accept them from the arbitrator.

The end result was that, through the use of remedy powers, Wallen treated arbitration as an integral and active part of the collective bargaining process, rather than as an odd appendage to the process to be used only when the more normal channels had failed.

Notes

1. Harold Davey, "The Arbitrator Views the Agreement," *Labor Law Journal* 12 (1961): 1166–68; Crane, "The Use and Abuse of Arbitral Power," p. 70.

2. R. W. Fleming, "Arbitrators and the Remedy Power," *Virginia Law Review* 48 (1962): 1220. As an example, see arbitrator Harold Davey's holding in Lagomarcino-Grupe Co. (1964), 43 LA 453 at 460. See also Meyer S. Ryder's Comments. In Mark Kahn (ed.), *Labor Arbitration and Industrial Change* (Washington, D.C.: BNA, 1963), pp. 68–70.

3. Stuart Bernstein, Comment. In Barbara Dennis and Gerald Somers (eds.), *Labor Arbitration at the Quarter-Century Mark* (Washington, D.C.: BNA, 1973), p. 80; Lawrence Kearns, Comment. In Barbara Dennis and Gerald Somers (eds.), *Labor Arbitration at the Quarter-Century Mark* (Washington, D.C.: BNA, 1973), p. 89; Emanuel Stein, "Remedies in Labor Arbitration." In Jean T. McKelvey (ed.), *Challenges to Arbitration* (Washington, D.C.: BNA, 1960), pp. 48–49.

4. Crane, "The Use and Abuse of Arbitral Power," p. 68.

5. Ibid., pp. 73 and 75; Carl Warns, Jr., "Arbitration and the Law," *Arbitration Journal* 15 (1960): 11; Frank Elkouri and Edna Elkouri, *How Arbitration Works*, 3rd ed. (Washington, D.C.: BNA, 1973), pp. 246–47.

6. For a study of the prevailing arbitral views on this subject, see Richard Shore, "Conceptions of the Arbitrator's Role," *Journal of Applied Psychology* 50 (1966) 172–78.

7. Sidney Wolff, "The Power of the Arbitrator to Make Monetary Awards." In Mark L. Kahn (ed.), *Labor Arbitration—Perspectives and Problems* (Washington, D.C.: BNA, 1964), pp. 177–78; Fleming, "Arbitrators and the Remedy Power," p. 1212; Robert Stutz, "Arbitrators and the Remedy Power." In Mark L. Kahn (ed.), *Labor Arbitration and Industrial Change* (Washington, D.C.: BNA, 1963), p. 57.

8. Wolff, p. 188; Robert Gorske, "Arbitration Back-Pay Awards," *Labor Law Journal* 10 (1959): 22.

9. George Bodle, "New Techniques and Remedies in the Grievance and Arbitration Process." In Virginia Shook Cameron (ed.), *Proceedings of the Fifteenth Annual Institute on Labor Law, The Southwestern Legal Foundation* (New York: Mathew Bender, 1969), pp. 199–204. See also a discussion of this problem in Josef Sirefman, "Rights Without Remedies in Labor Arbitration," *Arbitration Journal* 18 (1963): 17–35.

10. Alto B. Cervin, Charles J. Morris, Saul Wallen, and Jerre S. Williams (Lennart V. Larson, moderator), "Selected Problems in Arbitration — A Discussion." In *Proceedings of the Twelfth Annual Institute on Labor Law, The Southwestern Legal Foundation* (Washington, D.C.: BNA, 1966), p. 261.

11. Crane, "The Use and Abuse of Arbitral Power," pp. 68, 70, 74; Peter Seitz, "Problems of the Finality of Awards, or Functus Officio and All That." In Mark L. Kahn (ed.), *Labor Arbitration —Perspectives and Problems* (Washington, D.C.: BNA, 1964), pp. 169–70.

12. General Tire and Rubber Co., Waco Plant and United Rubber, Cork, Linoleum, and Plastic Workers of Am., CIO, January 24, 1949, p. 2.

13. Crane, "The Use and Abuse of Arbitral Power," p. 73.

14. Sylvania Elec. Prod., Inc. and Int'l Union of Elec., Radio, and Mach. Workers and Its Affiliated Local No. 352, January 10, 1962, pp. 9–10.

15. Trans World Airlines, Inc. and Air Line Stewards and Stewardesses Ass'n (TWU), Local 550, March 29, 1967, pp. 1 and 13–15.

16. Bell Tel. Laboratories, Inc. and Communication Workers of Am., May 4, 1967, pp. 4 and 16–17.

17. Aluminum Co. of Am., Warrick Works and Aluminum Workers Int'l Union, Local 104, May 24, 1965; The B. F. Goodrich Co. and United Rubber, Cork, Linoleum, and Plastic Workers of Am., CIO, Local No. 5, September 25, 1953; John Flynn and Sons Leather Co. and Leather Workers Int'l Union, Local No. 21, January 11, 1957.

18. American Brass Co., Am. Metal Hose Branch and UAW-CIO, Local 1251, June 21, 1954; Beggs and Cobb, Inc. and Int'l Fur and Leather Workers Union, Local No. 22, November 15, 1954; Western Air Lines, Inc. and Air Line Pilots Ass'n, Int'l, November 2, 1966.

19. Triangle Publications, Inc. and Television Broadcasting Studio Employees, Local No. 804, IATSE, June 3, 1960, p. 5.

20. Scott Paper Co. and Int'l Bhd. of Elec. Workers, Local 1768, September 15, 1966, pp. 1 and 4.

21. General Tire and Rubber Co. and United Rubber, Cork, Linoleum, and Plastic Workers of Am., Local No. 9, CIO, September 26, 1949; Farrington Mfg. Co. and Int'l Ass'n of Mach., Lodge No. 860, April 5, 1957; General Tire and Rubber Co. and United Rubber, Cork, Linoleum, and Plastic Workers of Am., Local No. 9, October 5, 1959.

22. General Tire and Rubber Co., October 5, 1959.

23. Firestone Tire and Rubber Co., Pottstown Plant and United Rubber, Cork, Linoleum, and Plastic Workers of Am., Local No. 336, October 26, 1960; Creese and Cook Leather Co. and Int'l Fur and Leather Workers Union, Local 21, October 14, 1954; The Budd Co. and United Auto. Workers, Local 813, September 7, 1967.

24. The B. F. Goodrich Co. and United Rubber, Cork, Linoleum, and Plastic Workers of Am., Local No. 5, January 8, 1952, p. 5. See also p. 7.

25. Walworth Co. and United Steelworkers of Am., CIO, Local No. 2394, June 18, 1956, p. 8.

26. Beggs and Cobb, Inc. and The Int'l Fur and Leather Workers Union of Am., Local No. 22, May 15, 1946, p. 3.

27. Puritan Leather Co. and Int'l Fur and Leather Workers Union, Local No. 21, CIO, January 30, 1947; Firestone Rubber and Latex Prod. Co., Fall River Plant and United Rubber, Cork, Linoleum, and Plastic Workers of Am., CIO, Local No. 261, March 5, 1953; Triangle Publications, Inc., June 3, 1960; Kaiser Aluminum and Chem. Corp. and United Rubber, Cork, Linoleum, and Plastic Workers of Am., Local No. 339, May 16, 1958; Eastern Air Lines, Inc. and Int'l Ass'n of Mach., District 100, May 5, 1964; Textron, Inc., Waterbury Farrel Div. and United Steelworkers of Am., Local 3381, May 14, 1965, pp. 8–9.

28. Union Twist Drill Co., S. W. Card Mfg. Co. Div. and United Steelworkers of Am., AFL-CIO, December 31, 1956; The B. F. Goodrich Co. and United Rubber, Cork, Linoleum, and Plastic Workers of America, CIO, Local No. 5, June 30, 1952; Beggs and Cobb, Inc. and Int'l Fur and Leather Workers Union, Local 22, January 30, 1953.

29. Beggs and Cobb, Inc., January 30, 1953; B. F. Goodrich Co., June 30, 1952; Universal Tanning Co. and Int'l Fur and Leather Workers Union, Local 21, October 9, 1953.

30. American Airlines, Inc. and Transport Workers Union of Am., January 20, 1964.

31. Stowe-Woodward, Inc. and United Rubber, Cork, Linoleum, and Plastic Workers of Am., Local No. 525, May 12, 1959.

32. Eastern Airlines, Inc. and Int'l Ass'n of Mach., April 8, 1963, p. 7; Eastern Airlines, Inc. and Air Line Pilots Ass'n, Int'l, June 23, 1967.

33. United States Envelope and Fed. Labor Union No. 20681, AFL-CIO, February 9, 1966; The B. F. Goodrich Co. and United Rubber Workers of Am., Local No. 43, December 19, 1963. As late as 1973, such a counseling requirement received notice in the *Daily Labor Report* as being a novel remedy, although there the ad hoc arbitrator then proceeded to go even further than Wallen ever did by requiring in addition that the union and the company establish an alcoholic referral service for other similarly afflicted employees. "Discharge of Alcoholic Produces Novel Remedy," *Daily Labor Report*, No. 103 (May 29, 1973): A5–A7.

34. Lynn Gas and Elec. Co. and United Gas, Coke, and Chem. Workers of Am., CIO, Local 497, September 28, 1955; United States Steel Supply Co. and United Steelworkers of Am., Local 3746, CIO, September 19, 1949; Borg-Warner Corp., Warner Gear Div. and United Auto. Workers of Am., Local 287, June 12, 1967.

35. Eastern Airlines, Inc. and Int'l Ass'n of Mach., Dist. 100, September 28, 1966, p. 10; Eastern Air Lines, Inc. and Int'l Ass'n of Mach., Dist. 100, December 15, 1965.

36. See p. 98.

37. FMC Corp., Ordnance Div. and Int'l Union of United Auto., Aerospace, and Agricultural Implement Workers of Am., Local 348, October 11, 1967, pp. 34–35; Fabet Corp. and Gloucester Sea Food Workers Union, Series 1572-1, Int'l Longshoremen's Ass'n, June 23, 1949, p. 9.

38. Arlington Mills, William Whitman Co. and United Textile Workers of Am., Local No. 113, AFL, July 15, 1947; Connecticut River Mills, Inc. and United Textile Workers of Am., AFL, Local 94, Issue No. 3, February 21, 1947, p. 11; Merrimack Leather Co. and Int'l Fur and Leather Workers Union, Local 212, CIO, March 24, 1947, p. 8; Fabet Corp., June 23, 1949, p. 9; Twitchell-Champlin Co. and Int'l Bhd. of Teamsters, Chauffeurs, Warehousemen, and Helpers of Am., Truck Drivers Local 340, AFL, July 30, 1947, 8 LA 448 at 449; FMC Corp., October 11, 1967, p. 34.

39. FMC Corp., October 11, 1967, p. 35.

40. The General Tire and Rubber Co., Waco Plant and United Rubber, Cork, Linoleum, and Plastic Workers of Am., Local No. 312, December 14, 1962, p. 3; Ford Motor Co., Cincinnati Automatic Transmission Plant and United Auto. Workers, Local 863, p. 2.

41. Kaiser Aluminum and Chem. Corp. and United Rubber, Cork, Linoleum, and Plastic Workers of Am., Local 339, September 13, 1967, p. 5.

42. Shack's Clothing Co. and Amalgamated Clothing Workers Union, April 21, 1964; Kennecott Wire and Cable Co. and Int'l Bhd. of Elec. Workers, AFL, Local Union No. 1450, March 7, 1955.

43. American Sugar Refining Co. and Local Industrial Union, CIO, No. 1660, January 26, 1955 (hearing date), p. 4; Raytheon Mfg. Co. and Int'l Bhd. of Elec. Workers, AFL, Local No. 1505, May 15, 1955, p. 6; G. L. Brownell, Inc. and United Steelworkers of Am., AFL-CIO, Local 2936, July 29, 1957, p. 4; J. Flynn and Sons, Inc. and Leather Workers Int'l Union of Am., Local No. 21, January 28, 1957, p. 4; Narragansett Hotel and Hotel, Restaurant, and Culinary Employees Union, CIO, February 4, 1957, p. 10.

44. General Tire and Rubber Co., Waco Div. and United Rubber, Cork, Linoleum, and Plastic Workers of Am., February 15, 1949, pp. 5–6; Republic Steel Corp., Chicago Dist. and United Steelworkers of Am., Local Union No. 1033,

December 26, 1967, p. 3; Sylvania Elec. Prod., Inc., Huntington Plant and Int'l Union of Elec., Radio, and Mach. Workers, AFL-CIO, Local No. 608, June 9, 1957; Firestone Tire and Rubber Co., Pottstown Plant and United Rubber, Cork, Linoleum, and Plastic Workers of Am., CIO, Local No. 336, August 23, 1955, pp. 3–4; Tubular Rivet and Stud Co. and Int'l Ass'n of Mach., AFL, Granite Lodge No. 1451, December 3, 1952, p. 9; Firestone Tire and Rubber Co., Pottstown Plant and United Rubber, Cork, Linoleum, and Plastic Workers of Am., Local No. 336, May 2, 1958, p. 4; The General Tire and Rubber Co., Waco Plant and United Rubber, Cork, Linoleum, and Plastic Workers of Am., Local No. 312, December 12, 1961, p. 2; The General Tire and Rubber Co., Waco Plant and United Rubber, Cork, Linoleum, and Plastic Workers of Am., Local No. 312, December 13, 1961, p. 2; Firestone Tire and Rubber Co., Fall River Plant and United Rubber, Cork, Linoleum, and Plastic Workers of Am., Local No. 261, July 1, 1957, p. 6; The B. F. Goodrich Co. and United Rubber, Cork, Linoleum, and Plastic Workers of Am., CIO, Local No. 5, January 8, 1954, p. 3; Curtiss-Wright Corp. and United Auto. Workers, Local No. 669, Grievance No. 28354, 1963, pp. 10–11.

45. Landers, Frary, and Clark and United Elec., Radio, and Mach. Workers of Am., CIO, Local 207, April 29, 1946; National Standard Co., Athenia Steel Div. and United Steelworkers of Am., June 30, 1960, p. 4; Davidson Mfg. Co. and United Furniture Workers of Am., CIO, July 18, 1947, p. 5; Hudson Worsted Co. and United Textile Workers of Am., AFL, Local No. 96, April 6, 1953, p. 3; Narragansett Hotel, February 4, 1957, p. 10.

46. Curtiss-Wright Corp. and United Auto., Aircraft, and Agricultural Implement Workers of Am., AFL-CIO, Local No. 669, April 8, 1956, p. 2.

47. Ibid., p. 3.

48. Goodyear Decatur Mills and United Textile Workers of Am., AFL, October 2, 1953, pp. 5–6.

49. Firestone Tire and Rubber Co., Pottstown Plant and United Rubber, Cork, Linoleum, and Plastic Workers of Am., AFL-CIO, Local No. 336, December 23, 1970, p. 3.

50. Firestone Tire and Rubber Co., Fall River Plant and United Rubber Workers of Am., Local No. 261, October 13, 1962, p. 3.

51. Firestone Rubber and Latex Prod. Co. and United Rubber, Cork, Linoleum, and Plastic Workers of Am., CIO, Local No. 261, March 5, 1953, p. 4.

52. Goodyear Decatur Mills and United Textile Workers of Am., AFL, Local 88, October 2, 1953, pp. 5 and 7.

53. Beggs and Cobb, Inc. and Int'l Fur and Leather Workers Union, Local 22, September 16, 1953, p. 3.

Chapter VIII

Conclusions and Comments

CONCLUSIONS

The preceding chapters have illustrated the degree to which Saul Wallen as an arbitrator ventured beyond mere disclosure of the intent of the parties' agreements in his decision making and instead relied on his own values — his own conceptions of what was proper, reasonable, and practical — in establishing arbitral procedures, the parties' basic substantive rights, and the appropriate remedies to be awarded. The precise degree to which he ventured beyond a traditional interpretive role and determined the parties' present and future behavior as a rule-making legislator or a decision-making manager can be illustrated, but cannot be summarized in a single sentence. What to some observers constitutes the mere discovery of the parties' unwritten, but clearly implied, intent is to other observers the rank and rampant imposition on the parties of the arbitrator's own values and brand of industrial justice.

A large part of the problem in labeling Wallen arises from the lack of a precise, commonly held yardstick defining the limits and meaning of contractual intent. A few observers of the arbitral process might argue that the parties themselves obviously intended that considerations of efficiency, equity, and stability would be factors to be considered in any decision under any labor agreement; that the various preambles and management's rights, recognition, and seniority clauses either mention or imply such considerations; and that Wallen's decision making as outlined in this study merely reflected these intentions. A much more limited, judicial view of the intent of the parties, more closely approximating the general arbitral view, was stated in a leading text on labor arbitration:

Whatever may be the inaccuracy of expression or the inaptness of words used in an instrument in a legal view, if the intention of the parties can be clearly discovered, the court will give effect to it and construe the words accordingly. It must not be supposed, however, that an attempt is made to ascertain the actual mental processes of the parties to a particular contract. The law presumes that the parties understood the import of their contract and that they had the intention which its terms manifest. It is not within the function of the judiciary to look outside the instrument to get at the intention of the parties and then carry out that intention regardless of whether the instrument contains language sufficient to express it; but their sole duty is to find out what was meant by the language of the instrument. This language must be sufficient, when looked at in the light of such facts as the court is entitled to consider, to sustain whatever effect is given to the instrument.[1]

Using this definition as a basic yardstick, it is possible to answer questions raised here about the appropriate role of personal values and expertise in arbitration. With respect to Saul Wallen, the facts indicate the following:

(1) Wallen often relied on personal values and his own expertise where no clear evidence of any contractual intent existed in cases on virtually all subjects. He also did not hesitate to rely on his own values and expertise even where considerable evidence of intent did exist if the plain words of the written agreement did not positively dictate a solution and if the issue at hand had important implications for a firm's economic well being, the bargaining ability of a union, an individual worker's safety or job security, or public safety. In a very few exceptional instances, he was even willing to ignore the agreement's clear written terms where the result of those terms was repugnant to his personal values. In general, where the weight of the evidence of the parties' intent was not overwhelming, but nevertheless clearly pointed to a result different from a result he deemed reasonable, practical, or just, he was willing under many circumstances to ignore that evidence and rely instead on his own values.

(2) In terms of his values, Wallen was particularly concerned with considerations of productive efficiency, industrial relations stability, and equity, including the recognition of workers' growing human investment in their jobs and the public's right to safety of product and service.

(3) Wallen behaved as a consultant to the parties in many instances and was concerned with the future conduct of the parties. He did not hesitate to offer advice to the parties on how to solve a problem or on how they should conduct themselves in the future, particularly where such advice might either provide needed expertise or else nudge a recalcitrant party into accepting a practical solution. He also did not hesitate to exercise his remedy powers and order such solutions. His touchstone was not whether the agreement's terms pointed to a particular remedy so much as whether they prohibited that remedy. Where repeated violations of clear contract

terms occurred, Wallen was not loathe to use threats and penalty remedies to insure future contract compliance.

As has been demonstrated, there existed no discernible difference between Wallen's behavior as a permanent and ad hoc arbitrator. This fact in itself indicates the importance that Wallen placed on his own values or goals, since arbitrators concerned primarily about their acceptability might well act more circumspectly, more in the manner of a judge, in those instances where they served in an ad hoc capacity. By relying on values and expertise only in those permanent relationships where arbitrators know that the parties will tolerate such behavior, they minimize the potential risk to their acceptability that a reliance on personal values might create. Wallen chose not to play it safe, but instead introduced his own opinions a great deal in both ad hoc and permanent situations, indicating that his own values were so strongly held that he was willing to risk his future acceptability.

As an indication of the frequency that extracontractual value considerations arose in Wallen's decision making, ten categories of cases were selected and his use of value judgments tabulated for cases in each category. No differentiation was made between ad hoc and permanent arbitration cases. The process for selecting the cases was as follows: (1) All of Wallen's cases were reviewed and those falling into one of the ten categories to be examined were indexed. The categories are mutually exclusive, no case falling into more than one category. (2) In each of the ten categories, all cases were numbered. (3) Through the use of a table of random numbers, 50 cases were selected in each category from all of the cases in that category. The total sample for all categories was 500 cases.

The cases selected in this manner were then analyzed to determine which extracontractual values were explicitly considered by Wallen. Only clear statements of these values by Wallen were counted. The tabulated results appear in the Table. The tabulation indicates in each instance the number of cases in the category, out of a total of 50, in which Wallen evaluated extracontractual considerations of efficiency and productivity, equity and justice, or industrial relations stability. What is tabulated is whether Wallen considered and evaluated these extracontractual sources, not whether they were the sole or determining factor in his decision. In most cases, it cannot be said with certainty that any one single factor, contractual or extracontractual, was the basis for the decision, since most arbitral decisions are the product of a balancing of several considerations. As a result, in any single case, Wallen might have considered one of these extracontractual values, more than one, or none at all, relying instead solely on evidence of the parties' intent.

The statistics in the Table demonstrate that more than one value consideration influenced a number of his cases. For example, in the discipline

Table.   The Incidence of Wallen's Value Judgments in His Decisions

Case category	Total number of cases	Efficiency	Equity	Stability	Total of all values
Discipline and discharge: vocational handicap	50	41	37	3	81
Subcontracting and transfer of work	50	48	21	13	72
Discipline and discharge: misconduct	50	18	35	7	60
Discipline and discharge: work refusals	50	21	10	29	60
Administrative discretion	50	15	28	12	55
Crew size and manning provisions	50	29	13	8	50
Arbitrability	50	4	32	8	44
Promotions	50	14	17	4	35
Piece-rate adjustments	50	7	19	9	35
Layoff and transfer	50	19	8	6	33
All categories	500	206	220	99	525

and discharge for vocational handicap category, the decision in the majority of cases involved the consideration of more than one extracontractual value. Here, the considerations of equity and efficiency were arguably antithetical. In the category of discipline and discharge for work refusals, many cases again involved a consideration of more than one value, although here the primary value considerations of efficiency and stability arguably reinforced one another.

The total number of value considerations arising in all 50 cases of each category are tabulated in the right-hand column, the total number of considerations of efficiency, equity, and stability are tabulated at the bottom of the table, and the total number of all value considerations in all cases is at the lower right-hand corner. As one can readily see, the total number, 525, averages out to slightly better than one significant extracontractual consideration per case arbitrated.

Extracontractual value considerations arose most frequently in those cases involving the discharge or suspension of persons suffering vocational handicaps, including physical injury, serious illness, alcoholism, or mental disabilities. The primary value considerations here by Wallen were those of equity for the worker, that is, the protection of job investment, and the company's need for efficiency. Safety considerations were also considered as being aspects of equity. The high incidence of value considerations in these cases, coupled with the fact that these values frequently conflicted with one another, made these cases among Wallen's most difficult to decide. Wallen once claimed for himself a "self-conferred degree of F. S.W.—Frustrated Social Worker," and related how personally difficult these cases were for him because of value conflicts.[2]

Subcontracting and out-of-unit transfer of work cases were decided to a great degree on the basis of Wallen's own personal values, his goal of efficiency balanced against those considerations of the individual worker's job security and the protection of the bargaining unit. Discipline cases also involved a large number of value judgments, primarily considerations of equity or simple justice. Those cases involving the specific misconduct of work refusals or wildcat strikes were decided to a great degree based on considerations of bargaining stability.

The category administrative discretion included those cases involving management's discretion in administering overtime, call-in time, and other similar provisions. Here, equity considerations arose most frequently. Cases involving management's right to determine crew size and manning provisions were influenced to a substantial degree by considerations of efficiency and to a lesser degree by considerations of equity, most notably the concept of a fair day's work. Cases over arbitrability were influenced to a substantial degree by considerations of equity, of granting a grievant a forum for redress unless it could be established with certainty that the agreement precluded this right. The remaining case categories, including the issues of promotion rights, piece-rate adjustments, and layoff and transfer rights were influenced to a lesser degree by Wallen's own personal values. In these cases, the relevant contract provisions were generally more plentiful and more specific and detailed than were the provisions governing those categories such as discipline and subcontracting, where Wallen's own values exerted a considerable influence on his decision making.

With respect to the conclusions that can be drawn about the arbitration process in general, it becomes clear from Wallen's example that (1) competent arbitrators can allow certain personal values to influence their decision making and still remain generally acceptable as an arbitrator; (2) concerns for efficiency, industrial relations stability, and equity for all affected individuals are among these values; and (3) arbitrators can play a large role in influencing the parties' future behavior through the creative and assertive use of remedy powers.

Whether an arbitrator successfully can flout the conventional wisdom of the profession to an even greater extent than did Wallen by relying on their personal values and influencing the parties' future behavior is still not clear. Neither is it clear whether yet other extracontractual personal values can be relied upon by arbitrators without harming their future acceptability to the parties. Insights into these absolute limits of an acceptable style can be gained best through further research of yet other arbitrators. A deeper look into some of the possible reasons for Wallen's success, however, does give some additional insight into the *probable* limits of an acceptable style of arbitration.

THE REASONS FOR WALLEN'S SUCCESS

Before analyzing the reasons for the success of Wallen's particular style, it is interesting to note some of Wallen's views concerning the degree to which arbitrators can insure their acceptability and success by any means other than simply rendering competent decisions designed to meet the needs of the parties. Wallen expressed his thoughts in a defense of the arbitration process[3] delivered in response to a post-Trilogy attack on arbitration by Judge Paul R. Hays.[4] The most serious criticism leveled by Judge Hays was not that arbitrators paid too little attention to the intent of the agreement and too much attention to their own notions of right and wrong, but rather that arbitrators tended to ignore the agreement and its intent and instead render those decisions most likely to please one or both of the parties and assure or enhance their own survival as arbitrators.

Why was Wallen the first and most vocal arbitrator to answer these charges? It is at least possible that he recognized that the Hays' charges raised questions about his own style of decision making. While Wallen stated, in fact probably overstated, the premise that arbitrators in general and himself in particular respected clear contractual intent and were not freely roaming problem solvers, he did reveal and justify some of his views on the appropriate role of considerations not precisely embodied in the agreement. In one article, he said that

Labor arbitration is more than the interpretation of contracts. It involves their interpretation in the context of an on-going relationship in which the rights and the wrongs are weighted against the parties' needs and aspirations which may transcend the immediate case. It requires of the decider a sensitivity to the parties' whole relationship precedent and antecedent to the case at hand. This is not to say that such considerations dominate arbitral decisions. It is to say only that they may temper them in cases where other factors are in balance.[5]

In another reply to Hays, he wrote,

But a good arbitrator is more than an "ad hoc judge...expert in analyzing issues, in weighing evidence, and in contract interpretation." He must do that in the specialized context of labor relations, in the special community of an industrial plant and a local union. To be meaningful and convincing to the parties, his decisions should impart an understanding and comprehension of that atmosphere and should convey to them the conviction that their controversy is being decided not with reference to abstractions remote from their ken but with reference to the realities which govern their day-to-day in-plant lives.[6]

He further stated that the test of the marketplace, the arbitrator's need to remain acceptable to the parties, tended not to prostitute the arbitral decision-making process, but rather tended, if anything, to insure the continuing integrity of the process. He wrote that

Arbitrators nearly always are the mutual choice of the parties. No matter how much an arbitrator pleases the winner, the irate loser can veto him for the future. And if he writes a decision that has a little bit in it for each party but not enough for either to accomplish justice, his cowardice becomes immediately apparent to both, and he courts the likelihood that both will axe him.[7]

• • •

Hays thus views arbitrators as cravens interested only in their survival in the field and little or not at all in their own integrity or self-respect. But the pressures on arbitrators are not primarily from the parties; they are from within. With each decision, an arbitrator lays his integity on the line. Few have failed to meet the challenge. The external pressures are countervailing. The need for living with himself is inexorable. If some arbitrators fail the test, they do not long survive. And those who do survive have met a test judges are not called upon to meet—the test of acceptability in an area where two contestants freely make him their mutual choice.[8]

While he did not refer to it in his rebuttal to Hays, his own willingness to shut out totally considerations of his future acceptability was clearly demonstrated when he rendered a decision that he well knew would cost him one of his most prestigious and lucrative umpireships — that with General Motors and the UAW — and possibly affect his career as an arbitrator.

Why was Wallen able to succeed to such a great degree both as an ad hoc arbitrator and as a permanent chairman or umpire? The most obvious answer is that the "truism" that the parties nearly always prefer a judge rather than a consultant is drastically overstated. There appears to have been, and hence presumably still exists, a significant demand for, or at the very minimum a tolerance of, the competent, limited, and restrained problem-solving type of arbitrator which Wallen epitomized, who respected the clear requirements or limitations on their role, but otherwise do not really hesitate to dispense their own brand of industrial justice. This would imply that a significant number of subscribers to arbitration do not regard the labor agreement as "a lengthy document, with every conceivable situation covered,"[9] to be strictly interpreted as the Braden-Morse-Crane models of arbitration suggest, but rather hold the agreement to be more in the nature of a constitution, with admitted and even intentional gaps left to be filled by arbitral legislation, and with the expectation that some flexibility and creativity will be needed to apply the document to reality, just as the courts (as a gross generalization) tend to be less literal in their interpretations of constitutions and legislation than in their interpretations of private contracts.[10]

This answer would also question the assertion that the vast majority of agreements are so specialized, and their drafters such a corps of specialists[11] whose particular expertise so exceeds that of the arbitrator, that the arbitrator's reliance on his or her own expertise or value judgments and creative remedial efforts will be not only resented by the parties, but also potentially damaging to them. The basic question here is whether under such circumstances the parties object to being "limited by an arbitrator's imagination or his limited knowledge of the available technology."[12] At least in Saul Wallen's case, there were a very large number of parties who did not object. Whether a relatively inexperienced arbitrator could operate in a manner similar to Wallen's and still escape objection is much more open to question. The great leeway given to Wallen would indicate either that the parties to arbitration appearing before him were not as uniformly expert as is asserted by some students of the process or else that the ambiguities and gaps with which he was frequently faced were purposeful.

Several authorities on arbitration, such as Paul Prasow and Edward Peters, Gabriel Alexander, and Meyer Ryder, have pointed out the prevalence of such intentional gaps and ambiguities.[13] Harry Shulman theorized that, inasmuch as one of the basic functions of collective bargaining and the labor agreement was to reduce unfettered discretion, the parties did not object to the arbitrator similarly reducing the parties' discretion by codifying principles and policies that fill those gaps that necessarily have to be filled for the enterprise to function, so long as the arbitrator was competent and rather discreet about doing so.[14] In one of his studies on arbitration, Wallen pointed out that in some situations, it was safer, politically or otherwise, for the parties to place the burden of decision or legislation on the arbitrator;[15] in some of his cases, he quite frankly asserted that, with respect to the issue he was asked to interpret, the parties had in their agreement essentially "agreed to disagree."[16]

Finally, the answer to why Wallen's style was in such demand also implies that Wallen's values in the long run either coincided with the values of a large number of the parties themselves or else became acceptable values to the parties after they pondered the results. This is not to say that every party found his results acceptable, but that the evidence is overwhelming that a great number of them did. His arbitral success over nearly a quarter-century could not have occurred had there not been a basic acceptability of those particular values upon which he relied so heavily. Not only do the immediate parties gain knowledge very rapidly of the arbitrator's manner of operation, but through published cases, word-of-mouth recommendation or condemnation, and subscription to services specializing in the evaluation of arbitrators, potential future parties also are apprised of the arbitrator's manner and holdings.[17]

Why were Wallen's values acceptable? First, they appear to be conservative values with which few businessmen or trade unionists would quarrel. By conservative it is meant that these values are consistent with the principles of democratic, representative government, with the free enterprise economic system, and with the concept of collective bargaining. As is apparent from plain common sense and from the many demonstrated applications of these values in the preceding chapters, however, efficiency is primarily a management consideration. Equity considerations usually favor the employee or the union. Stability is primarily a neutral value, or at most slightly "pro-management" since in several cases those acting against stability were wildcat strikers or individual employees who bypassed the proper grievance procedures. Thus, Wallen, on the one hand, had in these values of efficiency, equity, and stability the tools that could be used together to satisfy in appropriate circumstances the needs of the employer, the employee, and the union. On the other hand, an uneven application of these values could have caused resentment, and such resentment could have hurt his future acceptability.

Wallen's application of his values thus appears to be the second factor behind their acceptability. Wallen demonstrated no apparent bias against either party to arbitration; this neutrality is demonstrated by an examination of the results of the random sample of his cases presented in the Table. In all 500 cases, efficiency factors were considered 206 times and equity factors were considered 220 times. The slight pro-management effect that may have resulted from the consideration of issues of stability in 99 cases makes this small difference even more insignificant.

In conclusion, even from a thorough examination of 500 of Wallen's decisions covering ten varied categories, it is impossible to detect or measure any bias resulting from his use of personal values. This even-handedness of application, together with the basic conservative nature of these values, goes far to explain why Wallen was able to rely on his own personal extracontractual values and still remain acceptable to the parties.

IMPLICATIONS FOR FURTHER RESEARCH

Before one can generalize on the variety of acceptable arbitral roles, and the prevailing demand for each of the myriad of possible styles of performance, it is obvious that many more very detailed studies of other arbitrators are needed. It would not require an inordinate number of such studies of other arbitrators to encompass a very respectable percentage of the total number of cases that have been decided in the last few decades, since several other full-time arbitrators have also decided thousands of cases in their careers. The careers of arbitrators who performed solely or largely in ad hoc capacities should be explored to determine if these parties do generally demand a more restrictive style of arbitration. As has been stated throughout this study, Wallen's arbitral procedures, his value judgments, the degree to which they affected his decision making, and his use of his remedy powers did not differ in his various roles. Wallen was employed from the very beginning of his career as a permanent umpire, and simultaneously handled many ad hoc cases. It is possible that his general approach to arbitration might have been different if he had served solely as an ad hoc arbitrator or at least had so served for several years before receiving permanent positions. Similarly, if possible, it might be useful to examine the numerous brief careers of those who failed as arbitrators, or who tried and failed to become full-time, "mainline" arbitrators,[18] to determine if any common threads exist.

How accurately written arbitration opinions reflect the true motivating thoughts of the arbitrator in reaching a decision and remedy is a question raised by arbitrator Peter Seitz.[19] James Gross suggests that if arbitrators' opinions do not reflect their thoughts accurately and truthfully, the profession is in serious trouble.[20] Further, if the arbitral process and the arbitrators themselves are deemed worthy of study, they are similarly worthy of the presumption of basic honesty absent any indication to the contrary. Such a presumption does no injustice to the proper approach of scholarly skepticism in this type of analysis.

As a final potential issue for future study, it is apparent that only too little is known about the degree to which an arbitrator can truly educate, reorient, or influence the values and behavior of the parties in the long run. What has been examined to date, as in this study of Wallen, has really been the arbitrator's intentions, that is, how much Wallen tried to influence the parties. The few studies that do exist in this area, centering primarily on the effect of the arbitrator reinstating terminated employees, seem to indicate that the arbitrator in general has not been very successful here as a problem solver.[21] Does the same hold true of the arbitral guidance offered the parties, either through dicta or through creative remedies, concerning other issues in arbitration? This is one area in which the arbitrator and the parties, as well as students and observers of the process, are in the dark and could benefit greatly from research.

Notes

1. Elkouri and Elkouri, 3rd ed., p. 303.

2. Saul Wallen, "Society in Crisis," a speech delivered to the Staff Conference of the Middle and North Atlantic Regions of the Family Service Association, November 15, 1968, p. 1, personal files.

3. Wallen, "Arbitrators and Judges—Dispelling the Hays' Haze"; Wallen, Book Review of Hays, *Labor Arbitration.*

4. Paul R. Hays, *Labor Arbitration—A Dissenting View* (New Haven, Conn.: Yale University Press, 1966). See also Paul R. Hays, "The Future of Labor Arbitration," *Yale Law Journal* 74 (1965): 1019–38.

5. Wallen, Book Review of Hays, *Labor Arbitration,* p. 510.

6. Wallen, "Arbitrators and Judges—Dispelling the Hays' Haze," p. 166.

7. Wallen, "Book Review of Hays, *Labor Arbitration*," pp. 510–11.

8. Ibid., p. 511.

9. Donald Strauss, "Labor Arbitration and Its Critics," *Arbitration Journal* 20 (1965): 197.

10. Archibald Cox, "Reflections Upon Labor Arbitration," *Harvard Law Review* 72 (1959): 1482–1518; Robben Fleming, "Reflections Upon the Nature of Labor Arbitration," *Michigan Law Review* 61 (1963): 1245–72; Meyers, "The Task of the Labor Arbitrator," p. 28. For an examination of such "legislation," see Elkouri and Elkouri, 3rd ed., pp. 299–302.

11. Prasow and Peters, "The Development of Judicial Arbitration in Labor-Management Disputes," p. 14.

12. Crane, "The Use and Abuse of Arbitral Power," p. 75.

13. Prasow and Peters, *Arbitration and Collective Bargaining,* p. 57; Alexander, "Discretion in Arbitration," pp. 100–101; Meyer Ryder, "The Impact of Acceptability on the Arbitrator." In Charles Rehmus (ed.), *Developments in American and Foreign Arbitration* (Washington, D.C.: BNA, 1968), p. 107.

14. Shulman, "Reason, Contract, and Law in Labor Relations," pp. 1005–11.

15. Charles Killingsworth and Saul Wallen, "Constraint and Variety in Arbitration Systems." In Mark L. Kahn (ed.), *Labor Arbitration—Perspectives and Problems* (Washington, D.C.: BNA, 1964), p. 77.

16. Southern Airways, Inc. and Air Line Stewards and Stewardesses Ass'n, September 14, 1966, 47 LA 1135 at 1141.

17. Wallen, "Arbitrators and Judges—Dispelling the Hays' Haze," p. 167.

18. For an interesting discussion concerning this term, see Prasow and Peters, *Arbitration and Collective Bargaining,* pp. 284–93.

19. Peter Seitz, Communications, "Value Judgments in the Decisions of Labor Arbitrators," *Industrial and Labor Relations Review* 21 (1968): 427.

20. James Gross, Communications — Reply, *Industrial and Labor Relations Review* 21 (1968): 431.

21. Dallas Jones, *Arbitration and Industrial Discipline* (Ann Arbor, Mich.: University of Michigan Press, 1961); Arthur Ross, "The Arbitration of Discharge Cases: What Happens After Reinstatement." In Jean T. McKelvey (ed.), *Critical Issues in Labor Arbitration* (Washington, D.C.: BNA, 1957); Dallas Jones, "Ramifications of Back-Pay Awards in Discharge Cases." In Gerald Somers (ed.), *Arbitration and Social Change* (Washington, D.C.: BNA, 1970).

Bibliography

MANUSCRIPT COLLECTIONS

The Saul Wallen Collection. Personal arbitration files of Saul Wallen, containing notes, exhibits, transcripts, decisions, and correspondence for all cases decided between 1946 and 1968. Labor-Management Documentation Center, Martin P. Catherwood Library, Cornell University, Ithaca, New York.

The Saul Wallen Papers. Newspaper clippings and articles, books, pamphlets, National War Labor Board materials, and correspondence. Labor-Management Documentation Center, Martin P. Catherwood Library, Cornell University, Ithaca, New York.

BOOKS AND BULLETINS

Bernstein, Merton. *Private Dispute Settlement.* New York: The Free Press, 1968.

Braun, Kurt. *Labor Disputes and Their Settlement.* Baltimore: Johns Hopkins Press, 1955.

Brooks, George. *The Sources of Vitality in the American Labor Movement.* Ithaca: New York State School of Industrial and Labor Relations, Cornell University, 1960. Bulletin No. 41.

Coulson, Robert. *Labor Arbitration: What You Need to Know.* New York: American Arbitration Association, 1973.

Elkouri, Frank. *How Arbitration Works.* Washington, D. C.: Bureau of National Affairs, 1952.

Elkouri, Frank, and Edna Elkouri. *How Arbitration Works.* 3rd ed. Washington, D.C.: Bureau of National Affairs, 1973.

Fleming, Robben. *The Labor Arbitration Process.* Urbana: Illinois University Press, 1965.

Hays, Paul. *Labor Arbitration: A Dissenting View.* New Haven, Conn.: Yale University Press, 1966.

Jones, Dallas. *Arbitration and Industrial Discipline.* Ann Arbor: University of Michigan, 1961.

Kellor, Frances. *American Arbitration.* New York: Harper and Row, 1948.
————. *Arbitration in the New Industrial Society.* New York: McGraw-Hill, 1934.
Phelps, Orme. *Discipline and Discharge in the Unionized Firm.* Berkeley: University of California Press, 1959.
Prasow, Paul, and Edward Peters. *Arbitration and Collective Bargaining.* New York: McGraw-Hill, 1970.
Simkin, William. *Acceptability as a Factor in Arbitration Under an Existing Agreement.* Philadelphia: University of Pennsylvania Press, 1952.
Stone, Morris. *Labor-Management Contracts at Work.* New York: Harper and Row, 1961.
————. *Managerial Freedom and Job Security.* New York: Harper and Row, 1964.
Witte, Edwin. *Historical Survey of Labor Arbitration.* Philadelphia: University of Pennsylvania Press, 1952.

PERIODICAL, JOURNAL, AND LAW REVIEW ARTICLES

Aaron, Benjamin. "Arbitration in the Federal Courts: Aftermath of the Trilogy." *UCLA Law Review* 9 (1962): 360–80.
————. "Labor Arbitration and Its Critics." *Labor Law Journal,* 10 (1959): 605–10 and 645.
————. "Some Procedural Problems in Arbitration." *Vanderbilt Law Review* 10 (1957): 733–48.
Abelow, Robert. "Standards of Evidence in Arbitration Proceedings." *Arbitration Journal* 4 (1949): 252–59.
Baer, William. "Precedent Value of Arbitration Awards." *Personnel Journal* 45 (1966): 484–88.
Bailer, Lloyd. "The Right to Assign Employees in One Job Classification to Jobs in Another Classification." *Industrial and Labor Relations Review* 16 (1963): 200–204.
Banta, William. "Labor Obligations of Successor Employers." *George Washington Law Review* 36 (1967): 215–23.
Benewitz, Maurice. "Discharge, Arbitration, and the Quantum of Proof." *Arbitration Journal* 28 (1973): 95–104.
Blumrosen, Alfred. "Public Policy Considerations in Labor Arbitration Cases." *Rutgers Law Review* 14 (1960), pp. 217 — 63.
Braden, J. Noble. "The Function of the Arbitrator in Labor-Management Disputes." *Arbitration Journal* 4 (1949): 35–40.
Cox, Archibald. "Reflections Upon Labor Arbitration." *Harvard Law Review* 72 (1959): 1482–1518.
Dash, G. Allan, Jr. "The Arbitration of Subcontracting Disputes." *Industrial and Labor Relations Review* 16 (1963): 208–20.
Davey, Harold. "The Arbitrator Speaks on Discharge and Discipline." *Arbitration Journal* 17 (1962): 97–104.
————. "The Arbitrator Views the Agreement." *Labor Law Journal* 12 (1961): 1161–76.

————. "Hazards in Labor Arbitration." *Industrial and Labor Relations Review* 1 (1948): 386–405.

————. "Labor Arbitration: A Current Appraisal." *Industrial and Labor Relations Review* 9 (1955): 85–94.

————. "The Proper Uses of Arbitration." *Labor Law Journal* 9 (1958): 119–26.

————. "The Supreme Court and Arbitration." *Notre Dame Lawyer* 36 (1961): 138–45.

DeVyver, Frank. "Labor Arbitration after Twenty-five Years." *Southern Economic Journal* 28 (1962): 235–45.

Doyle, Charles. "Precedent Values of Labor Arbitration Awards." *Personnel Journal* 42 (1963): 66–69 and 95.

Finley, Joseph. "Labor Arbitration: The Quest for Industrial Justice." *Western Reserve Law Review* 18 (1967): 1091–1121.

Fleming, Robben. "Arbitrators and Arbitrability." *Washington University Law Quarterly* 1963 (1963): 200–221.

————. "Arbitrators and the Remedy Power." *Virginia Law Review* 48 (1962): 1199–1225.

————. "Problems of Procedural Regularity in Labor Arbitration." *Washington University Law Quarterly* 1961 (1961): 221–49.

————. "Reflections on the Nature of Labor Arbitration." *Michigan Law Review* 61 (1963): 1245–1272.

————. "Some Problems of Due Process and Fair Procedure in Labor Arbitration." *Stanford Law Review* 13 (1961): 235–51.

Foster, Howard. "Disloyalty to the Employer." *Arbitration Journal* 20 (1965): 157–67.

Freidin, Jesse, and Francis Ulman. "Arbitration and the National War Labor Board." *Harvard Law Review* 58 (1945): 309–60.

Garrison, Lloyd. "Proposal for a Labor-Management Board and a Charter of Fair Labor Practices." *University of Chicago Law Review* 14 (1947): 347–62.

Gitelman, Morton. "The Evolution of Labor Arbitration." *DePaul Law Review* 9 (1960): 181–95.

Glick, Leslie. "Bias, Fraud, Misconduct, and Partiality of the Arbitrator." *Arbitration Journal* 22 (1967): 161–72.

Goldberg, Arthur. "A Supreme Court Justice Looks at Arbitration." *Arbitration Journal* 20 (1965): 13–19.

Gorske, Robert. "Arbitration Back-Pay Awards." *Labor Law Journal* 10 (1959): 18–27.

————. "Burden of Proof in Grievance Arbitration." *Marquette Law Review* 43 (1959): 135–79.

Gross, James. "The Labor Arbitrator's Role: Tradition and Change." *Arbitration Journal* 25 (1970): 221–33.

————. "Value Judgements in the Decisions of Labor Arbitrators." *Industrial and Labor Relations Review* 21 (1967): 55–72.

Hafen, Bruce. "A Study of Labor Arbitration: The Values and the Risks of the Rule of Law." *Utah Law Review* 1967 (1967): 223–50.

Handsaker, Morrison. "Arbitration of Discipline Cases." *Personnel Journal* 46 (1967): 153–56 and 175.

_____. "Grievance Arbitration and Mediated Settlements." *Labor Law Journal* 17 (1966): 579–83.

Harris, Philip. "Arbitration and the Selection and Retention of Supervisors." *Personnel Journal* 46 (1967): 231–37.

_____. "The Arbitration Process and the Disciplining of Supervisors." *Labor Law Journal* 16 (1965): 679–84.

_____. "Labor Arbitration and Technological Innovation." *Labor Law Journal* 17 (1966): 664–70.

Hays, Paul. "The Future of Labor Arbitration." *Yale Law Journal* 74 (1965): 1019–38.

_____. "The Supreme Court and Labor Law." *Columbia Law Review* 60 (1960): 901–35.

Hepburn, William, and Pierre Loiseaux. "The Nature of the Arbitration Process." *Vanderbilt Law Review* 10 (1957): 657–65.

Jensen, Vernon. "Notes on the Beginnings of Collective Bargaining." *Industrial and Labor Relations Review* 9 (1956): 225–34.

Johnson, Frederick. "Contrasts in the Role of the Arbitrator and of the Mediator." *Labor Law Journal* 9 (1958): 769–73.

Jones, Edgar. "Power and Prudence in the Arbitration of Labor Disputes." *U.C.L.A. Law Review* 11 (1964): 675–791.

Leonard, John. "Discipline for Off-the-Job Activities." *Monthly Labor Review* 91 (1968): 5–11.

McDermott, Thomas. "Arbitrability: The Courts Versus the Arbitrator." *Arbitration Journal* 23 (1968): 18–38.

_____. "Enforcing No-Strike Provisions via Arbitration." *Labor Law Journal* 18 (1967): 579–87.

McKelvey, Jean. "Sex and the Single Arbitrator." *Industrial and Labor Relations Review* 24 (1971): 335–53.

McLaughlin, Richard. "Custom and Past Practice in Labor Arbitration." *Arbitration Journal* 18 (1963): 205–28.

Meltzer, Bernard. "Ruminations about Ideology, Law, and Labor Arbitration." *University of Chicago Law Review,* 34 (1967): 545–61.

Meyers, Frederic. "The Task of the Labor Arbitrator." *Personnel Administration* 22 (1959): 24–29.

Moore, Ernestine, and James Nix. "Arbitration Provisions in Collective Agreements." *Monthly Labor Review* 76 (1953): 261–66.

Morgan, C. Baird. "Adequacy of Collective Bargaining in Resolving the Problem of Job Security and Technological Change." *Labor Law Journal* 16 (1965): 87–99.

Morse, Wayne. "A Realistic Approach to Labor Legislation." *University of Chicago Law Review* 14 (1947): 337–46.

Morvant, Robert. "The Nature of Industrial Arbitration." *Labor Law Journal* 18 (1961): 1042–52.

Platt, Harry. "The Arbitration Process in the Settlement of Labor Disputes." *Journal of the American Judicature Society* 31 (1947): 54–60.

Plaut, Frank. "Arbitrability Under the Standard Labor Arbitration Clause." *Arbitration Journal* 14 (1959): 51–72.

Prasow, Paul, and Edward Peters. "The Development of Judicial Arbitration in Labor-Management Disputes." *California Management Review* 9 (1967): 7–16.

————. "New Perspectives on Management's Reserved Rights." *Labor Law Journal* 18 (1967): 3–14.

Rose, George. "Do the Requirements of Due Process Protect the Rights of Employees Under Arbitration Procedures?" *Labor Law Journal* 16 (1965): 44–58.

Rubin, Milton. "The Right of Management to Split Jobs and Assign Work to Other Jobs." *Industrial and Labor Relatons Review* 16 (1963): 205–7.

Schmertz, Herbert. "When and Where an Issue of Arbitrability Can Be Raised." *Labor Reporter Bulletin* 3 (1966): 2–16.

Seitz, Peter. "Value Judgments in the Decisions of Labor Arbitrators." *Industrial and Labor Relations Review* 21 (1968): 427–30.

Seitz, Peter, and George Moskowitz. "The Arbitrator's Responsibility for Public Policy." *Arbitration Journal* 19 (1964): 23–44.

Seligson, Harry. "Minority Group Employees, Discipline, and the Arbitrator." *Labor Law Journal* 19 (1968): 544–54.

Seward, Ralph. "Arbitration and the Functions of Management." *Industrial and Labor Relations Review* 16 (1963): 235–39.

Shore, Richard. "Conceptions of the Arbitrator's Role." *Journal of Applied Psychology* 50 (1966): 172–78.

Shulman, Harry. "Reason, Contract, and the Law in Labor Relations." *Harvard Law Review* 68 (1955): 999–1024.

Sirefman, Josef. "Rights Without Remedies in Labor Arbitration." *Arbitration Journal* 18 (1963): 17–35.

Smith, Russel. "The Question of 'Arbitrability'—The Roles of the Arbitrator, the Court, and the Parties." *Southwestern Law Journal* 16 (1962): 1–42.

Smith, Russel, and Dallas Jones. "The Impact of the Emerging Federal Law of Greivance Arbitration on Judges, Arbitrators, and Parties." *Virginia Law Review* 52 (1966): 831–85.

Stein, Emanuel. "Arbitration and Industrial Jurisprudence." *Monthly Labor Review* 81 (1958): 866–67.

Straus, Donald. "Labor Arbitration and Its Critics." *Arbitration Journal* 20 (1965): 197–211.

Summers, Clyde. "Individual Rights in Collective Agreements and Arbitration." *New York University Law Review* 37 (1962): 362–72.

Taylor, George. "The Arbitration of Labor Disputes." *Arbitration Journal* 1 (1946): 409–14.

————. "The Factual Approach to Industrial Arbitration." *Arbitration Journal* 2 (1938): 343–47.

————. "The Voluntary Arbitration of Labor Disputes." *Michigan Law Review* 49 (1951): 787–804.

Teele, John. "But No Back Pay is Awarded." *Arbitration Journal* 19 (1964): 103–112.

————. "The Thought Processes of the Arbitrator." *Arbitration Journal* 17 (1962): 85–96.

Teller, Ludwig. "Specific Remedies in Labor Arbitration." *Arbitration Journal* 3 (1948): 176–80.

Tobias, Paul. "In Defense of Creeping Legalism in Arbitration." *Industrial and Labor Relations Review* 13 (1960): 596–607.

Van de Water, John. "Growth of Third Party Power in the Settlement of Industrial Disputes." *Labor Law Journal* 12 (1961): 1135–60.

Waks, Jay. "Arbitrator, Labor Board, or Both?" *Monthly Labor Review* 91 (1968): 1–5.

Warns, Carl. "Arbitration and the Law." *Arbitration Journal* 15 (1960): 3–16.

Weiler, Paul. "The Role of the Labor Arbitrator: Alternative Versions." *University of Toronto Law Journal* 19 (1969): 16–45.

Wortman, Max, and Fredrick Luthans. "Arbitration in a Changing Era." *Labor Law Journal* 15 (1964): 309–15.

Yaffe, Byron. "The Protected Rights of the Union Steward." *Industrial and Labor Relations Review* 23 (1970): 483–99.

EDITED VOLUMES

*Aaron, Benjamin. "The Uses of the Past in Arbitration." In *Arbitration Today.* Ed. by Jean T. McKelvey. Washington, D.C.: Bureau of National Affairs, 1955.

*Alexander, Gabriel. "Discretion in Arbitration." In *Arbitration and the Public Interest.* Ed. by Gerald Somers and Barbara Dennis. Washington, D.C.: Bureau of National Affairs, 1972.

*Bernstein, Stuart. Comment. In *Labor Arbitration at the Quarter-Century Mark.* Ed. by Barbara Dennis and Gerald Somers. Washington, D.C.: Bureau of National Affairs, 1973.

Bodle, George. "New Techniques and Remedies in the Grievance and Arbitration Process." In *Proceedings of the Fifteenth Annual Institute on Labor Law, The Southwestern Legal Foundation.* Ed. by Virginia Shook Cameron. New York: Matthew Bender, 1969.

Brown, Douglass. "Management Rights and the Collective Agreement." In *Proceedings of the First Annual Meeting of the Industrial Relations Research Association.* Ed. by Milton Derber. New York: Industrial Relations Research Association, 1949.

Cervin, Alto, Charles J. Morris, Saul Wallen, and Jerre S. Williams (Leonard V. Larson, moderator). "Selected Problems in Arbitration — A Discussion." In *Proceedings of the Twelfth Annual Institute on Labor Law, the Southwestern Legal Foundation.* Washington, D.C.: Bureau of National Affairs, 1966.

*Cox, Archibald. "Reflections Upon Labor Arbitration in the Light of the Lincoln Mills Case." In *Arbitration and the Law.* Ed. by Jean T. McKelvey. Washington, D.C.: Bureau of National Affairs, 1959.

*_____. "The Place of Law in Labor Arbitration." In *The Profession of Labor Arbitration*. Ed. by Jean T. McKelvey. Washington, D.C.: Bureau of National Affairs, 1957.

*Crane, Louis A. Discussion of "Arbitrators and Arbitrability." In *Labor Arbitration and Industrial Change*. Ed. by Mark L. Kahn. Washington, D.C.: Bureau of National Affairs, 1963.

*_____. "The Use and Abuse of Arbitral Power." In *Labor Arbitration at the Quarter-Century Mark*. Ed. by Barbara Dennis and Gerald Somers. Washington, D.C.: Bureau of National Affairs, 1973.

*Crawford, Donald. "The Arbitration of Disputes Over Subcontracting." In *Challenges to Arbitration*. Ed. by Jean T. McKelvey. Washington, D.C.: Bureau of National Affairs, 1960.

*Fleming, Robben W. "Due Process and Fair Procedure in Labor Arbitration." In *Arbitration and Public Policy*. Ed. by Spencer D. Pollard. Washington D.C.: Bureau of National Affairs, 1961.

*Fuller, Lon. "Collective Bargaining and the Arbitrator." In *Collective Bargaining and the Arbitrator's Role*. Ed. by Mark Kahn. Washington, D.C.: Bureau of National Affairs, 1962.

*Howlett, Robert. "The Arbitrator, the NLRB, and the Courts." In *The Arbitrator, the NLRB, and the Courts*. Ed. by Dallas L. Jones. Washington, D.C.: Bureau of National Affairs, 1967.

*Jones, Dallas. "Ramifications of Back-Pay Awards in Discharge Cases." In *Arbitration and Social Change*. Ed. by Gerald Somers. Washington, D.C.: Bureau of National Affairs, 1970.

*Jones, Edgar. "Problems of Proof in the Arbitration Process: Report of the West Coast Tripartite Committee." In *Problems of Proof in Arbitration*. Ed. by Dallas Jones. Washington, D.C.: Bureau of National Affairs, 1967.

*Justin, Jules J. "Arbitrability and the Arbitrator's Jurisdiction." In *Management Rights and the Arbitration Process*. Ed. by Jean T. McKelvey. Washington, D.C.: Bureau of National Affairs, 1956.

*Kearns, Lawrence. Comment. In *Labor Arbitration at the Quarter-Century Mark*. Ed. by Barbara Dennis and Gerald Somers. Washington, D.C.: Bureau of National Affairs, 1973.

*Killingsworth, Charles, and Saul Wallen. "Constraint and Variety in Arbitration Systems." In *Labor Arbitration — Perspectives and Problems*. Ed. by Mark L. Kahn. Washington, D. C.: Bureau of National Affairs, 1964.

Luskin, Bert. "Arbitration Comes of Age." In *Third Annual Arbitration Conference*. Amherst, Mass.: Labor Relations and Research Center, University of Massachusetts, 1968.

*Mittenthal, Richard. "Past Practice and the Administration of Collective Bargaining Agreements." In *Arbitration and Public Policy*. Ed. by Spencer D. Pollard. Washington, D.C.: Bureau of National Affairs, 1961.

Morse, Wayne. "The Judicial Theory of Arbitration." In *Unions, Management, and the Public*. Ed. by E. Wight Bakke and Clark Kerr. New York: Harcourt, Brace, 1948.

Pound, Roscoe. "Jurisprudence." In *The History and Prospects of the Social Sciences.* Ed. by Harry Barnes. New York: Knopf, 1925.

*Ross, Arthur. "The Arbitration of Discharge Cases: What Happens After Reinstatement." In *Critical Issues in Labor Arbitration.* Ed. by Jean T. McKelvey. Washington, D.C.: Bureau of National Affairs, 1957.

*Ryder, Meyer S. Comments. In *Labor Arbitration and Industrial Change.* Ed. by Mark L. Kahn. Washington, D.C.: Bureau of National Affairs, 1963.

*_____. "The Impact of Acceptability on the Arbitrator." In *Developments in American and Foreign Arbitration.* Ed. by Charles Rehmus. Washington, D.C.: Bureau of National Affairs, 1968.

*Seitz, Peter. "Problems of the Finality of Awards, or Functus Officio and All That." In *Labor Arbitration—Perspectives and Problems.* Ed. by Mark L. Kahn. Washington, D.C.: Bureau of National Affairs, 1964.

*Seward, Ralph. "Arbitration in the World Today." In *The Profession of Labor Arbitration.* Ed. by Jean T. McKelvey. Washington, D.C.: Bureau of National Affairs, 1957.

Shulman, Harry. "The Role of the Impartial Umpire." In *Unions, Management, and the Public.* Ed. by E. Wight Bakke and Clark Kerr. New York: Harcourt, Brace, 1948.

_____. "The Role of Arbitration in the Collective Bargaining Process." In *Collective Bargaining and Arbitration.* Berkeley: Institute for Industrial Relations, University of California, 1949.

*Smith, Russel A. "Arbitrators and Arbitrability." In *Labor Arbitration and Industrial Change.* Ed. by Mark L. Kahn. Washington, D.C.: Bureau of National Affairs, 1963.

*Sovern, Michael. "When Should Arbitrators Follow Federal Law?" In *Arbitration and the Expanding Role of Neutrals.* Ed. by Gerald G. Somers. Washington, D.C.: Bureau of National Affairs, 1970.

*St. Antoine, Theodore. Discussion of "The Role of Law in Arbitration." In *Developments in American and Foreign Arbitration.* Ed. by Charles M. Rehmus. Washington, D.C.: Bureau of National Affairs, 1968.

*Stutz, Robert. "Arbitrators and the Remedy Power." In *Labor Arbitration and Industrial Change.* Ed. by Mark L. Kahn. Washington, D.C.: Bureau of National Affairs, 1963.

*Taylor, George. "Effectuating the Labor Contract Through Arbitration." In *The Profession of Labor Arbitration.* Ed. by Jean T. McKelvey. Washington, D.C.: Bureau of National Affairs, 1957.

*Wallen, Saul. "Procedural Problems in the Conduct of Arbitration Hearings: A Discussion." In *Labor Arbitration —Perspectives and Problems.* Ed. by Mark L. Kahn. Washington, D.C.: Bureau of National Affairs, 1964.

*_____. "The Silent Contract vs. Express Provisions: The Arbitration of Local Working Conditions." In *Collective Bargaining and the Arbitrator's Role.* Ed. by Mark L. Kahn. Washington, D.C.: Bureau of National Affairs, 1962.

*Wirtz, W. Willard. "Due Process in Arbitration." In *The Arbitrator and the Parties.* Ed. by Jean T. McKelvey. Washington, D.C.: Bureau of National Affairs, 1958.

*Wolff, Sidney. "The Power of the Arbitrator to Make Monetary Awards." In *Labor Arbitration—Perspectives and Problems*. Ed. by Mark L. Kahn. Washington, D.C.: Bureau of National Affairs, 1964.

Yaffe, Byron (ed.). *The Saul Wallen Papers: A Neutral's Contribution to Industrial Peace*. Ithaca: New York State School of Industrial and Labor Relations, Cornell University, 1974.

STANDARD PUBLISHED ARBITRATION REPORTS

American Labor Arbitration, Prentice-Hall, Inc., Englewood Cliffs, New Jersey.
Labor Arbitration Awards, Commerce Clearing House, Inc., Chicago, Illinois.
Labor Arbitration Reports, Bureau of National Affairs, Inc., Washington, D.C.

---

*Proceedings of the National Academy of Arbitrators.

INDEX